ALSO BY JONATHAN MOONEY

Learning Outside the Lines (coauthor)

The Short Bus

The Short Bus

A JOURNEY BEYOND NORMAL

JONATHAN MOONEY

HENRY HOLT AND COMPANY ▇ NEW YORK

Henry Holt and Company, LLC
Publishers since 1866
175 Fifth Avenue
New York, New York 10010
www.henryholt.com

Henry Holt® and ® are registered trademarks of
Henry Holt and Company, LLC.

Library of Congress Cataloging-in-Publication Data
Mooney, Jonathan.
    The short bus : a journey beyond normal / Jonathan Mooney.—1st ed.
    p. cm.
    ISBN-13: 978-0-8050-7427-7
    ISBN-10: 0-8050-7427-9
    1. Mooney, Jonathan.   2. Mooney, Jonathan—Travel.   3. People with
disabilities—United States—Case studies.   4. Learning disabled—United
States—Biography.   I. Title.
HV1568.25.U5M66 2007
362.196'8588900972—dc22
[B]   2006052588

Henry Holt books are available for special promotions and premiums.
For details contact: Director, Special Markets.

First Edition 2007

Designed by Kelly Too

Printed in the United States of America
1 2 3 4 5 6 7 8 9 10

To Becky—my life, my love

The judges of normality are present everywhere. We are in the society of the teacher-judge, the doctor-judge, the educator-judge, the social worker-judge; it is on them that the universal reign of the normative is based; and each individual, wherever he may find himself, subjects to it his body, his gestures, his behavior, his aptitudes, his achievements.

—MICHEL FOUCAULT

contents

The Short Bus

Prologue: The Short-Bus Story

I have to admit, in the spirit of full disclosure, that I once harbored aspirations of becoming an after-school special. On June 2, 2003, I was waiting in the lobby of the Waldorf-Astoria hotel in Manhattan for Ernest, an independent movie producer interested in optioning the story of my life. We were to have breakfast that morning with a producer from Merv Griffin Entertainment, during which I was to "pitch" myself as the subject for an after-school special.

Shifting my weight back and forth, I turned over the situation in my mind. In less than twenty-four hours, I would be leaving New York to fly to Los Angeles, where I had grown up, to pick up an old short school bus (the kind used to take some kids with disabilities to special ed programs). My plan was to transform this vehicle into a makeshift RV and depart from California on a two-month journey around the United States.

On the road I'd interview and spend time with people, like myself, who had once been labeled "abnormal" or "disabled." I wanted to see how they overcame—or didn't—being labeled different. I wanted to see the lives they fashioned for themselves. Waiting for Ernest, watching old ladies with plastic faces and big diamonds pass by, I suddenly realized that my trip really wasn't after-school-special material. I wanted to empower people, but I also wanted to be real, completely honest, and unsentimental.

A short-bus rider myself, I had grown up in special education, having been labeled learning disabled with attention problems at the end of third grade. I was one of *those* kids who grew up chilling out with janitors in the hallways; one of *those* kids who were always on a first-name basis with Shirley, the receptionist in the principal's office; one of *those* kids who grew up hiding in the bathroom to escape reading out loud. I dropped out of school for a while in sixth grade and had a plan for suicide by the time I was twelve. A high school guidance counselor confided that people like me ended up flipping burgers. That prediction did not come true; I eventually graduated from Brown University with an honors degree in literature and published a book, in part about my experiences. I had believed, when I arranged to meet the producer, that all this could be the subject of a movie. Now I was realizing I had to tell it my way.

Ernest, who had a handlebar mustache and wore a blue western vest, tapped me on the shoulder and escorted me to the restaurant, where we were to wait for the producer whom I thought of as the Man. Kind and quiet, Ernest looked like a fusion of accountant and, given the mustache, retired porn star. As we sat and drank coffee, he told me about his work. He had read my first book, *Learning Outside the Lines*, and thought my story was pretty inspiring stuff. "You are an American success story," Ernest said. I mulled that over as I ate my fancy eggs. Is that what I wanted, to be what television considered "inspiring"? After about fifteen minutes, the producer arrived, and Ernest rose to stand at attention. It was clear the Man made all the decisions.

I was used to selling myself, selling my story. So after the pleasantries, I leaned forward to deliver my well-rehearsed pitch, but something strange happened: when I opened my mouth nothing came out. My old song and dance about overcoming my "disability" seemed like a fraud. I had wanted this meeting but just couldn't do it. I couldn't speak about my resilient mom, or my determination to be successful, or even the injustice I faced in school. "Did I tell you all that I'm about to leave for a trip around the country in a special ed school bus?" I asked. Ernest looked downcast. After a little explanation of what a short bus was and who rode it, the conversation stopped. The Man adjusted his belt and said, "Why the hell would you do that?"

I did and did not have an exact answer to this question. My reasons for this trip shifted around like the sides of a Rubik's cube; the moment I thought I had something pinned down, the other side was screwed up, jumbled, and needed to be rearranged again. Why would I go back to my experiences of disability when I had transcended all that? What did I hope to find out there back in the bus? Sitting at that table, I was at a loss. What emerged, however, was as close to an answer as I could muster: "I'm going because of two kids, named Bobby and Clay."

I first met Bobby in the fall of 2000, somewhere in the middle of America, shortly after graduating from college, on my book tour. *Book tour* was actually an optimistic term. I'd personally planned this jaunt during a summer spent holed up in my pathetic apartment "spamming" disability Web sites and contacting unsuspecting moms. I'd offered to come to their towns, free of cost, sleep in their homes, and lecture to any audience that they could scrounge up. After managing to get some invitations, I packed my bags, perfected my authoritative yet sincere speaking voice, and set off for self-help stardom. I wanted to sell my book and cap off my rise-to-success story. (From hiding in the bathroom to Ivy League student to best-selling author.) I was under the illusion that I would be healed by fame, that recognition would save that little kid who used to hide in the bathroom during reading class.

Then I met Bobby Glass. I'd been standing in a school gym, answering questions, but I could not take my eyes off this young kid in the back of the line. He was no more than five feet tall, and while I autographed books, I watched him snake back and forth with the rhythm of the line. I couldn't take my eyes off his colored eyeglasses. They were a deep purple, and they seemed custom-made for him. I nodded as people asked me questions: *So what is the best medication for ADD? You're so normal; most kids aren't like you. How can my Jane go to an Ivy League university?*

When Bobby had introduced himself he said, "You ever seen these?" He gestured at his glasses. I laughed. "Seen 'em? I was told to wear a pair, man." These colored glasses were often prescribed as a way to "fix" dyslexia and other reading problems. I hadn't seen them in a long time. They took me back in time. "No shit?" Bobby said. "I'm sixteen now; they prescribed these for me when I was ten. Don't need these things anymore, never did, but I keep them as a reminder of how they tried to fix me all the time: the shrinks, the school, my parents." Minutes later, after our bond had become undeniable, Bobby made a confession. He took off his glasses for a second, then said, "You know I snapped once. I had had enough."

Bobby was in sixth grade the day that he decided to just give up. His mom had dropped him off at the bottom of the gravel pathway that led to school, hoping he would walk to class by himself. His clothes didn't feel right that morning, although every day he wore almost the same thing: the same hat, the same pants, and the same red shirt.

At school, Bobby walked up and down the hall looking for that one spot where he could hide. This happened almost every day, and the teachers always laughed at Bobby. Sometimes other things would be said, things he would never forget. With him, teachers could say anything. All he could ever see of one teacher was a big dot. This was because of all the dots that she put on his work—a dot on every word that was not written nicely, two dots for the misspelled ones.

That day, the air was filled with the kind of silence that comes before a snowstorm or a lightning storm. Bobby felt the snow starting as he headed down the road home that day. I saw Bobby in my mind as he described walking home, visualized his purple eyeglasses moving silently through the snow. He entered the house the way he always did, past his dog, Jake. No one was home, and he knew no one would be there for a while, unless the snow got bad and his mom left work early. But it was quiet.

Bobby Glass's note was found in his backpack after he tried to kill himself, after he was discovered, just in time. He had fashioned a noose above his bed.

When Bobby finished telling me his story, the cafeteria had long emptied. But he kept on talking. "Did I tell you I just got into college, early admission to study math? It had nothing to do with those purple eyeglasses or anything they did to fix me. You know, they've come up with a lot of fancy diagnoses, a lot of talk about disorders and disabilities, but not much has changed, has it? Why? Jon, that's my question because we seem more disabled than ever."

The fall turned into the winter, and I was still on the road, but because of the way Bobby's tale sank into me, all the other stories seemed more vivid and important. These weren't so-called success stories like mine, but the testimonies of kids who still locked themselves in bathrooms and threw up during reading class; memories from those who hid under their beds and had ulcers; tales of others who pulled out their hair and scratched their faces until they bled. I heard stories of people who grew up in segregated schools—in institutions for the disabled. I heard firsthand accounts from people who were sterilized.

But I also heard stories of transcendence—of artists who attributed their creativity to their disabilities, of people who learned to think beyond the labels pinned on them. What I was learning was the notion of disability as, inherently, a social construct. These experiences were not those of people intrinsically defective or broken but were tales of human variance, differences, and diversity.

All the stories that were coming to me as I traveled were so different. But something I couldn't yet name held them together. I realized what this glue was, months later, when I gave a lecture at a special education class and came upon what could be the essence, symbol, and vehicle of my journey: the short bus.

It was terrifying to be back in a special education classroom, the kind that I spent countless hours in as a kid. The irony of the situation was not lost on me: I had graduated from Brown less than a year earlier and now I was back in special education. I remember dreading my special education teacher's condescending smile and her patronizing voice as she said, "Try to act normal today, OK." I was there to give a lecture, supposedly no longer a short-bus rider but rather a role model of success for these kids. But I sure as hell didn't feel that way. Sitting in that classroom waiting for the kids, my skin still crawled like it had almost twenty years earlier and my stomach filled with anxiety that felt like bees stinging my insides. I had a few minutes before I had to talk, as kids from other local schools arrived, so I found a seat in the back of the room, hoping to disappear.

I wasn't alone for long, though. I could see out the window that the school buses were slowly arriving. Not big buses, like most kids rode to school, but short ones, the symbol of disability and pain in my life. I knew it well. Kids started filing into the classroom, filling it with the white noise of childhood. One voice, though, broke through.

His name was Clay, and he was probably about eleven or twelve years old. Clay got off his short bus, walked into the class, and went right to the back of the room and found a seat next to me. He was humming the tune to "If You're Happy and You Know It Clap Your Hands." He turned to me and, laughing, said, "The tard bus is always late." I laughed. He continued, "It has ADD. We're working on getting it some Ritalin. That's what the normal kids say anyway. Might as well beat them to the punch, don't you think?"

I reached my hand out. "I'm Jon." I said. "I'm Clay. You're the guy who's talking, right." I shrugged. "I guess so." For the next fifteen minutes as we waited for the rest of the students, Clay and I shot the shit. Then we were quiet and watched the other students filling up the classroom. Sitting there with Clay was like looking at a ghost of myself. Clay was a punk with an attitude. He was the kind of kid who grew up in the hallway but had spirit that couldn't be destroyed. Because he moved around too much, his teacher sometimes strapped him to his chair with "seat belts" that cut into his waist and made him bleed. Clay's experience and his attitude reminded me of the kid I used to be. Before I started elementary school, I used to run around with cowboy boots and kick people in the shins. I used to yell at the top of my lungs, "Normal people suck!"

I looked around the special ed room and out to the short bus in the parking lot. Even at this point in my life, I couldn't get "try to act normal" out of my head. I wasn't like *these* kids who were really fucked up. I was past that now. I tried not to look at them. Clay tapped me on the leg and broke me out of my trance. A giant head wearing a helmet floated in front of me. He sat facing me with his arms crossed, like a little man, smiling from ear to ear. He didn't say anything. "He wants to give you a hug," Clay said. "That's his deal. He gives people hugs in the morning."

Stunned, I shrugged my shoulders, and the boy in the helmet leaned over and hugged me. He held on tight. Then, without saying a word, he left. For the rest of the time before my lecture, the boy in the helmet went from seat to seat and hugged every kid. I couldn't take my eyes off him. His smile just kept getting bigger and bigger. Sometimes he had to stop and brace himself. Sometimes he fell over. But he got up and moved on to the next kid. Clay told me the jocks called him "Helmet Boy" and beat him up. His doctors told his mom he was retarded and should be institutionalized. In a different era, he might have been lobotomized or sterilized.

That little man broke something inside of me. I looked around the room and saw faces that were so familiar. The people I had forgotten about from my journey in special ed came rushing back to mind. I saw Steve, my best friend from junior high school, who could hardly read. I saw the way he looked at me the day I gave him the nickname "Stupid Steve." I saw all the people I had tried to act like I wasn't like, trying to be normal. In this classroom were faces that drooped with Down syndrome, faces that twitched uncontrollably, faces that were covered by the straps of their helmets, faces of the kids who threw up most days in reading class but held it in so the teacher wouldn't know. There were faces of kids who were told every day that they needed to be normal, had to be normal, had to change themselves. These kids, beyond our surface differences, were very much like me.

Sitting in that class, lost somewhere between the past and the present, for the first time in a long time, I felt part of something. I had never felt a part of anything trying to be normal. I just felt like an outsider. But there were no outsiders in the special ed room and on the short bus because we are all considered to be freaks. But in this community being a freak was normal.

This united feeling went away, though, as the teacher quieted the classroom in preparation for my lecture. The room became dead silent. It was a bone-dry silence that seemed to crack. This was the silence of shame, and the only thing that broke it was the sound of these kids trying to disappear. Once the class was quiet, the teacher stood up and began her introduction. "Now students, we are honored to have Mr. Mooney here." My eyes glazed over as I stood up and prepared to talk. But the teacher continued. "Mr. Mooney *used* to be like you. Be respectful of Mr. Mooney. Try to act normal, OK?"

I stood in front of the class shocked. In that small moment, something shifted inside of me. I wanted to shake that teacher and tell her to tell them that they were beautiful. I had usually begun my lectures to kids by recounting my academic success at Brown University. But not that day. "Good morning," I said to the class. "The first thing I want people to know about me is that I think normal people suck, guys, they suck." I had not said that for a very long time. The teacher was already giving me that "You're in trouble, Mister" look. The rest of the kids were saying, "Normal people suck" over and over again.

Needless to say, the lecture did not last all that long. When it was over, I found Clay again and gave him my e-mail address. As I walked away, I heard Clay's voice. He was singing what he had been humming earlier that morning, first quietly, then as loud as he could:

If you ride on the short bus clap your hands
If you ride on the cheese bus, clap your hands
If you're a tard and you know it,
and you're not afraid to show it,
If you're a tard and you know it,
clap your hands.

What a simple, common, and destructive message: *You're not normal.* How many people have been told, regardless of who they are, *You're not normal*? But where did the idea of normalcy come from? How many lives has that idea screwed up? And how do people learn to reject the message that they have to conform to this way of being? In that moment, an idea was forming inside of me.

It would be easier to say that I left Clay and bought a short bus the next day, but that is not how life unfolds. I embarked on a different trip, departing for New Zealand in June of 2001, almost a year to the day after I graduated from Brown. The trip was set up over e-mail with a woman named Moira, whom I hadn't spoken to until the morning of my departure when she called at 4:00 a.m. and said, "Jonathan, bring your winter woollies; it's winter in New Zealand." That was it, nothing more, and I boarded a plane and flew for two days.

When I arrived at the Wellington airport, I expected to be welcomed with a traditional Maori greeting, which included a band and fifteen dancers. ("For such a distinguished and honored guest, nothing less would be acceptable," Moira had written.) But when I got off the plane there were no dancers, no signs with my name; in fact there was nobody to greet me. I wandered around the Wellington airport for an hour, alone, waiting for a woman I had never met. I began to get nervous until I heard "Jonathan Mooney" over the intercom. I finally found Moira, who was short (about five feet tall), stout (round like a kettle), with gray hair and gray wandering eyes. She greeted me and seemed nice enough, but when she spoke I couldn't understand a word. She mumbled something and then motioned in the direction of the parking lot. I followed her to the car, a filthy two-door Commodore. The seats were ripped, and the interior reeked of smoke. When I got in, she talked as I watched the Wellington sky turn colors and wished I were a cloud speeding back toward the other side of the world.

She lived with her chain-smoking eighty-year-old mother in a middle-income housing project on the outskirts of Wellington. Coughing, I listened to this old broad talk about the labor strikes of the 1920s and '30s, the Cook Islands, and the fundamentally unjust outcome of the treaty of Wanganui. After the history lesson, we went to a rugby match. Finally, I was taken to my room for the night at Moira's friend's house, where I was to sleep in an open room on a crazy-looking pull-out bed. Before we parted, Moira said, "Tomorrow you'll meet our traveling crew" and "You should think about what you're going to say, dear." That night I lay on the mattress on the floor, watching the night sky, terrified and lonely. This wasn't the trip I was supposed to be on.

The next day I met my traveling companions. I learned that Moira had a traumatic head injury that affected, among other things, her sense of time, organizational abilities, and general personality stability.

I also met my crew. There was Allen, our driver—a retired cop who I quickly learned was a recovering alcoholic. (Over the course of our six weeks together, Allen got it in his head that I, too, was in recovery. I didn't have the heart to tell him that, in fact, I quite enjoyed drinking. But Allen was my only friend here, so for weeks I accompanied him many nights in small towns across New Zealand to AA meetings.) Then there was Mary, who, according to Moira, was my "warm-up," an eighty-year-old spelling expert whose act consisted of a large phonics cube that was somehow relevant to teaching the structure of language. Mary had severe flatulence, so whenever she bent over—whether to get into the car or to pick up her beloved cube—she passed gas.

I had traveled all the way around the world to tell my story in some glamorous, triumphant way but found myself aboard a ship of fools. What a freak show, I thought to myself as we set sail from Wellington up to Auckland. As we pulled out, I did what I always did: I put on my headphones and detached myself from what was going on. I stared out the window, in my own world, and watched the country pass by.

I was furious at this trip, at the world, at all that had led me here. But then, in my mind's eye, I saw them again, out in the dry winter New Zealand grass: Bobby of the purple glasses. I saw Clay singing his song of resistance. I shook my head to get them out. I turned up my headphones, but those bastards were taunting me, mocking me. How much of my life had I missed because I had invested in that idea of normalcy? How much do we all miss when we conform?

When the batteries on my CD player died, I looked ahead and out the window as if nothing had happened, bobbing my head slightly to some imaginary music. But then I saw it. I heard it. Out of the corner of my eye, I saw Allen's lips moving, his entire mouth was open, and his jaw opened like a fish sucking air. Oh God, yes, he was singing. He was singing Bette Midler's ballad that I so hated. *Did you ever know you're my hero? You're everything I would like to be.* To my utter horror, Mary chimed in, first softly, then quite loudly. Then, as if God wanted to punish me for my foolishness, Moira joined them: *Fly Fly Fly so high against the sky / so high I almost touched the sky.* I stared at them, these freaks, these fucking freaks. Allen looked at me and said, "Come on now, mate, join us," and he tilted his head back, let go of the steering wheel, and fluttered his arms like he was flying. He burst out laughing. "You have to enjoy the ride, mate."

There, on the other side of the world, it hit me. I had spent the past year unconsciously seeking out these situations. I was looking for people like Allen, Moira, and Mary, because a long time ago, I used to be someone who didn't give a shit about what other people thought. I had once shared that utter abandon, that disregard for what was normal, that unruly energy that I recognized as they sang their horrible rendition of that melodramatic song. I started to laugh. Who the hell was I to call anyone a freak? Sitting in that car, listening to Moira and Allen and Mary sing at the top of their lungs, I actually felt more at home than I had ever felt trying to be normal. I took a breath, and I decided to just take this trip, as absurd, as terrifying as it was, without judgment, to experience whatever ride I was on.

I left the Waldorf in New York that long-ago morning without a movie deal. I walked home to pack for this new journey. It had taken me well over two years to set it all up, to get the money, to plan and deal with setbacks and life. I would be gone over four months, two months longer than my original estimate. I would travel thirty-five thousand miles, in one huge loop around the country from L.A. back to L.A. again. I would spend all my money on this trip, decimating my savings account and going into debt. But this ride on the short bus would fundamentally change my life.

The next day I flew out of JFK. On that plane speeding at thirty thousand feet, high above the cloud line, I had no idea where I was going. In all honesty, the trip was in shambles. I didn't know if my short bus worked. My plans for whom I would visit had partially fallen through.

But out there waiting was Ashley, an eight-year-old deaf and blind girl who likes to curse out her teachers in sign language. Out there was Cookie, a reclusive Maine artist saving up money for a gender-change operation. Out on the road was Butch Anthony, a self-taught artist and proud founder of the Museum of Wonder where he has a telepathic chicken. Out there were people from my past life, people whom I had lost touch with, treated poorly, and demeaned because of my own obsession with being accepted "in the real world." Out there was Kent Roberts, a college friend who is a brilliant performance artist and also labeled, among numerous other things, ADD. Out there was my uncle Bill, an insane brilliant priest whom I'd lost and wanted to find again. Out there was also my future. In my pocket was a little toy ring that I had bought on eBay for five dollars. I hoped it would serve as an engagement ring for my girlfriend, Becky, who was joining me on the first leg of the trip.

As the plane descended through the clouds into Los Angeles, where I was to pick up my short bus, I sat back and started to hum a song I learned from Clay. The woman next to me on the plane stared at me, but I didn't care, I was on a new journey now. Floating between flying and landing, I sang to myself: *If you ride on the short bus clap your hands / if you're a tard and you know it, and you're not afraid to show it / if you're a tard and you know it, clap your hands . . .*

PART ONE

Everyone in Their Right Place

Los Angeles, CA–New York, NY

1

You Are Responsible for the Safe Operation and Cleanliness of This Vehicle

On June 3, 2003, I was standing out in front of Margo's house, chilling with Conor, my four-year-old nephew, and my mom. We were waiting for my mom's pal Margo, a dyslexic ex-stripper who had transformed herself into a mover and shaker in the L.A. world of social services. Margo had grown up in Indiana Catholic schools and still had small scars on her knuckles from where she was smacked with the thin metal edge of the Catholic reading remediation program known as "the ruler."

Among Margo's many other business ventures was a bus company. The previous December, over coffee at her home in the "Black Beverly Hills," she had offered to find me a short school bus to live out of for the next four months. "I get shit done," Margo had said as my mom chimed in with an inspired "uh huh." As we left, I was told to ask no more questions. Margo would take care of the bus. Five months and eighteen thousand dollars later, she had lived up to her promise, and the proof was sitting in front of her house: one hell of a *short* school bus.

Margo had the keys, however, and as was often the case, she was well over an hour late. So Conor and I stared at the bus. Newly painted, it looked slightly unstable, parked on the hill, its weight leaning in a way that seemed somewhat precarious. But it was what I had wanted, a short bus, yellow and black, twenty feet long, and ten feet tall.

Drawing his face up like he had just eaten a lemon, Conor asked, "What is your bus's name, Jonny?"

"I have no idea, man," I said.

"Well, Jonny," Conor said in his adult voice, "you know, things need a name."

He was right. So as we waited I thought of all the names kids have for these vehicles: the tard cart, the cheese box, the short bus. None of them fit anymore, but I had no idea what did.

"That's OK, Jonny," Conor said. "You can name it later."

A more pressing problem: My trip was in complete disarray. I was supposed to depart in three weeks but had no idea where I was going or how to get there. I'm one of those folks for whom large things (like driving around the country in a short school bus) seem easy. But now my optimism seemed ephemeral, flimsy. As the sun broke through the L.A. mix of the marine layer, smoke, and stale air, Conor turned to me and said, "Jonny, why do you have to go live in that bus?"

I had been diagnosed as dyslexic at the end of third grade. I had faked reading most of my life and had actually dropped out of school for a time in sixth grade. In high school a guidance counselor gave me a fifty-fifty chance of graduating. I slipped into my first university, Loyola Marymount in Los Angeles, as a soccer player on scholarship. And yet "miraculously" I managed to graduate in 2000 from Brown University with a 4.0 GPA in English literature, despite having the phonic awareness and reading rate of a seventh grader and being a third-grade-level speller. In most people's minds and, in all honesty, mine as well, I had overcome. What the hell was I doing waiting for an ex-stripper to bring me the keys to a short school bus?

On the most obvious level, the bus represented a path set in motion when I was eight years old and labeled learning disabled. I was drawn to the short bus because it was a public symbol of disability and special education. The bus emerged out of federal legislation, the Individuals with Disabilities Education Act (IDEA) of 1975, which mandated that children with disabilities be educated in a public school setting. It was a historic moment for my tribe, but there were problems: Schools were not required to fully integrate students with disabilities, and a segregated system of special education programs was created. Then along came segregated transportation: the short bus. Thrown together under the rubric of special education, these passengers included kids with physical disabilities, Down syndrome, learning disabilities, autism, as well as emotional problems. Special education and the short bus grouped together all these different students, expanding our culture's definition of *disabled*. The short bus as a symbol of special education says as much (or more) about that culture—its values, beliefs, fears, aspirations, and injustices—as it ever did about people with disabilities.

Conor and I stood at a respectful distance from the bus. As I eyed it, the magnitude of the situation struck me: This would be my home for the next four months. This vehicle was supposed to transport me from L.A., through the southern states, up to Maine, across the Great Plains, over the Rocky Mountains, to the shores of the Pacific Northwest, down the coast riding Highway 101 and then Highway 1 back home.

Conor tapped my leg and said, "Jonny, I don't think I would want to live in that thing if I was you."

"No shit," I said, taking a seat on the pavement. Conor, talking to himself, flew Buzz Lightyear around the universe in his mind. Sometimes I think of Conor as the kid that I lost in special ed. He reminds me of the full-of-life version of me who was obsessed with the show *Roots* and who used to run around the house yelling, "Kunta Kinte!" He's like the three-year-old me who had tapped on the window of a doughnut shop until a young woman came up to him, and then demanded, "Give me a fucking jelly doughnut, you bitch." I looked at Conor and then at the short bus, and I knew that buried somewhere in that yellow siding was the kid I wanted back.

When Margo's car finally pulled up, Conor pointed Buzz Lightyear at her and said, "It doesn't matter if you're black, Margo, because I'm green."

"Really. OK, green man," Margo said. "Here comes Wes's black ass right now with them keys."

Wes was the man Margo had put in charge of finalizing our transaction. After parking his car, he walked up and I shook his hand. "Let's go see your bus," he said. So we stood there, staring at the thing.

Conor said, "Jonny, you can't drive that. You have no license. The cops took Jonny's license for driving like a drunk."

The little man was right. In part because of a 1996 DUI, I hadn't had a license for over five years. But in 2003, I had passed my road test and been issued a temporary license. I was still smarting from the experience. When I had confused a right from a left turn, the DMV evaluator insulted me by asking if I was "retarded." On my temporary license were disparaging comments such as driver is "distracted" and "shows poor decision-making in traffic."

"Here you go," Wes said, handing over the key. "You got yourself one short school bus." I stepped inside and sat down in the driver's seat. The air conditioner, for which I had paid an extra $1,500, hummed. The bus was cool and smelled like rubber and disinfectant. But, more than anything else, it smelled like school, and I felt a mixture of fear and shame. I looked at the speedometer—it read 150,000 miles, not 15,000 as promised.

But at that moment none of that mattered. Two years of work had led me here, and now I was sitting in the bus, in the driver's seat, alone. I waited for my mom to pull out in front of me. Here it was, the first mile, to Raintree, my family's apartment complex. I put the bus in drive, took my foot off the brake, and felt the bus jerk forward with a force that sent me back into my seat. It was out of control. I turned the wheel both ways, and the bus didn't respond. It felt like I was driving a boat speeding down La Cienega Boulevard. I was going only thirty-five miles per hour, but it sounded and felt like I was going eighty.

I couldn't see out of the side mirrors. I kept thinking thirty thousand miles, thirty thousand miles, thirty thousand miles. A long way to go. Pulling into the apartment complex, past the guard gates, toward the guest parking, I spotted a parking space and turned the bus toward the curb, crashing into a tree. Conor got out of my mom's car, pointed

Buzz up over his head, and said, "Maybe they shouldn't have given Jonny a new license after all."

I woke up the next morning, my first full day in L.A., to my dog, Max, pissing in the corner of my makeshift bedroom in the middle of my parents' den. Running over to my futon, he licked my face. Max was not a youthful creature, though my mom had insisted that he was nine years old for the past six or seven years. At one point, we were told that he was a fifty-fifty mix of golden retriever and yellow Lab. But after my mom got a dog calendar for Christmas featuring different exotic breeds every month, she became convinced that Max was really a Rhodesian ridgeback—our family's last hope for a pedigree.

I wasn't mad that Max had almost pissed on me. No one really got angry at any of our insane dogs. My family's carpets always reeked of urine. It wasn't until I went to Brown and visited my college friends' houses that I realized it was not the norm to have the carpets smell like a zoo. I quickly learned that there are two types of people in this world: those whose carpets reek and those whose carpets do not. I accept the fact that my family falls into the first category, and I'm more comfortable around people who know this sort of secret shame.

I grabbed a cup of joe and prepared to face my first full day in L.A. My plan was to drive to my former school, Penny Camp Elementary, and get my old records if they hadn't been discarded or buried at some storage facility. I wasn't in the best of moods that morning. The night before, when I arrived, my pops had already started on the Jack Daniel's. My dad waits all day for that designated time to drink. Then he sits alone in his cheap faux-leather chair, listening to a rotating selection of classical music. He's always had this kind of chair. Families like mine buy this stuff to look respectable. My dad's chair has shiny synthetic leather and fake wood arms, and it faces armies of Conor's toy robots and soldiers, battalions ready to fight off an invisible sadness.

I had breakfast with my sister Kelly and this put me in a better mood. Kelly was ten years older than me, my best friend, and someone I admired more than words. Kelly was in a time of transition in her life.

She had quit her job at my mom's nonprofit, sold her apartment, and moved in with my folks. Kelly's plan was to go into the Peace Corps. But first she was going to ride the bus with me for a month, in August. Kelly has always been the wild one, the freak. Though she was labeled "gifted" and is the smartest among us, she missed almost a year of high school because of depression. After weaving in and out of college (she started at the University of California, San Diego, and transferred to UCLA), she ultimately graduated with a theater degree and committed herself to becoming an actor and a writer.

Like many actors and artists, Kelly had a difficult road but she devoted all of herself to her work. Kelly produced her own plays that dealt honestly with complicated issues such as child abuse. She never made it, though. Kelly didn't care about this material success—what I admired most was my sister's commitment to staying true to herself. Without her, I would not be the person I am today.

After breakfast, I headed out, not in my fucked-up bus but in my mom's more compact Subaru, pointing the car south on Sepulveda Boulevard toward Manhattan Beach, where my family had moved in 1978 from San Francisco. We had arrived in an old station wagon named *The Incredible Hulk* in search of a new life. My mom had raised my half brother, Billy, and my two half sisters, Kelly and Michelle, on welfare, in the Squares, a housing project, in San Francisco. Then, in the mid-1970s, she met my father, an upwardly mobile attorney. I was born in San Francisco, but an old beach house on Seventeenth Street in Manhattan Beach is what I recall as my first home. It sat on the crest of the last hill before the world rushed down into the Pacific Ocean.

On that June day in 2003, I found Manhattan Beach more rich, more white, more gated than I remembered. The only people of color were maids. My house was gone. But that didn't stop me from remembering being in a rubber swimming pool with my mom's dress floating in the water like a drifting flower. She was young and strong. I recalled being maybe three, watching my mom stir tuna fish in a big bowl with a wooden spoon. The sky was shaking by like a mirage outside our big bay window. Fog was rolling in for the night. *Pinocchio* was on the TV.

I felt OK, stable, safe, and permanent like a stone. These images matter to me because they represent brief moments of safety with my place in the universe secure. It was later, in school, that I developed suffocating anxiety. I still recall feeling seized by that beast crawling up my stomach and into my lungs and my head. By third grade, I had developed a series of nervous tics.

After Seventeenth Street I made my way to my family's second house on Nelson. Our house there was like the one from *Grey Gardens*, a documentary about two old ladies living in a decaying mansion in the Hamptons. Our place wasn't a mansion. It didn't have a doorknob, and through the hole where the knob should have been, a visitor could have glimpsed a world of chaos—some bad, some good.

This visitor might have glimpsed my primal scenes. At four years old, I'm sprinting down the long hallway naked but for my socks. Running as fast as I can, I jump on the slick tile and launch myself sliding—and suddenly I'm in sixth grade, labeled learning disabled. I can hardly read, and special ed is my territory. I'm depressed, I have an eating disorder, and I'm wearing checkered pants, checkered shirt, checkered hat. I remember heading down the long stretch of Nelson from Peck Street to our yellow house on the end of the block on my checkered bike, trying to find a way out, wishing I was flying away.

I headed to Penny Camp Elementary as the sun broke through the marine layer. I could still feel the approaching-school terror, even after all these years, in the tips of my fingers. As I walked up the tarred ramp into an old hallway covered with concrete, I remembered one of my last days here. I don't know what grade I was in, but in my vision the sky is large, huge and open. The sun is out, and I feel like an old man, but I'm singing to myself, *No more schoolbooks, no more teachers' dirty looks*, and I'm filled with relief, utter relief spreading through my body like warm water. Shame and anxiety had filled my life, *were* my life, for so long.

My struggles in school started the first day in kindergarten. At recess there were these small metal bikes that I had never seen before, and I loved them. The rules were that you had to ride them in a practical pattern traced on the concrete; I couldn't follow the lines, so I was banned from all the bikes. I also couldn't tell time. One day, when it was my turn in the time-telling circle, I guessed ten o'clock. I was right. From that day on, no matter what time it actually was on the toy clock the teacher held up, I blurted out, "Ten o'clock." All the kids laughed. I learned quickly that it was better to be the funny kid than the stupid one.

In second grade we all had desks lined up in a row, like work stations in a factory. I tried to sit still, but I couldn't. Five seconds into class my whole body was moving—hands, feet, and arms—and then I was pointed at, ordered to stop moving, to control myself. Miss C., my teacher, yelled, "Jon, what is wrong with you?" The rest of my day was spent out in the hallway, my spirit evaporating into the thin air.

I was the bad kid, the stupid one with terrible handwriting, spelling, and reading. Everyone knew that I was in the slow reading group. The black birds, the blue birds, and the sparrows; why do we bother? My reading group might as well have been named after a bird that did not fly: an ostrich trying hard just to keep up. By second grade I was reading *See Spot Run* while the rest of the kids tackled real books. By the end of that year, I was asking my mom, "Why am I stupid?"

Toward the end of third grade, my mom was called in to a meeting with a team of professionals: my teacher, an aide, and a third person who would now be known as a learning or LD specialist. They were lined up behind a desk like a jury of inquisitors. My mom sat across from them in a small child's chair, the kind used during story time. They looked down on my mom as they talked in educational jargon about my learning disabilities and attention problems. After about fifteen minutes, my mom said, "Excuse me, but perhaps he is not the problem—he was fine in kindergarten and preschool."

She was right; in any environment where I did not have to sit still and read, my learning problem disappeared. "Mrs. Mooney, perhaps you should take a parenting class" is what my mom was told. "We are experts; we know how your son learns." Upon hearing that statement, my mom, a woman who had struggled in school and wanted nothing more than to be accepted, grew silent. It was recommended that I be taken for weeklong psycho-educational testing. And so, with that week of testing, the machinery of disability was set in motion in my life.

On Monday of the first day of testing, I slept in, and my mom and I went out for breakfast. I had French toast, and we didn't really talk. My mom had hated school, as an institution of power and conformity, and she knew that it was the environment, more than my mind, that was broken. She had learned to work the system in her own way, rising from a volunteer to executive director of a nonprofit organization. She was faced with the fact that I did not fit into the school's notions of intelligence (pinned to reading and writing) or good character, which it linked to compliance and obedience. Accepting the label LD, however, was a deal with the devil, and my mom knew it. But she had no idea how to get out of it. That morning at breakfast she ranted against school, explaining that we had to learn to "play the game."

After breakfast we drove down Sepulveda in the fog past Redondo Beach to Torrance, and we sat in a musty office waiting for the educational shrink, a kind woman who put her arm around me. She told me that for the next week I would take some tests, without any right answers. This was bullshit; she knew it and I knew it. Every test has right answers, and all the questions and answers and exams have consequences. During the testing I stared at the blue wall behind the quiet lady holding up ink blots and imagined it was the sky underneath the heavy smog and smoke of L.A.

A week later, my world changed. I found myself in the heart of special ed, spending most of my day in a different classroom, bearing the pseudo-scientific medical label of learning disabled with attention problems. My experience is a textbook case of a medical model being used to understand the experience of disability. My parents and I were told I was broken, and that my deficits should be diagnosed, treated, and cured. But the medical model gives the doctor all the power and dehumanizes the "patient."

My mom understood that what was happening was an injustice, and she instilled this idea in me every day. After school, I would sit and listen to her—a five-foot-tall Irish woman—giving my teachers hell. I struggled horribly with spelling and dreaded the weekly exam every Friday. For a while, I got my words on Monday and spent hours drawing the words in the sand, building the words with blocks, and even doing interpretive dance to learn. But I always failed the test.

For most of one year, my mom and I ditched school on Fridays, and we went to the zoo. Before school every morning she read to me a book called *Leo the Late Bloomer,* a work demonized in hard-core LD professional circles for telling parents of "different" kids that life could go on without professional intervention. When my mom finished, I would turn to her and say, "Leo would have been fucked if he was in Miss C.'s class." The words in that book, those moments with my mom when she helped me understand that the system was broken, saved my life . . . but just barely. By the time I was in sixth grade I was being held together by a thin thread, which finally broke one day, about halfway through the school year, in the principal's office. I dropped out of school that day. But something more happened in the principal's office, something that I never truly understood.

I had come back to Penny Camp to try to figure out why I dropped out of sixth grade. I walked into the office and was greeted by a harried-looking secretary. "How can I help you, sir?" the secretary asked. She must have been in her late thirties, not the fleshy old secretary I remembered, but nice enough.

"I'm here to see about some of my old school records," I told her. "I was a student here a long time ago."

"Let me ask someone in the administration," she said.

When I sat down I realized I was sitting in almost the same seat that I had sat in on a life-altering day in sixth grade halfway through the year. I had a new teacher, who had given our class an assignment to write a story. But I couldn't write. Literally. I had a hard time putting pen to paper, couldn't spell, and the process of writing made me so nervous that all my ideas got jumbled. So I decided to dictate a story to my mom. This was the first time that I had ever done anything like that.

Two days after I turned in my story I was called to the principal's office. I foolishly believed that I was going to receive an award, and I could feel my chest swell with pride for the first time in my life. I walked to the office, sat in the chair next to the secretary, and waited. But I was not being awarded Penny Camp's declarative prose plaque.

I was being accused of plagiarism. My mom had been called in, too. I held her sweating hand in mine as the teacher said, "People like you, Jonathan, can't have ideas like this."

We left school that afternoon and never went back. Something fundamental changed. I folded in on myself, ashamed. I disappeared and would not come out for quite some time.

The secretary came back into the room. "I'm sorry, but those records, if they exist, are at the district office. I can give you the phone number." I thanked her and took down the information, but the records weren't a real concern of mine. I thought of the bus, sitting unnamed out on the sidewalk, and I felt as if I were about to set off on that bike again down Nelson Street, moving between what was lost and what is to come. When I got home, I spent some time with my dad. We got drunk on wine and watched sports in our cheap chairs, which we've never managed to get rid of, no matter how many times we've moved, no matter how hard we've tried.

The next morning, I drove to my mom's organization, the South Bay Center for Counseling, where I would spend a week mapping out the route for this trip. It felt good to be back in the center. I grew up there, really; the space was as much a part of me as my family home. It still felt the same: musty, a little dirty, the hallways filled with the smell of bad coffee. I found a room and locked myself in for the next week, going through all of the stories that I had collected over the past year and figuring out where the hell I was going on this bus.

After dropping out of Penny Camp in sixth grade, I went to the center every day with my mom for the rest of the school year. I was so embarrassed that I wasn't in school that I made fake conversations about school holidays with the people who worked with my mom. They knew me and knew that I was lying, but they were kind and played along. I loved movies, and the center had three rooms with VCRs. I could watch films all afternoon. I dodged different therapy sessions, moving from therapy room to therapy room, surrounded by old cheap pillows and stained couches where people talked about their lives. The old furniture felt soft and warm to me as I lay there and watched old movies about knights. I loved *King Arthur*, about a group of outcasts, searching for something to save themselves. A hero's quest for this little sad boy. But I was determined to make a new plan, something to chase, like the Knights of the Round Table, a new myth for myself. I had to overcome all that was wrong with me.

Now I was back at the center, trying to get ready for my trip. Over the next week, I wrote down on large note cards selected information about the people I would visit on my travels. I spread the cards over an old map of the United States that I had purchased at a yard sale. The map was brightly colored, with reds and yellows and blues, and most U.S cities and interstates weren't even on it. This seemed appropriate. Here was a blank slate, on which I'd create a new map of a minority community that was connected by the shared experience of oppression, discrimination, and marginalization. I would be mapping not only a community but also a culture: the values, beliefs, and unique forms of knowledge that arise not *despite* disability but *from* the experience of being disabled in America.

With five days until I shoved off, it was time to stop screwing around. My bus had to be transformed into an RV, though recreational vehicle wasn't exactly an apt description. "TV is more like it," I told Kelly the morning I decided to tackle the task of construction: "tard vehicle." But behind the jokes, I was in a panic. All of it—the bus, the idea of driving around the country in the bus, living out of the bus— terrified me. There was also the minor problem that I was not handy at all. So I called Christopher Klonecke, Kelly's friend, a man whom I barely knew. Christopher was a full-time filmmaker who had spent time building sets. I needed help and we struck a deal. "Just come on down," I said over the phone. "It will take an afternoon, tops."

For the next five days, twenty hours a day, Christopher and I lived in the Home Depot parking lot, arriving with migrant workers in the early morning and leaving after midnight. Christopher had elaborate plans requiring complicated structural modifications. Soon, it was clear that Christopher was a card-carrying member of the freak club. He wanted to build two desks, a loft bed, attach solar-powered showers, and install a full-scale generator. By the end of our work, we were sleep-deprived, dirty, and I had spent over two thousand dollars, the last of my savings. We had installed one desk, not two as planned, and two shower bags that ripped after the first mile of the trip. On the last day, after twenty hours of construction, we sat on the bumper, exhausted, drinking beers. Christopher got up. "I'll be right back," he said, but before walking away he turned to me and said, "So what are you going to name this thing, man?" I still didn't know.

Later, I was standing alone by the bus when someone tapped me on the shoulder. Turning around, I saw this huge head of dreadlocks floating behind purple glasses.

"What you got here, man?" the man said. He was a somewhat deranged-looking black man who spoke quickly and moved in a jagged and angular way like an untrained boxer. He was smeared with paint; it covered his hands, his purple pants, his face.

"Shorty, man?" he said.

"Yeah," I said. "It is a short bus."

He looked at me and turned his head toward the other side of the parking lot. "I got me one," he said, pointing across the concrete to a purple short bus sitting out in the distance. "I'm Bob Henry," he said as he extended his smeared hand. I reached out and felt his calluses, scars, and cuts.

"I live in that bus, man. You know what that bus means?" he paused and looked at me intensely.

"I think I do," I said. "It is a special ed bus."

"That's right, man," he said. "I rode one, I grew up in that, you know—and now I live in mine. I'm a handyman, fix things, got all my shit and tools and life in there."

"Do you know what that bus means, man?" Bob Henry repeated. I could see now that he was pointing to the sign above the driver's seat. "That bus is the police, man. The police." Then he left. I walked around the bus and read the sign above the driver's seat that Bob Henry had pointed to: *You are responsible for the safe operation and cleanliness of this vehicle.*

I realized what the short bus is all about: It serves a social function. Our myth of who we are, who we should be, is actually created by categorizing people with disabilities. Disability is inherently a negation. In our culture, people with disabilities stand more for what they are *not* than what they are—not normal, not whole—a negation that calls into being its opposite: the normal. The normal looms over all of our lives, an impossible goal that we are told is possible *if*: if we sit still, if we buy certain consumer goods, if we exercise, if we fix our teeth, if we . . . The short bus polices that terrain; it patrols a fabricated social boundary demarcating what is healthy and sick, acceptable and broken, enforcing normalcy in all of us. What had I lost in trying to belong to the other side?

The night before I departed, I drove up to a bluff that overlooked the city of L.A. The horizon was a flattened-out plane, and the city lights were fragmented and disconnected: balls of light radiating like halogen lamps, exploding sideways and backward. A new story of myself was unfolding in the fog and scattered lights, in the short bus below me. I looked out one last time on L.A., out on my past, took a breath, and prepared to hurl myself somewhere new. I left the next day, on June 24, well over a month behind schedule. Becky, my girlfriend of five years, arrived in the morning, and we packed. My dad was home, and when he saw Becky he rushed over to her, hugged her. He knew I was hoping to get engaged on this trip.

I always thought my dad was ashamed of me, that somehow I let him down because I couldn't read well and because I wasn't good enough at soccer. As I watched him standing there, bent over and looking weepy, I saw an old man whose life must have been profoundly shaped by the same struggles I had. I've seen pictures of him. He was a sad kid with big ears and coal-black hair. When he was little his mom taped his ears behind his head because they stuck out too much.

And then, before I could get too sentimental, we were off. Just like that. Nothing fancy, nothing big, just the quiet turn of the key, and something new was set in motion. The goal was to get out into the desert, somewhere in Arizona, and spend the night. We picked up sandwiches for lunch and found I-10, heading east, suffocating with traffic. After an hour or so, my hands were sweating and the bus felt tenuous, unstable. When we hit the grapevine, a mountainous pass outside of L.A., to take us up into the high desert, the bus slowed to a near stop. I pulled over to the slow lane and the bus limped along. People honked. The bus spewed white smoke out its tailpipe and shook.

I thought about the past month, about how much the trip had already changed in me. This was my bus, a part of my life and who I was and who I was going to become. "Let's call the bus Bob Henry," I said.

2

The Lightning Field

It soon became apparent that Bob Henry was a sputtering sort of obstacle standing between white-haired men in Porsches and Las Vegas. We received our share of obscene hand gestures. As we drove, the bus heated up, the temperature gauge slowly tipping into that red zone on the dashboard display. As the temperature rose, the speedometer fell, forty . . . thirty-five . . . twenty-five. I pulled over as far as I possibly could after we were bombarded with honking, shouts, and what seemed to be a shoe thrown in our general direction. One middle-aged man pulled up beside the bus, slowed down, rolled down his window, and said, "Get that fucking tard car off the road."

It was going to be a long trip.

I had thirty-five thousand miles in front me, and much of the euphoria of the departure was wearing off. It felt like much of my life had come full circle. I was on the same road that my folks and I had traveled when we headed off into the great West that year when I left school. That summer, we had packed up the minivan for a trip to the western national parks. As we drove out of L.A., up over the grapevine, I turned to my mom and asked her why I wasn't "normal." That was the first time I had ever said that about myself.

My journey on the short bus has to be understood within the context of my family's history of insane vacations, which sort of represented pathetic attempts at middle-class conventionality. My father used to take off on some whim or time-share deal where, if we sat through a series of pitches, we stayed for free. When I was three or four, Dad packed the family—me, my brother Billy, sisters Kelly and Michelle, Major, our dog, and Big Kitty, our cat—into the station wagon and headed out into the desert toward Scottsdale and the Grand Canyon. On the first night, we found the only hotel on a long lonely desert street in the middle of Arizona, but it did not accept pets. My job was to distract the owners, to make some sort of scene in the lobby, as Billy and Michelle smuggled Big Kitty and Major around the back. Kelly put Big Kitty in her shirt, Billy hid Major in a sheet, and they piled into an elevator as I "ran cover" in the lobby. But the plan was a failure, and we were promptly ejected, forced to drive through the night to Scottsdale.

The thing is that my dad hadn't rented the kind of time-share you find in Scottsdale or the Grand Canyon or anywhere else. My dad, as always, had gotten a deal, and our destination was just a regular motel surrounded by nothing but empty desert. He loved the place and sat outside by the small sea-green pool with algae on the bottom, tanning and drinking beer. Michelle and Kelly played Miss Pacman late into the night. I fell into the hot tub but, because I couldn't swim, sank to the bottom and swirled until Billy jumped in and saved me. Our vacations, our trips, our attempts to be like the Joneses never, ever worked.

The summer after my sixth-grade disaster was no different than my family's other trips. On this outing, we stayed in shady ranches and low-budget campsites, but it didn't bother me. My life was changing; I was almost thirteen. "Ice Ice Baby" came out that summer, and often when we drove within range of any small town or city, the song came on the radio. I tried to memorize the lyrics until the reception disintegrated into static. I wanted to disappear into the mountains; I was a hurt kid, obsessed with cowboys, horses, and a straw hat and old gun holster I bought in Big Sky, Montana.

I slept in my purchases, hoping I might wake up and fight off whatever was in the dark with my six-shooter. I was afraid—terrified, really—of what was coming the next year. I didn't think I could fake it anymore. I had thought of suicide, but during our camping trip my mom and I put together a new plan. Our family had recently moved to a new house in a different school district. In the fall, I'd be going to a new school, in Hermosa Valley, and would start over. I'd go back to school as someone new.

As we drove home down the 405 that summer, I tried to think of all the parts of myself that I was ashamed of, that I thought didn't fit: I talked too fast, cursed, couldn't spell, couldn't sit still, mispronounced words, and interrupted people. I cried for a minute and then told myself to stop. I decided, at twelve years old, as dramatic as this sounds, that I would be a soccer player, nothing more. Just be that dumb jock. I made a very concrete and detailed plan: my training schedule, what teams I would play for, what camps I would go to. This was the only way I could envision my life.

In that moment, I drew a line separating what was acceptable in my life and what was not—a clean line between what needed to be fixed, expelled, and "treated." But what happens to a person who is split in two by that invisible line? How do you bring the two back together? I had no idea then—I thought chasing normal would bring me back together, and I wasn't sure now, as I drove into the desert.

After about an hour of driving in the slow lane up the grapevine from Los Angeles, I decided to turn off the road Becky and I had been traveling on and head north toward Flagstaff. I felt better. The other drivers' crude gestures, the heat, and the falling speedometer seemed less dire. We crossed a border between the last fragments of L.A.'s expansion and the last bit of desert that refused to be pulled into the city's orbit. The billboards and traffic evaporated like everything else in the desert sun, and the road flattened out, the sky opened up, and the freeway narrowed into two small lanes snaking out into the red horizon.

As I drove, I thought about that word *normal*. Before leaving on this trip, I had come across a great book called *Enforcing Normalcy* by Lennard Davis, who makes a strong argument that the word *normalcy* did not enter the English language until around 1860. Before then, we had only the concept of the ideal, which no one could ever hope to obtain. In the United States, *normal* arose within a cultural context as the nation sought to control a growing urban population and Americanize immigrants from around the world. Normalcy, though, is first and foremost an idea that arises from statistics. The normal, norm, or normalcy do not exist in the real world of people, despite the fact that we are told that we can modify our behavior and train our bodies and minds to reach it. We are told to chase it—in our culture, in our families, in our lives. But when we chase it—as I did—it disappears. Normalcy is like a horizon that keeps receding as you approach it.

The sun set behind the bus, and I knew the weather would soon turn cold because it wasn't summer yet in the high desert. By the time we got to Joshua Tree National Park, it was dark and the traffic was gone. We rolled up all the windows, and Becky sat in the back and watched the desert, and we didn't talk. The horizon was gone too; there were no cars in front of me, none behind me, nothing to chase, only Bob Henry's headlights streaking into the distance, illuminating the road. I felt the heat of the engine crawl up my legs and fill in the space around the driver's seat. I felt OK, for that moment.

"We're not making it to Flagstaff tonight," I said over the hum of the engine.

"No shit," Becky said. "I'll look at the map." She found a small town named Seligman where we could spend the night. I exited on Route 66, the old trade route that ran through the Southwest. The road was a caricature of itself, old motels wrapped in the ephemera and nostalgia of the past. We pulled into the first one we found in Seligman, the Route 66 Motel.

The place was clean enough but strange, stuck in time and clinging to its past. On the wall of the lobby were signed head shots of old B-movie stars. They smiled their fake smiles down on nothing but the lime green carpet and dust from the desert night air. I had never heard of most of them; their fame was gone now, and they were just pretty faces lining the walls of a motel on a dying road, their stars faded into the horizon.

It was cold the next morning when we got up before sunrise and packed Bob Henry in the clear desert air. Becky went to check out of our room, and I sat on Bob Henry's bumper, still feeling the vibrations of the previous day in my back and neck. I watched the sky turn colors and the stars fade back into the universe, and I drank a cup of bad coffee in a white Styrofoam cup. We were already well behind schedule. I had—as I would continue to do and had always done—drastically underestimated the timing. I was supposed to be halfway around the country, but I was sitting less than three hundred miles outside of L.A.

The goal was to get to Albuquerque, New Mexico, in two days; there I would meet a twelve-year-old boy named Brent whose struggles were very familiar to me. He struggled with reading; he spent a lot of time in the hallway and hiding in the bathroom.

But as we drove down I-15, Brent felt far away. My mind was on other things. We had another stop before Albuquerque—Quemado, New Mexico, a small town on Highway 60. In Quemado was a work of conceptual art called *The Lightning Field*, created by an eccentric artist named Walter De Maria. One of the rock stars of earth art, conceptualism, and minimalism, De Maria had bought a huge tract of land on an arid desert plain in the late 1960s. He spent the next ten years building a rigid grid of steel polished rods, each roughly twenty feet tall, driven into the ground in a pattern laid out over one square mile.

De Maria believed that art should be experienced, not just looked at, that it should be transformative. The rules of *The Lightning Field* were that you had to stay with four strangers in a cabin perched on the edge of the field for twenty-four hours. This was the only way to experience the work. It was there, in this cabin on a high desert plain, that I was going to ask Becky to marry me.

I looked at Becky; she was watching the sun and the road as I turned her ring around in my pocket. It was a plastic toy decoder ring, the kind that you could get in a cereal box. It was all I had, though. Becky was so different from me, at least on the surface. As a kid she did not stare out of the window of the special ed room; school had been easy for her. I used to say that her whole life had been easy. But she was the rebel in her prosperous, suburban, clean-carpet family. Her mom is fond of telling stories about Becky's defiance. Compared to the rest of her clan, she was actually pretty radical; she used to think she was adopted.

The first summer we dated, I found an old picture of Becky, the kind that captures the light and essence of a person like a still life. In it, she is four, maybe five, and she and her sister are at a pumpkin patch near her family's summer house on Long Island. It's getting dark, and the girls are posed near a scarecrow. Her sister is smiling and looking straight into the camera, but Becky is sticking her fist out, her lips pressed together and her face turned in on itself. She might as well be giving her parents the finger. It is her tough-cookie face, and looking at that picture, I fell deeply in love.

Now, as I drove, turning my plastic ring around and around in my hand, I was filled with fear. What if she said no? I had always felt like a little bit of a fraud around her. I had been so good at faking it, lying to people about whether I could read or not, acting like I was OK when I wasn't. I also still believed, somewhere deep inside myself, that I was that broken kid who wasn't right and never fit. Did I deserve to be with someone like Becky? Was I good enough? Maybe I was just full of shit. So much of what we are taught about ourselves never seems to completely go away. Even though I knew these feelings were old, and didn't define me, they lingered.

Becky and I arrived in Quemado by midday, and the sun was high and tight and spread out over the western sky. Quemado is a tiny town, with a population of under one thousand. It's filled with short white stucco buildings to keep out the heat, in the middle of New Mexico, between everything and nowhere. *The Lightning Field*, we were told, was an hour or so outside of the town center, up a private gravel road. We decided to eat lunch at a small Mexican restaurant, the only one in town actually, where old Native American men sat in booths and drank steaming coffee out of chipped mugs. We found a seat across from an elderly man whose face was brown with deep creases like a worn saddle. He looked as if his life had ridden him to this town in the middle of nowhere and left him to drink bad coffee from a stained white cup.

After lunch we met our companions for the next twenty-four hours. George was an artist from Santa Fe, and he wore the kind of cowboy hat that yuppies in New York buy at the Ralph Lauren vintage

store for a thousand dollars. He was a "conceptual landscape painter."
His traveling partner, Jeffrey, was a lighting designer who was living in
the Santa Fe area working on a local opera. Jeffrey was from Pennsylvania but had spent time in London, where he'd acquired an affected
British accent and British-looking teeth as well. Jill was a nondescript
single mother from California. Jill's traveling "partner," however, was
Meredith, a photographer from Albuquerque and a professor at the
University of New Mexico. She had wiry rough hair that curled out of
her head like springs. She was rail-thin and gave off a bad vibe. A
pedometer on her belt recorded the number of steps she took each day.
Why anyone would want to record this information is a mystery to me.

We left Bob Henry in downtown Quemado and drove to *The Lightning Field* with our new crew in an SUV. The road was rough, and we
all made awkward conversation, knowing in the back of our minds that
we were about to share a small cabin for twenty-four hours. All of us
were polite, chatty, and somewhat wary; I was definitely nervous. I had
lured Becky to *The Lightning Field* with the guarantee that we'd be staying in a bona fide cabin, with indoor plumbing and even a private bathroom. (She is the kind of tough Jewish cookie who is definitely not
down with outhouses.) As we pulled up, Becky's arm around my neck
tightened. Pointing into the distance, she yelled, in a voice a little too
loud for her proximity to my eardrum, "Is that a fucking outhouse?"

The car stopped and in front of us was nothing but a clear sky. The
landscape was flat, grassy, with what looked like small silver toothpicks
stuck into the ground by some giant child. "Is that *The Lightning Field*?"
I asked.

"Yep. And there is the cabin," the rancher's wife said, pointing to a
rustic log structure. There were three bedrooms and two bathrooms
(much to my relief). The rancher's wife gave us a brief tour, using as
few words as possible, opening the fridge and pointing out our dinner:
chicken enchiladas that we had to reheat. She then walked us back
outside and pointed us to the field and said, "You can walk anywhere
you like. It's nice to walk that way as the sun sets." She pointed clock-
wise, adding, "And then it's nice to walk that way in the morning," as
she pointed in the other direction. Then she continued, "The field will
change," and headed to the car.

Step-counting Meredith seemed nervous and wore a high-strung look that signaled desperation. I shared her anxieties. "Is there anything else we should know?" she asked. We had all come here looking for something transcendent, and we were faced with a dry field littered with toothpicks. The reply she got was not comforting. "Watch for rattlesnakes."

Things got worse from there as a dispute emerged over which "couple" would take the bedroom that had its own bathrooom. A very uncomfortable ten minutes passed as each pair tried to sway the other that they deserved the room with no bathroom. Their argument boiled down to this: The room with no bathroom had one king-sized bed, so Becky and I should take it. (Apparently only heterosexual couples can share such a bed in America.) It got ugly and Becky, always the tough cookie, was forced to drop what she believed to be the rhetorical trump card. "Well," she said to this group of strangers, "this is a little awkward, but I actually have my period . . ." and then stared bravely into the silence waiting for their capitulation. "I don't care," the step counter replied quickly and decisively.

After things got settled, Becky sat down on our bed and looked out at the desolate plain, full of rattlesnakes and small silver poles planted by an insane man who wore black leather pants. Was this the perfect place to begin a life together? I asked myself. Would she even say yes?

"Should we take a walk?" I said. I always walk when shit is bad, having come from a family of epic walkers. Becky and I had walked together, exploring more of the world than I had ever seen with anyone else. An hour or so before the sun set, we headed out into the field. The ground was dry and hard like baked clay and covered with knee-high shrubs.

As we stood on the edge of the field, in front of us was a line of poles shooting out straight ahead, and then to the right and left a line of poles that marked the edge of the field. We were alone. Becky was, obviously, underwhelmed. I felt the floor drop out from under me. I was a short-bus-riding fool with a fake ring standing on the edge of an absurdly pretentious work of conceptual art. But there was nothing to do about that, so we held hands and took our first steps onto *The Lightning Field*.

Becky and I didn't talk as we walked. We were looking for some hint of the poles' beauty. After about twenty minutes or so, Becky turned to me and asked, "What do you think?"

"Poles in the ground," I said.

"Yep," she said.

As we walked, I thumbed the ring in my pocket. This wasn't the right place for a marriage proposal.

Then Becky grabbed my arm. "Do you see?" she said, pointing into the distance where the light was shifting, hitting the poles in a different way. "What?" I said. "The way the poles are changing." "Are you high?" I asked. "Look," she said as she pointed toward the sun setting over the last line of poles.

I stopped walking and looked out toward the setting sun. It filled the sky with soft light and the last heat of the day, the kind of heat I used to nap in as a kid. The poles on the edges of the field were turning shades of blue-purple like glacier water. The poles next to us hummed with vibration. Then all the poles were on fire, reflecting the setting sun. The field exploded outward in each direction. The straight lines of poles were gone, the world expanded outward, and everything was changed. Becky was like *The Lightning Field* in my life. I had spent so much time without any hopeful image of myself. But with Becky, my world was beautiful and expansive. We stopped walking and I got down on one knee, cleared my thoughts, and said, "This is a three-carat, slightly imperfect, slightly occluded, plastic toy decoder ring . . ."

She said yes.

That night Becky and I had dinner with the rest of the crew, usually a feat that would require generous amounts of alcohol to lubricate my social anxiety. But in *The Lightning Field*, this feeling of restlessness, was gone. We all ate green chili enchiladas and drank warm beer and talked about how art like *The Lightning Field* can help us see the world differently. After dinner Becky and I walked out and sat on the porch. It was dark and there was no moon and we stood with our necks tilted toward the sky, the heat around our hands clasped together keeping out the cold desert air. I felt the soft plastic of Becky's decoder ring on her finger, twisting around itself, to meet itself on the other end. There was no moon so the sky was alive with exploding stars and orbiting satellites. There was no horizon, only the infinite universe visible. Something had changed, and something had just stayed the same. This is what Becky had always meant in my life: she brought the horizon to me, it stopped moving, and I stopped chasing.

By ten the next morning the sun sat above the field and the poles looked the way they did when we arrived—flat and dull. The world had looked different for that moment, back in the field; I had felt different, had seen a different way to think about myself, my life, but now it was gone, covered in heat and sweat, with the horizon and the rest of country out in front of me again. After breakfast, we packed up and rode back to Bob Henry. I felt anxious again, unsettled. I hoped I could find a way on this trip to hold on to the lightning field. But the horizon was already back, and I was striving again to find out what was on its other side.

My anxiety returned and stayed with me the rest of the day as we drove down U.S. Highway 60, through the mountainous spine of New Mexico. Then we shot back out into the first of many long valleys that would empty us into the low desert. After an hour, the bus felt more like a part of me. The road rose and fell rhythmically, and the sky shed its blue color with each passing cloud, slowly dimming into evening.

Out of the mountains by six or so, we spilled into a valley filled with heat. Here were twenty or so giant satellites, each a few hundred feet tall—round half-circles pointing toward the sky. I pulled Bob Henry over and parked next to a plaque that said these satellites were searching for life out in the universe. The satellites emitted a low hum that created a field of vibration. I could feel the humming and the heat collected from the day radiating from the steel and wire and paint of these beautiful searching machines.

I always thought of myself as a striver not a searcher. Maybe that will change at some point. As I stood in front of these satellites, I hoped that during this trip I could finally end my years of trying to fit someone else's idea of a meaningful life. But I knew that this journey was not going to be like others—change is a slow, hard, bumpy road, especially when you're rocking a short bus. Things would have to fall apart before I could put myself back together again. I pointed the bus toward Truth or Consequences, New Mexico, our last stop before Albuquerque and Brent.

T or C is a small town named after the game show, as a publicity ploy by the city, to bring in tourists. This innovation, however, was definitely not a success. T or C isn't much of a town; it sits off of I-25 between El Paso to the south and Albuquerque to the north, which is like lying naked between two people you don't want to have sex with. There is a reservoir that is slowly evaporating in the town and a few restaurants and old adobe houses with rusted cars adorning some dry and dying lawns. What had brought us here was a beautiful hotel called the Sierra Grande Lodge and Spa that I had stayed in some time back, when I had fled El Paso after a lecture. It is run by a man named Serge, who also runs a famous New York restaurant called Raoul's; this hotel was his vanity project. The Grande, once abandoned, was restored by Serge, and it now sits in T or C waiting for game-show tourists. Or crazed but hopeful short-bus drivers.

It was dark when we arrived, and we found our room and unpacked and then went down to the pool where natural hot springs run. I sat in the pool and then dipped underwater holding my breath to wash away the desert and the road. Becky held her fake plastic ring close to her heart, like it was a two-carat trophy ring. It didn't matter to her that it wasn't at all the ring her sister or friends would wear. She looked beautiful. She looked happy. Later, in the middle of the night, I had a recurring nightmare that woke me up. I was chased across the state of Wisconsin by this little kid with long reddish brown hair. When this kid finally caught me, I could see that he was me—before I started rubbing my eyebrows and legs raw. When the kid caught me, he said, "You're superman."

I had told myself that I needed some time to get things together before we headed up to Albuquerque to see Brent. That was a lie. In reality, I was terrified to see Brent. I didn't know why, but when I thought of him I felt hollowed out, unsure. Brent, as his tutor had said in her e-mail, was so similar to me in many ways, a kid caught in the middle of that machine of disability. He was a dyslexic soccer player with a single mom living in the burbs. The label "learning disabled" may seem minor in a world full of labels, but in the context of normalcy and self-acceptance, it matters deeply. A kid who on every other level appears normal and could pass for normal is pulled out of the crowd and told, in essence, that he isn't right, isn't like everyone else. Normalcy is created and lives and breathes in the middle-class world that both Brent and I come from. The same line was drawn around Brent that was drawn around me, the same machinery was slowly spinning him around.

The Hole in the Door

Brent and Sara

ALBUQUERQUE, NM

I was supposed to meet Sara and her twelve-year-old son Brent in the lobby of my hotel at 1:00 p.m. to talk about our day together, but I wanted to stay in my room, curl up in a ball, and disappear. Albuquerque had put me in a foul mood. We drove up early that morning, and after an hour on I-25 the desert was gradually transformed by the suburban sprawl that constitutes the horizon of most western American cities. After exiting I-25, we drove aimlessly around looking for a hotel amid the car repair shops, supermarkets, and TGI Fridays. We found one, near a mall, a few miles from the base of the mountain range that rises steeply behind Albuquerque's low skyline.

As I got in the Hilton elevator on the third floor and pushed *Lobby*, I felt like I couldn't breathe. Something hard, like a small bone spur, had lodged in the middle of my chest and wouldn't go away. I felt this knot expand as I rode the elevator down to the lobby. Looking up, I caught a glimpse of myself in the mirrored ceiling—full beard, unruly hair. I felt, at that moment, like a fraud. I knew that one reason Brent and Sara had agreed to be a part of this trip was that Brent wanted to spend time with me. Sara had written, in one of our first e-mail exchanges, that I was a role model for Brent, who was learning disabled and dyslexic, like me. But I didn't know if that was such a good thing.

I found a seat in the lobby and waited. I had no idea what they looked like, but from across the lobby I heard, "Jon! It's me, Brent!" and I saw a short boy, just under five feet tall, pointing in my direction. He walked over and said, "It's me, Jon, do you remember me?" Brent wore a white shirt that said *ABQ Soccer Academy* and had on tan shorts and black soccer sneakers. His skin was a deep brown, from playing soccer outside all summer, as I knew from my own experience. "Brent, what's up, man?" I said as I reached down to shake his small hand. Standing behind him, a few feet back, smiling through the glare of fluorescent lights, was Sara, his mom. I couldn't tell how old she was; she was wearing pleated jean shorts and a loose shirt and sunglasses, pretty, with short steel-colored hair, the shade of rusted antique tin. Brent stood in between me and his mom. Yes, I did remember Brent. We had met, a long time back, after a lecture I gave.

That day, who knows how long before, Brent had stood in front of me in the Albuquerque convention center, bathed in fluorescent light and the sound of the air-conditioning. His mom hovered a few paces back. His hands covered and uncovered his face as he talked to me, telling a story about when he was in second grade and had to write a few paragraphs on a Christmas tradition in another country. He chose Denmark, which made sense for the holidays, with the snow and all. But writing even one paragraph was tough. Words didn't make much sense for him, nor did school, really. Doing things with his hands felt more right. Digging tunnels, holes, playing catch with his dad on a warm desert evening—these were his paragraphs. That year, a friend of his helped him a lot in class, dipping over and reading the next page when they read out loud so Brent could get a sense of the material and not humiliate himself.

He didn't really write the Christmas-in-Denmark paper. He talked it out to his mom, trying to find a logical ordering of his ideas. His dad believed that his mother helping him wasn't right; Brent could sense this as his dad paced in the background. After Brent and his mom finished, Brent stayed up well into the night to memorize the floating words that were more like movies than anything else. The next day, he stood up in front of his class. All the other moms and dads were there. When it was his turn, he couldn't slow down the movies running through his head. He couldn't read a word. His teacher came up and put her arm around him, and said, "Come on, Brent, all the other kids read." That didn't help. Sara was in the back of the room, and she started to cry; he wanted to cry, too, but held back the tears. That is the kind of day that permanently changes a kid in ways no one ever really understands—even the kid.

When Brent had finished telling me this story on the day we met, I watched him twisting his body around as he talked. "Man, I got teased," he said. He looked angry and then said, "Those rug munchers," and he laughed, his anger coloring the surface of his skin.

"God, man, you're tan. It's been a while," I said to Brent as we stood in the Hilton lobby. I put my hand on his head and then gave him a high five. He smiled wide as though his face would crack. Although we had met before, I extended my hand toward Sara and introduced myself. She shook firmly. I motioned to the sofa, and we all sat down. I went through my speech about how we would spend the day together. As I talked to Sara, though, I sensed that she was waiting for a break in my monologue to jump in.

When she found that break, she said, "Well, I would love to tell you about the lawsuit. I don't know how much you can write about, but in the morning we can talk about that." This sounded familiar; something was mentioned to me in an e-mail about a lawsuit filed against the Albuquerque public schools, but in all honesty, I hadn't taken it in. And I wasn't listening very closely to Sara. I was watching Brent. He couldn't sit still; he moved to his left, then to his right, then stood up, and then sat down again. It was a familiar kind of restlessness, the sense of never being quite comfortable. I thought about his anger and his life here in the middle of the suburbs, where I was sure he was told he had nothing to be angry about, where life is normal.

"In the afternoon," Sara said, "Brent wants to take you paint-balling." The moment Brent heard the word *paintball*, he stood up and started shooting an imaginary gun. "Yeah, paint-balling," Brent said, coming to life. "Can't wait."

Sara grabbed a napkin off the table and drew me a map to get to her house. While Sara drew, I put my hand on the top of Brent's head.

The sharp tips of his crewcut locks were like shocks of electricity hitting the palm of my hand. Brent's body felt electric, and he moved his hands with the speed of flickering fluorescent lights. Sara handed me the map, a few lines in pen, including maybe three or four streets. "It's easy," Sara said as she left, "three turns from here, almost a straight line. You can't possibly get lost."

The next morning, after twenty minutes of driving, contrary to Sara's confidence, I was lost. I have no trouble reading maps. In fact I have a very good visual memory. The problem was that Sara's map was not as simple as she thought. While it was only four lines, the same gas station she told me to turn at could be found on every street corner. Everything in this place looked the same: the houses, the streets, the corner gas stations, and the landscape. This was a fitting way to begin my day with Brent and his story of growing up with a learning disability.

Most people and even some professionals in the field assume that LDs were discovered over time as our knowledge improved. Many people think that they are clear-cut medical entities like head colds or gallbladder ailments. This is just not true; LD is far more complex than something like a virus. The term *learning disabled*, in fact, did not enter our culture until the 1960s.

What we now know as LD was originally called *word blindness*. James Hinshelwood, a Scottish ophthalmologist, first used the latter term in a British medical journal in 1895. He developed this theory in a series of publications in the same journal, concluding with an article in 1907 that demonstrates the biases and errors inherent in the concept of *word blindness*. Hinshelwood wrote about four brothers, who, according to their headmaster, could not manage to read, in spite of their obvious intelligence. Hinshelwood assumed that the root of these reading problems was to be found in the defective neurology categorized by his newly coined terminology, and concluded that it was the cause of the brothers' struggle *before* actually examining them.

According to Professor Gerald Coles in his book *The Learning Mystique*, many factors were ignored in Hinshelwood's conclusion. The overcrowded and substandard school environment was pushed aside as an explanation for the students' struggles. The fact that one of the boy's reading drastically improved when the reading material was of personal interest (magazines about English football) was minimized, and the general living conditions of this working-class family were ignored.

Running parallel to the research and theory set in motion by Hinshelwood is the work of Alfred Strauss in the 1930s and 1940s. Strauss worked from 1937 to 1946 at the Wayne County Training School in Michigan, a residential program for children we would now label retarded, or in the charming language of the times "defective." Strauss's work was concerned with diagnosing, through mental testing, two types of defectives: those with brain injury and those whose problems stemmed from family or genetic factors. Strauss concluded that learning problems stemmed from neurological deficits. According to sociology professor James Carrier, "Strauss injected into the basis of learning disability the idea that incorrect, false, or improper behavior and thought is a sign of illness, which of course has the corollary that correct, true, or proper behavior and thought is the sign of health."

This history is brief, but in these two founding pieces of research are all the seeds of the current LD framework. The school environment was never questioned. The fact that many LD students are very good learners in alternative environments was ignored. And neurological deficits were presupposed but never proven.

Most of the neurological research, which attempted to tie LD to a deficit in the brain, did not pan out. And so, in the 1960s, the field shifted to an argument that basically traded a hard neurological basis for LD for an almost completely subjective definition. As a result of the rapid development of psycho-educational testing, the field began using an educational standard of underachievement (based on academic potential measured by IQ) to categorize a kid as LD. In short, an LD individual was now someone who had the potential to be successful in school, but was not.

This brings us to the present. Many researchers have hoped that advances in brain scans such as Functional MRIs (FMRIs) and other brain imaging technology would finally give us the holy grail of LD theory: concrete neurological proof of a brain deficit or lesion. But technology has not supplied unequivocal proof. Let me be very clear: Many good research studies using brain imaging do show that LD and dyslexic brains do have a different structure than so-called normal brains. Often the brains of people like Brent and me have smaller left hemispheres than most, the part of the brain responsible for processing language. However, the way we interpret this structure makes all the difference. We may also find that, while the left hemispheres are smaller, the brain is such an elastic organ that other parts of the brain are stronger and have grown larger as a result. This is hardly proof of a defective neurology. These neurological differences are not inherently problematic or patho-logical. LD is not a thing or material fact in the world like bacteria. LD is an *idea* and an *interpretation* of cognitive difference.

The reality is that there are many different ways we can interpret this cognitive difference. Is LD inherently a deficit, when emerging research shows that many LD brains have larger visual cortexes? A broader view of LD, incorporating research about the plasticity of the human brain, might actually discover that LD plays a specific, though as yet unknown, role in creative thought. A dean at the Rhode Island School of Design, one of the top art schools in the country, once sug-gested to me that over 40 percent of the student body was or could be considered LD.

The interpretation of these cognitive differences as disorders has, I believe, drastic personal and sociological consequences. Blaming kids for their academic failures leaves our culture's definition of intelli-gence and learning unquestioned. Blaming defective neurology, not educational systems, keeps parents focused on the needs of their indi-vidual LD child, not systemic reform for all kids. Brent's marginaliza-tion, his public struggles in front of his class, gives all the kids the message that what it means to be smart is to read well, write well, when nothing could be further from the truth.

On a personal level, I know that the conflict inherent in LD has consequences. The message you get is that you are broken; you have to change and fix yourself to be OK. But there is nothing wrong with kids like Brent. That's not what we're told. It's not what I was told. It's not what Brent was told.

———

After thirty minutes or so of driving around lost, I finally found my way to Brent and Sara's house. It sat at the base of a mountain, halfway between the poor people in the valley and the rich on the top of the hill. Brent and Sara lived on a cul-de-sac in a tan town house, in the middle of other town houses, which all shimmered in the desert air like a mirage.

It was cold outside when I got out of Bob Henry and stood in front of Brent and Sara's house. The sky, open and swimming-pool blue, spilled out in all directions like a big western dream. I was about to ring the doorbell when I heard some noises behind the gate to their backyard. I walked close to the gate and heard heavy footsteps and deep breathing. It sounded like a huge dog. Through a tiny hole in the door, I could see black fur. A child stretching on his tiptoes could have flipped the latch and let the animal out.

Sara answered the door, and Brent stood behind her. "I'm sorry," I said as I walked in, "I got a little lost." "No problem," Sara said, smiling. "I'm cooking breakfast, waffles, Brent's favorite."

"What's up, dude?" I said to Brent, who was darting around. I was eager to talk to him alone.

The first order of business that day was the obligatory grand tour of the house. White is really the best way to describe it: white and clean. I'm sure that Brent and Sara had shined things up because I was coming over. Their house felt like no one really lived there; it had a slightly sterilized feel. I was relieved, however, to see a few rough edges, small stains here and there on the carpet, chipped paint near a media stand. So maybe Sara was not naturally a clean-carpets mom.

As she led the tour, Sara's gestures were apologizing for something, and I could tell she wasn't from this place of soccer games, minivans, and Carnival Caribbean cruises. I imagined her on the sidelines of this life, as the kind of suburban mom who wears jeans that are either too fancy or too cheap, and who stands at her son's soccer games envying the other moms because they seem born to all of this.

Sara was originally from a small rural town in southern New Mexico. Her parents were in the tourism industry. She described a household filled with chaos and sadness. Sara was a good student, though;

school was easy for her, and education was the way out: out of the house, out of the town she grew up in, and maybe out of herself to someone new. After graduating from high school near the top of her class, she went to a state college, where she studied business. It wasn't what she was passionate about but it was a way to get a decent job. After college she moved to the big city: Albuquerque. She has always worked in purchasing; she is good at it, she told me. Tracking things, buying things—this type of activity gives her a sense of safety and control. Sara met Brent's father in Albuquerque while she was working at a home-furnishings store. But Brent's father was gone now.

"And this is Brent's room," Sara announced about halfway through the tour. The space was small but neatly organized and clean. It didn't seem like a room, more like a museum displaying the things that held Brent together: soccer and paintball, mainly. But there were also childhood mementos that said loud and clear, *This is Brent*. My eye stopped on a school picture on his desk. As Sara talked, I picked it up and stared at it. None of the kids looked particularly happy, but Brent's fake smile made him look like he was crying and he was clenching his fist. He looked like he wanted to launch himself into orbit, out of that room. If he clenched his fist hard enough, maybe he could make it happen.

Brent's struggles with school were apparent, according to Sara and his records, right from the beginning. Brent grew up in northeast Albuquerque, a mixed neighborhood both ethnically and socioeconomically. His parents, in many ways, were in transition from working-class to middle-class managers. After the first few days of school he hid under his bed. The outdoor world always made more sense to him: He was at peace outside, with anything that he could pick up, touch, or build. He had attended a day-care center and spent all his free time in the yard building blocks, digging holes. First grade hurt, physically: the desks, the chairs, the time and the clock on the wall marching in circles like a dog chasing its own tail.

Reading hurt the most. A word, a letter, a phoneme made his head feel heavy, as if it was filled with water. In first grade Brent was put in the slowest reading group, and he sat in the circle pulling the threads from the blue carpet and feeling himself unravel. He couldn't sit still, either. He would start moving one foot, then the other, then both hands, and before long he was standing up and talking out loud.

Right before it was his turn to read, Brent would raise his hand and ask to go to the bathroom. In the bathroom his stomach churned. He looked at the blue linoleum floor and counted the seconds on the clock until they were minutes, but they felt like hours. He tried to stay in the bathroom for as long as he could. But often he didn't stay long enough. He would come back from the bathroom to find that his teacher had waited for him. It was still his turn to read. Sometimes he would stand in front of his class for what felt like a lifetime stumbling over a few sentences. He wanted to disappear, a feeling that often never leaves a kid. It was obvious to Brent, his teachers, and his mom that he needed more help, and toward the end of first grade he was pulled out of class and sent to the library to read. Walking out of the real classroom, past all the other kids, felt like peeling off a layer of skin. But he thought reading in the library was OK, he told me; he got to sit there with a kind teacher and eat gingerbread cookies. That, at least for a moment, made things all right.

Sara and I walked out of his room toward the kitchen for breakfast. "Jon, this is José," she told me. Sitting at the breakfast table was a very large, handsome man who looked like a cross between a linebacker and a politician. When I extended my hand, he stood up and shook it a little too sternly. "José has helped me with the lawsuit," Sara said as we sat down and she served us heaping portions of waffles and eggs. Sara and Brent had been involved in litigation against the Albuquerque public schools for "discriminating against Brent because he is dyslexic," as José put it. It was clear that both Sara and José wanted to spend this time telling me about the litigation, and they started in almost before I could get a bite of my food down.

This is the history of their litigation: For almost three years Sara—on the recommendation of the school staff—paid for a very expensive form of reading remediation called Orton Gillingham for Brent. This tutoring, or as they call it "language therapy," occurred on school grounds for one hour a day, four days a week. It was helping Brent, but in the middle of his sixth-grade year, the school informed Sara that the tutoring could no longer take place on its grounds. After negotiations stalled, Sara filed a due-process complaint requesting that the school allow the tutoring to occur on school grounds. She believed, in short, that the school was incapable of meeting Brent's needs. So not allowing the tutoring violated his right to be appropriately educated.

After about twenty minutes or so, Sara stopped talking about the lawsuit. Brent was gone; my plate was empty. José looked at his watch and said his good-byes. The room was quiet for the first time since I had arrived. Sara looked tired; her struggle had drained her. She sat at the kitchen table staring out past the white kitchen up at the hills that lay over the horizon of their town house. "I just don't feel good," she said. "I have a headache." And then her words trailed off.

The battles for children who are different are brutal for everyone who tries to wage them. At this point Sara had spent close to twenty thousand dollars fighting for Brent. She was exhausted, like everyone connected to LD in our culture. None of us has the hours or the stamina to question anything because we are so preoccupied with the children's immediate problems. There is not a moment to question our culture's ideas about schooling or learning, or to consider whether the idea of LD is contributing to educational or social inequity.

Brent ran back into the room and slid on the linoleum floor. "Jon, do you want to see my room again?"

"Right on," I said.

Brent was passionate about two things: soccer and paintball. They held him up like the wires supporting a marionette. He expressed himself mainly through these two physical activities. Brent's passion for soccer was easy to understand. He spent his weekends shuttling between tournaments and sleeping in hotel rooms. The game made him feel good, alive, not dumb or broken. On the field, Brent wasn't anyone with a problem. He was just a kid. In all the literature on LD and in all the stories from kids like Brent that I've heard, the kids who survive have something that they care about, some place they go where all the talk of deficits and disorders disappears. His moments on the soccer field were, it seemed, the most important in Brent's life.

Back in his room, Brent pulled out a large poster that outlined all the differ-ent paintball guns that a particular company made. Jumping on his bed, he held his hands close to his side, moving his fingers like he was firing into the air. "I'm going to save up for this," he said as he pointed to one of the guns. Brent had an obsession with guns, but in a culture where the nightly news broadcasts video game–like footage of people dying in Iraq, this is not really too far outside of what we would con-sider normal. Yet Brent *was* filled with anger. Justifiably so, according to my way of thinking; he had enemies he had to fight.

Beginning in fifth grade, Brent was regularly teased. In our culture's discourse on bullying we often ignore the role that adults and teachers play in creating the problem. Brent and Sara will be the first to acknowledge that Brent was acting out because of his frustration with school. But Brent was also unfairly considered the "bad" kid, a label that often becomes a self-fulfilling prophecy. "Once you get on their list everything that happens is your fault," Sara said to me. Kids pick up on the teacher's bullying, as Brent knew all too well. "You know I'm way in the back of the classroom with my book and the teacher is reading to the other kids. I just feel left out." He put his hands on his chest and then spread his fingers out like a web. "The other kids make fun of me," he said as he looked up at me; his hands covered his face and then balled up into a fist that stopped under his chin like he was resting his entire body on his only form of self-defense. I looked right at Brent and his face teetered between sadness and anger, but not for long. "Fuck 'em," he said.

During the remainder of the day, Brent had no interest in talking about school or LD or anything like that. It was all just soccer and paint-ball. He had been forced to create a self that wasn't linked with school, an identity that wasn't all about what was wrong with him, in order to survive. I understood and respected him for it. So I dropped the inquisi-tion and said, "It's almost time to split for paintball, right?" His face lit up. I put my hand on his head again and felt his energy escaping like steam from a New York manhole cover. "You're going to kick my ass at paintball, aren't you?" I said. He nodded slowly, and then we went into the kitchen for peanut butter sandwiches on Wonder Bread.

Before paintball, however, Brent had to go to tutoring. He had been working with his reading tutor, Ann, four hours a week, almost twelve months a year, for well over three years. Brent claimed that he liked tutoring, but I found that hard to believe; it was the middle of the summer, and no kid wants to be carted off for an hour of phonics.

After we ate our sandwiches, we were late for tutoring, and Brent went outside and opened the gate to his backyard. A huge black Lab bolted out and jumped on my chest and almost knocked me down. Brent fell on the floor laughing and then chased the dog around. "He's locked up in the back most of the day," Brent said, "and man is he ADD!" When the dog finally calmed down Brent threw a tennis ball a few times and the dog ran and slid and brought it back and Brent's face lit up. I watched Brent throw the ball back and forth, and I wondered if he could hold on to all that was beautiful about himself in the face of being told he was broken. "It is time to go to tutoring," Sara yelled through the back door. Brent put his face down, and put his beautiful and wild black dog back behind the fence, "where," Brent said, "he belongs."

After about twenty minutes of driving, we pulled up in front of Ann's house and parked. I followed Brent and Sara inside, and we were greeted at the door by an older woman, maybe in her early fifties. She looked like a cross between a librarian and a Berkeley hippie. I followed her and Brent into her back room. Ann, professional yet kind, wore a blue dress that seemed childish for a middle-aged woman. Brent seemed to like her, and she seemed to genuinely care about him and believe in the work that she was doing. Her office was a teacher's office. But it also had the feeling of an intellectual's sanctuary—cluttered and serious. On the wall were a chart of the English language, a few world maps, and a table of world history. Dark and cool, it felt safe. I could see why Brent liked Ann. She was methodical, controlled, and predictable, all the things that can give structure to a life that might feel out of control. We sat down and Ann took a moment to explain what kind of work she was doing and what I would see.

Ann, who is a certified Orton Gillingham instructor (OG for short), practices what she calls "alphabet therapy." OG is an intensive form of reading remediation created by Samuel T. Orton. For professionals in the field, OG is both an after-school science club and a cult of personality. Many experts whose work is grounded in sophisticated neurological research hold Orton up to almost godlike status. And OG *is* very beneficial for many struggling readers. But at the same time it is very expensive and time-consuming.

"OK," Ann said, "let's get started."

The moment the tutoring began, I wanted to jump out of my skin. Part of this was just a personal visceral reaction; I remembered what I went through as numerous professionals tried to beat various reading programs into my mind. But I also wondered what Brent might have been doing instead of all this. He was a twelve-year-old boy, and here he was sitting in a room, in the summer, several hours a week. I wondered how that time and money could have been spent. Brent could have gotten an internship at a paintball company. He could have worked at a soccer store. He could have just been a kid. Would these activities have been just as productive?

About halfway through the session, Brent was told how to hold his pencil and given another command: "Feet on the floor, wrists bent, hands up." I thought of a passage in a book called *Discipline and Punish* by Michel Foucault. In one section the author describes how (in a French school system, around 1700) kids were told how to hold their pencils, not simply to ensure good penmanship but as a way to discipline the body. Brent, three hundred years later, was going through the same sort of process, and it seemed dangerous to me. If Brent, of all people, was sick and needed to be fixed, who was next?

"Dude, will this hurt?" I asked Brent later, as we pulled into the parking lot area of the "Field." Brent smiled. "Oh yeah," he said. The Field was a former parking lot covered by a net and splattered with paint. There, ten small and awkward teenage boys (and three not so small but equally awkward full-grown men) were lying on their stomachs, hiding behind cardboard cutouts made to look like buildings, and grunting what seemed to be commands, victory howls, or cries of pain.

"Two sets, OK?" Brent said to the pimply kid behind the counter.

My friend seemed different here on the Field. His skin fit him better; he had settled down and was in control of his hands and body. It is amazing how experiences that kids love can transform them, no matter how banal adults like me think they are. The guy behind the counter handed me a gun, some paintballs of varying colors, and a sweaty jumpsuit. "Rock on, you're ready to ball," he announced, nodding in the direction of the court.

Moments later, Brent was waiting for me, suited up, goggles on, making his air trigger motion. "Look at how many rounds I can get off," he said. Finger-reaction time, Brent explained to me, was the essential element of paintball. On the practice range, teenage boys polished their guns and shot tin figures. They talked exclusively about paintball: the equipment, tournaments, guns, paint.

"They're like some national team," Brent said. "Kind of stupid, huh?" He tried to laugh but he couldn't. "You know they told me I'm stupid," he said. He looked a little sad but then angry as he pulled the trigger on his invisible weapon. "But I'm not." "No," I said to him as I put my hand on his head, "you're not stupid at all." Brent smiled at me and then pointed back over to the group of pseudoprofessional paintballers. "They're going to kick our asses," he said. "Yeah," I said. "I don't think I'll be laughing at them in a few minutes."

Needless to say, I didn't last long in the paintball wars. I lay on the ground until I lifted my head and got shot right between the eyes. After falling, I was hit five more times, splattered like a Jackson Pollock. I lay there, watching all of the paintballs in my gun roll out onto the ground. Brent would have lasted much longer, but he jumped out behind his barrier, running cover for me. He was a goner, hit ten times, and then he fell down next to me. We walked off together, with me limping and he laughing. We were done fighting for the day. We took off our masks, and Brent looked at me, then off past the Field and the net that hung above us. "Man, this hurts," he said.

After paintball, I pointed Bob Henry toward the mountains, where we were headed to meet Sara and have dinner. We were on the same highway again, the one that holds the mountains to the desert, or keeps them apart, depending on how you look at it. He was different now; his mood was lighter and he talked as I drove.

"Man, you got your ass kicked," he said.

"No shit." My legs were bruised and my socks filled with paint.

"Man, when you jumped out of that bunker, I was, like, what is he doing?"

"I know, dude, it was painful, man."

Brent sat on the edge of his seat, tilting both forward and backward as we drove. I watched him through the rearview mirror, illuminated by the rust red of the desert and the gray synthetic leather of my old school bus. I watched Brent through the half image of myself. Brent was so much like me. Brent was at that place in his life where he would have to decide whether they were right about him: Was he broken? My mom had told me that the system was broken but I realized during my day with Brent that I haven't always believed that. I believed I was broken.

All the windows of the bus were open, and the wind was shaking Bob Henry back and forth. The desert blew all around us, and the houses on the hill were covered with dust. Brent looked at me in the rearview mirror like he was going to crack.

I didn't know what to say to him. I felt a deep empathy for Brent. I could feel in my chest the same knot that was there when I rode the elevator down to meet Sara and Brent the day before—I had lost so much of myself thinking I was broken. I wanted to tell Brent that this was all bullshit, but before I could open my mouth he took his seat belt off and put his head out the window, into the wind, the heat, and the desert air. Brent yelled into the desert as loud as he could, laughed, and then sat back down.

I didn't have to tell Brent anything.

He was fighting, like me when I was his age. But, unlike me, Brent wasn't fighting himself. This, I realized as I watched him, is the first step; it's all that really matters. I joined Brent in his primal scream. I opened my mouth like he did. I tilted my head back like he did and yelled as loud as I could.

"Fuck 'em," Brent said into the wind.

"Yeah," I said, following his lead. "Fuck 'em."

4

Steel Boxes, Crushed Cars

We left Albuquerque and Brent on July 2 in the early morning. It was still a little cold on the edges of the day, the sprawl of the city giving way to the desert. The goal was to get to Marfa, Texas, that night—though I had drastically underestimated the distance and time it would take. I had read about Marfa, a tiny town in west Texas. Donald Judd, a conceptual artist, had moved there in the 1970s and had taken it over. There was a museum in Marfa for conceptual art, and the spare landscape in the area was said to be stunning and unique. I justified the stop because it was on our way to Austin, but that was bullshit. Marfa was off Highway 90, a one-lane road that headed due south toward the Mexican border via the high desert and ultimately Big Bend National Park. It was certainly *not* on the way to Austin. Nowhere was really where I wanted to go, so Marfa was on the way.

Driving toward Las Cruces, New Mexico—between the two mountain ranges that I-25 cuts between like a concrete river—I was seized by the idea of disappearing into the desert and evaporating like water into the atmosphere and then raining down on the desert as something new or as nothing at all.

As I drove down the highway, I thought about Brent and the battles he was waging against normalcy. I did not fight as hard as Brent when

I was his age. A part of me had given in; I tried to be normal. I remembered, in seventh grade, I bought the right clothes. Parachute pants were in that year. So were Z Cavariccis, hideous and very expensive designer pants that had an absurd number of pleats on both legs and narrowed to ungodly tapers around the ankles. I put on the uniform. It is pathetic and almost embarrassing, but by the end of seventh grade I was voted most popular. I still have the yearbook, the only one I've ever kept, one of the only awards I remember.

But this, of course, didn't fix anything. That year and throughout eighth grade, I felt like I was splitting in half. On the surface I may have appeared normal, but in school, in the classroom, there was a continued assault on myself. I did not tell anyone about the reading, the passing, really. My way out, as for Brent, was soccer.

Wrapping myself up as the dumb soccer player held me together in middle school, but I still secretly had hoped for more. All throughout eighth grade I held out this dream that I would go to a private school for ninth grade. Halfway through the year I applied, and the day that I was rejected I sat on my oil-stained garage floor and burned the material from the school and sobbed. It scared me how I felt in that garage. I was crying uncontrollably and felt the heat from the small fire that I was watching slowly burn itself out. I was cold and numb.

By the next year my life was changing, but it was still built around soccer. My father had accepted a job in Colorado. My mom and I joined him in February after I finished my first two semesters at Mira Costa in Manhattan Beach—this in and of itself was crazy. I should have started ninth grade in Colorado, but we decided against it because I would have missed my window to play for the high school soccer team if we moved in the fall.

We moved in early February to a suburb outside of Denver and I did not enroll in my new high school, Green Mountain, until mid-April. On Friday of that first week in school, I sat in front of Green Mountain and waited for my dad, filled with a sense of shame and anger and numbness. As I waited, I hunted for hairs with split ends on my upper thigh. I was obsessed with split ends and when I found them on my leg, I pulled them out and held them up to the sun and stared at them. I liked the real fucked-up ones the best, the kind that split in all directions, growing in five different ways at the same time. I tried to pull them all out, one by one, for over an hour. When my dad pulled up he pointed to my upper thigh.

"What happened?" he said. I looked down and I was bleeding through my shorts. A small spot of blood was on my white pants. "Are you okay?" he asked. "Sure" was all that I could say. I was lying, maybe, I didn't know. I couldn't pull out all the split ends, but that year and for the rest of high school I was sure as hell going to try.

Around five in the afternoon, Becky crept up behind the seat and asked, "How far is Marfa?" "Oh not far," I said, lying. "But we should eat soon." She agreed, and so we pulled off I-25 in Las Cruces, a college town, and drove through its sprawl to a smaller town called Marfia. I had been here before, a long time ago when I had spoken in El Paso. It was supposedly where Billy the Kid had been killed. "This," I said to Becky as we drove past small adobes with broken-down cars in front, "is a *real* New Mexican town." "You have no idea what the hell you are talking about," Becky said.

After about fifteen minutes of driving, we passed a few orchards and the air filled with the smell of grass. We found the town of Marfia, parked, located a divey Mexican joint and ate burritos, talked, and swatted flies. I listened to two sorority girls from the local university talk about a party they had been to and watched a couple on what seemed like their first date. Then we walked out into the town square, which was really nothing more than a church and a few tourist shops. But there was a very cool old theater that showed art-house movies. It had a 1950s facade and, in the lobby, a poster for silent movies. I wanted to stay in Marfia and asked Becky if she could live there. "Are you kidding?" is all she said.

By the time we found I-25 again it was past six and we had five more hours, at least, in front of us. We hit traffic in El Paso, which is one of the worst places on earth. I would swear that it has the highest concentration of Chinese buffets per capita. The city sits on the edge of the United States and Mexico, and across this imaginary divide sits the city of Juárez, smoking across the highway that rides the line between these two worlds. Across the line is a third-world country where life is different: mud huts and neighborhoods without running water, electricity, or sanitation. That afternoon there was a UV advisory in El Paso. Huge electric billboards above the highway, normally used to announce traffic delays, warned, UV HIGH—STAY INSIDE.

Just outside El Paso we merged onto I-10, an interstate that could have taken us across the country through the South. But we weren't going to stay on it for that long. I felt the drive in my back, and in my hands, which were slippery with sweat. The afternoon traffic throbbed in my head. Bob Henry still felt like an arm that had fallen asleep and was slow to respond. It was getting dark, and there was construction on the highway, closing one of the lanes. Truck headlights floated off in the distance. The road was grated and grooved, and BH took to these small grooves like a train to tracks, following each one, shaking and swiveling and rocking back and forth.

Why was I going to Marfa? I was drawn to this town in the middle of nowhere, where Donald Judd moved after he became famous. It was a utopia, a place Judd had created, literally, his own world based on creativity and minimalism. He had designed many of the buildings. What was he looking for out in the desert? Was he hoping he would be different in Marfa? Hoping to change made sense to me; it made me feel a little less insane. I've always moved from place to place—hoping that something would be different about myself somewhere new.

"No more *Violator*, OK?" Becky said as we pulled off of I-10 onto Highway 90. *Violator* is a very dark Depeche Mode album that I had been playing over and over again since we left Albuquerque. The CD player we had hooked up was skipping, so we had bought whatever relatively "current" cassettes thrift stores along the way had. After Brent and my thoughts of split ends, *Violator* fit my mood. "Just one more time," I pleaded. *Violator*, however, did not fit Becky. That's how we were. I was a Radiohead kind of guy; she was a Lionel Richie kind of gal. "No," she said again very clearly as she ejected the tape. "We are driving to Marfa first with the sweet sounds of the *White Knights* soundtrack and then bringing it home with my boy Lionel!"

Highway 90 was empty. It was well past eleven and we had two hours to go. With the windows rolled down, we could hear the sounds of fields: the wind skimming the tips of the high grass. It felt like we had traveled back in time, and the monotony was broken only periodically by the rise and fall of the road and the occasional trucker pulling up behind us, headlights flooding the back of the bus, illuminating our silhouettes like X-rays.

When we pulled into Marfa, the town had the feeling of an empty movie set. The downtown was lined with solid symmetrical brick buildings, and there was an ornate nineteenth-century courthouse at the end of the main business district. After a loop through town, I pointed the bus forward, drove straight through the one stoplight, and found a motel.

Things looked different in the morning. We were up early, for us at least, at 7:30 to catch a 9:00 a.m. tour of the Chinati Foundation—which was really a museum. It is considered the first established viewing space for conceptual and minimalist art. We showered, checked out of the motel, and drove BH across a set of railroad tracks and back onto the main road. The town was beautiful and surreal in morning light surrounded by high desert. The desert looked prehistoric; there were high rolling hills on both sides of us, and open land that stretched into the horizon. The view was broken up by cacti and trees bent from the wind like contortionists. The light stretched out on the ground like a child resting, soft and warm and transitory, ready to change with the hours and movements of the sun.

About halfway through town, the heart of Marfa became readily apparent. In front of the bookstore stood several middle-aged men and women, dressed mostly in black, sipping espresso and gesticulating wildly. I knew this breed well: cool art tourist. But this is why I can't really hate hipsters: They make good coffee. After a great cup of Café Americano, we asked the clerk, who could easily have been from New York's East Village, for directions to the museum. "You mean the foundation?" he said behind black-rimmed specs. "Sure," I said as he pointed back in the general direction we had just come from.

Our tour guide at the "foundation" was a young woman named

Brooklyn, who wore an ironic T-shirt that said, "What goes around comes around." We followed her across an open field to an old building that had a glass roof and sides. Inside, lying on the floor, were thirty small steel boxes, no more than two feet high and a few feet wide, all lined up in a row. The morning sun was streaming in and the high desert was exploding on all sides of us. Each box was missing a different piece of itself. Despite, or perhaps because of, the missing pieces, the line of boxes was beautiful.

After viewing the boxes, we followed the tour back toward the main town over the railroad tracks to an old grain building that Judd had converted into a space to show John Chamberlain's works. Another total freak, I would learn—Chamberlain, I mean. Inside this building was his series of huge automobiles or parts of them, cars literally crushed into balls and balancing on their sides. Ugly, mangled, and discarded scrap metal had been transformed into complete, controlled, and still worlds of utterly surprising and compelling beauty. I wandered around the sculptures and felt their chaos like heat radiating from an engine. After a few minutes, I walked over to a book that held an artistic statement by Chamberlain. It was a somewhat incoherent but brilliant diatribe on the idea of cultivating laziness and losing, of all things, self-control. As I read this statement, my stomach rumbled. I heard the words *control yourself, Jonathan* echo in the empty building. *Control yourself* was said to me most days when I was a kid. It started in second grade. I would sit at my desk, and my hands would sweat and my face got red because I knew that I would fail the first test of educational purgatory: "sitting still."

I couldn't help it, but my foot bounced, then both feet started going, and then I busted out the drums with my pencil. After the drums, all my synapses were firing. I blurted out words and talked too fast. Miss C. would stop class, point at me, and say, "What is your problem? Control yourself." My body was always pierced by those words; it was as if lightning had shot out of her fingertips, shocking my system into compliance. I was so scared that once in class I pissed on myself, just a little. The kid next to me saw the wet spot, but he didn't laugh; he looked ashamed. I feared I couldn't control myself and that the rest of my life would be filled with people like Miss C. shooting their lightning through my body until I couldn't feel myself anymore.

Something had been lost in that command, *control yourself,* something I wanted back. I was grateful to Chamberlain for creating car sculptures that sat on the edge of themselves. I was glad to find someone who had invented his own art, his own standards of beauty. That, to me, was life's goal. Before I left that old grain building, I thought about Kent Roberts, the man I was on my way to see. Most people would consider Kent to be, at best, lazy and a little off. Or crazy and a degenerate. He was a conceptual artist, a humorist. He had moved from New York, via Gainesville, Florida, and was now living in Austin writing a book of "yo mama" jokes.

Kent and I had gone to college together, and I still didn't know what I truly thought about him. On the one hand, Kent—uncontrolled, lazy, and undisciplined—was all that I was told to hate about myself. On the other hand, Kent was brilliant and had managed, in his journey through school, to create or hold on to an essential self, a self that was his and his alone. Like me, Kent had been labeled with attention deficit disorder (ADD), an amorphous developmental/behavior disorder. But the paradox, to me at least, was that so much of what was good about Kent, especially his creativity, stemmed from his ADD. In Marfa, it struck me that the paradox surrounding Kent has relevance for all of us. Are our selves in some way twisted around, like Chamberlain's crushed cars and Judd's imperfect boxes? Are our deficits and disorders actually our strengths?

The next morning, Marfa felt like a hangover, the heat keeping its residents indoors and the art tourists in the bookstore drinking double espressos. The plan was to keep heading south, for another day at least, before setting off toward San Antonio and then Austin. Before we left Marfa, though, I had to check my e-mail, and so I left Becky in bed and walked out of the hotel plaza toward the public library. Distracted by a thrift store, I found myself sifting through old T-shirts and burned pans and other relics from people's lives. It was a tiny shop, manned by a single old woman whose name was Nelly. I bought a few T-shirts, one of them from a high school band that, when I put it on, made me look like a lesbian gym teacher.

When I got to the library, there was a child's theater performance in progress, and the moms and dads were watching the little kids on the stage. I didn't want to interrupt, so I stood out front and watched from outside through a pane of glass. I could see that the kids were singing. I put my ear to the window, straining to hear that sweet sound.

I stood out in front of the library and I thought to myself, Could I do what John Chamberlain had done? Could I transform my split ends into something beautiful? I went into the library and checked my e-mail. In two days, I would be in Austin, Texas. Kent Roberts was awaiting my arrival. According to an e-mail sent several days earlier, he was excited for my visit. He said he wanted to see "how fast that motherfucking short bus could go!"

We stayed that night in the Alpine Hotel, a historical building with an old gold rush facade masking shitty rooms and a low cream-colored flaky industrial-style ceiling. I felt a little better the following morning, the Fourth of July, and I spent most of the day at a college-type coffee shop acting like I was working. At about five in the afternoon Becky and I took a walk through the town and caught the tail end of the Fourth of July parade. Teenagers were hanging out in pickups, kissing as their parents drank beer from plastic cups. After the parade, we walked through the back side of town, filled with old dogs and rusted cars and boarded-up stores that lined the railroad tracks that used to bring life to this high desert city.

We found a Mexican restaurant crowded with people coming from the parade and drinking Bud from sweating bottles. While we waited for our food on the deck, a young woman brought out a small stereo and set it on the wooden railing. She pushed *Play*, but one of the speakers was broken, so mariachi music was carried through the air filtered like whispers over telephone wires. It was ghostly and beautiful, and she danced in small slow circles. She had on a flower-print, flowing dress that looked hand-stitched, and it spun around creating tight circles of color. Becky and I sat in the last of the afternoon's heat and had a few beers and watched. Holding Becky's hand made me feel OK, less anxious.

The next morning, back on the road, it was cold, but the sky was open like a mind after meditation. The road was empty, and I pointed BH toward Big Bend, though we would have to turn off before descending into that beautiful gorge. After about an hour of driving we decided to stop for lunch in a town called Marathon, the last town in the high western desert. After lunch we stopped in at an antiques shop. The store felt like a Victorian curiosity cabinet with high ceilings, old handbags, and masks. It was run by a quietly beautiful older English lady named Victoria. She projected a solid, oaklike sense of self, a trait that I have always envied in others. After chatting with her for a while, I became fascinated by her story.

Victoria had moved from London to west Texas because she had fallen in love with a cowboy (who came up and introduced himself to me). He looked like a character from a painting, his skin tanned like saddle leather. He was wearing scuffed boots and the well-known western plaid shirt with metal snap buttons running up the front. But their families didn't approve of the match. She moved to Texas anyway. "Back then," she said, "this was still the West. The *real* West."

He ran cattle, and she was a cattleman's wife. "We were happy," she said. I envied the way they seemed to fit so comfortably in their skin. Later, after a bit of browsing, I found an old mask—Mexican, Victoria said, used in birthing rituals. I bought it (impulse control has never been one of my strengths) because it reminded me of myself. One of my eyes is a little lower than the other one.

By now we were seriously behind schedule, and it was time to split. I was also exhausted, so Becky said she'd take the wheel. I know it's just my machismo, but it was hard for me to relinquish the driver's seat and so I bitched and made Becky feel insecure. "It is hard to drive this bus," I said. "Are you sure you're up for it?"

"Fuck off" was all she said.

She jumped into the driver's seat and piloted like a seasoned trucker. It was quite a sight to see: a five-foot-two-inch New Yorker in the middle of west Texas sitting on a pillow, lost behind the steering column, and piloting a short school bus. But when your skin fits, it fits you whatever you do. So I let it go. I put on my old mask and watched the desert float by through my imperfect eyes.

—————

It rained the rest of the way to San Antonio. By the time we got there, we were exhausted and wet. The bus, it seemed, wasn't held together as well as we thought. It leaked through all of its joints. Once in the city, we drove to the famed river walk and found a hotel for the night. (Austin would have to wait another day.) I parked BH, as it turned out, illegally. So I got back in the bus to move it, turned the key in the ignition . . . but BH was dead.

The next morning, I waited thirty humid minutes for the tow truck. Finally, it arrived, and I noticed the word *Tango's* written on the side. The man behind the wheel swung his truck around the bus like it was part of his body. When the truck had BH lifted, he leaned out of the passenger-side window, stretching past a young woman seated next to him, and said, "I can pull that bitch. Get in."

I got in, and the man told the woman to slide over as he shifted gears. She straddled the gear shift and put out her hand. "I'm Tamara, and he is Tango," she said.

"Tamara and Tango," I responded, "like some sort of variety show from the seventies?"

"That," she said as she lit a cigarette, "is funny."

In less than five minutes I had their story. Tango told me that he had moved to San Antonio when his life wasn't going too well back East, and that he had hooked up with "this here beauty," without filling in the blanks about how they met. "Yep" was all Tamara said about that. Then she talked about her life before she met Tango. "I found my fiancé with another woman, walked in, walked out, and just kept going west and found this here." She pointed to Tango, who smiled an ungodly smile of bulldog-esque teeth. "Once we bunked up together," Tamara said, between drags on her cig, "that fool kept on calling me, wanting me back, but I was with Tango here where I was supposed to be." Tango laughed. "Yuck yuck, man," he said as he navigated through traffic. Their lives had broken down, but they found themselves and each other in the shadow of the Alamo. I liked that.

Tango dropped me off at Pep Boys on North Military, a huge road with chain stores and cars rushing through an unbearable summer heat and haze. After a while, I couldn't take the waiting anymore, so I walked outside and called Kent to tell him that I would be at least a day late. His voice mail picked up, and all it said was "uh." I left him a message.

Kent was either a complete madman or an utter genius, or perhaps both, and my time with him would be about finding out how close that line really was in all of us.

5

The Sound of One Hand Clapping

Kent Roberts

AUSTIN, TX

The night before I was to spend the day with Kent Roberts—an individual diagnosed with attention deficit disorder, the coauthor of the book *A Portrait of Yo Mama as a Young Man,* a performance artist, an *Onion* contributor, and a self-proclaimed "freak"—I called him from my hotel, in downtown Austin, and asked for directions to his apartment. After some small talk, Kent got down to the business of giving me proper directions, which lasted well over half an hour. The direction-giving was punctuated, rather liberally, by pauses ("Huh, where was I?"), digressions on the nature of directions ("what does it actually mean to turn left?"), and tangential monologues/songs (such as the Kent Roberts original "I've Gone Country").

None of this, however, was going to get me to Kent's house the next day, so I interrupted my friend and encouraged him to try to "focus." And try he did. Giving it his best effort, Kent distilled his directions to their essence. From my hotel, I was to take a series of lefts, find the Colorado River, and follow it to his place. Though there were numerous problems with these directions—the streets to turn on, the specific address of his apartment remained mysteries—I chose to focus on what, to me at least, appeared to be most problematic. I politely pointed out that if I took four lefts, as Kent suggested, I would, in fact, end up back where I started. When I said this, Kent laughed and passed the phone to his girlfriend, Amanda, an Austin "native" (from college on) who proceeded to give me very precise directions to their apartment in the Shadow Oaks development.

The next morning, the drive to their apartment took between fifteen and eighteen minutes, as Amanda said it would. I took three lefts and then a right, sped five miles down a highway, took another left, a right, and a final left. (There was, however, one similarity between both Amanda's directions and Kent's: Both followed the Colorado River.) Minus the lefts, in a vague and circular way, Kent's directions fit the nature of Austin. Austin has highways within highways, exit ramps that curve in on themselves and loop back into traffic. It is a horrid place to drive any vehicle—not just a short school bus—but the city has a kind of beauty to it, twisting in on itself, its arteries rushing in no one direction.

Austin itself seemed flat to me, though Texans insist that the city is situated on one of the many rolling hills that run through the center of the Lone Star State. To hear natives, or transplants acting like natives, hype Austin's aesthetics, one would think Austin was like Rome—a city raised to the heights by seven mythic hills—and that the Colorado River flowed like the storied Tiber. Needless to say, neither the hills nor the river are mythic, but Austin is still a beautiful city, in a quiet kind of way, and the river does drift with a rhythm, pace, and purpose, leading nowhere in particular but still somewhere in general.

I arrived almost exactly on time—which meant absolutely nothing to Kent—so I don't know why it meant anything to me. Arriving on time is one of those ideas that matters only because we all collectively believe it matters. But Kent led his life according to a completely different set of values. What these were, exactly, I didn't know, but they were not ordinary. For example, once past the security gates of Shadow Oaks, I noticed that Kent lived on Jollyville Road. It would not have surprised me at all if Kent had chosen his apartment purely because of this street name. I could see Kent saying to himself, "Shitty apartment but great fucking street name. I'll take it." Sometimes, at Brown, Kent's life seemed to resemble a large performance art piece. Shadow Oaks, however, was not where I had imagined Kent living when he told me that he was moving from New York City to Austin. I guess I had watched too many slacker movies, but I imagined Kent living a faux hipster life: cool, run-down apartment, distressed yet fashionable clothes, beautifully ugly friends, and much witty sarcastic banter. Shadow Oaks was far from "cool."

But this suburban setting was actually quite fitting for Kent's story. Kent has never really fit any frame that I have ever used to make sense of his life. He is a paradox, and I was drawn to him for this reason. He is labeled ADHD, or *is* ADHD (we'll get to this linguistic splitting of hairs later), which stands for attention deficit/hyperactivity disorder.

Like many people with ADHD, Kent is profoundly gifted. He got a score of 1600 on his SAT, and has an unruly and intuitive mind. Digressions like the ones that occurred when he was giving me directions are quite common for Kent. At Brown, he began publishing a newsletter about himself—*the Kent*—that was at once a satire on the culture of celebrity and narcissism and yet also a very touching and honest look at his life.

One issue of *the Kent* had a poem called "Sad" that read: "Maybe I'm not so good at being in relationships. It's a possibility." Another poem was titled "I like to swim: When I get up in the morning, I like to go to the swimming pool by the office of our apartment complex . . . At first I had cut-offs, but now I have a bathing suit." Also at Brown, he was known for performing twenty-four straight hours of stand-up comedy. His experimental, edgy, and yet fairly sophomoric (in a good way) book of "yo mama" jokes consists of lines such as "Yo mama's so lupine, she chases rabbits." You get the idea.

What came hand in hand with these gifts, however, were profound personal and neurological weaknesses. Despite his creative triumphs, Kent almost failed out of Brown. He has the attention span of a gnat. For me, there has always been a question about whether Kent Roberts, like many ADHD artists and creative people, can live successfully in the world of conventionality. People labeled ADHD often have difficult lives; they struggle with social settings, with finding partners, with depression, and with their sense of who they are. Kent has grappled with all of these issues.

This paradox and struggle was a very personal issue for me, too. Professionals and lay people alike labeled me ADD. My mind does move like a spinning top and when I'm going full force nothing can break my momentum. But when I lose steam, lose interest, my mind wobbles around and wanders. I grew up ashamed of how fast I spoke, how I blurted things out, how I jumped from idea to idea with hardly a breath in between. By the time I met Kent, at Brown, I had learned to keep this spinning to myself. I was very conflicted about Kent, who was all performance, all spinning, like he was trying to appear by disappearing. At times I thought he was brilliant. Other times I thought Kent should just learn to sit still and control himself like I had.

I lost touch with Kent after graduation from Brown, though both he and I moved to New York. But Kent didn't last long in New York. He worked a series of odd office jobs and published *the Kent* from his Brooklyn apartment. He tried stand-up comedy, but—and this all depends on whom you ask—either he was too sophisticated for the mainstream comedy clubs or he just wasn't funny. During this attempt to make it as a comic, Kent spent all of the small inheritance that he had received from his grandmother, the last dollars he had to his name. After six months in New York, Kent left for Gainesville, Florida, where he lived with a few driftless and hard-drinking friends from Hanover, Indiana, his hometown. He continued to work on *the Kent* and got a job at the "Block," or Blockbuster Video. It is unclear whether he was fired from the Block or quit, but according to Kent he was hardly the ideal employee. He spent his time daydreaming or pulling bizarre jokes.

During his time in Florida, the satirical newspaper the *Onion* became interested in *the Kent*, and he and a friend got a two-book deal, *Yo Mama* being the first. He was back in New York by the spring before I departed for this trip, and when I saw him there, he was the same old Kent. He was late. He had on a black T-shirt with a pink pony silk-screened on the front. (Underneath the pony were emblazoned the words *Ride me.*) His hair was shorter than it was in college, but he wore his same old brown barn jacket that was too flimsy for an urban winter, and he was reading a book of religious philosophy that he had found on the street. He also had a new comedy act in mind. He would take the stage with a bag of random everyday objects—a cell phone, a cucumber, a slide rule—and pretend to stab himself in the face with one these objects. This was Kent, still planning his absurd acts and performances with no regard to earning a living. This was Kent, walking a line that seemed to embody the paradox of ADD: the line between utter foolishness and genius, the line between disaster and success.

As I headed toward Kent's stucco-sided apartment, I wondered: What is it like to walk that line? How does one have the courage to do that? I walked around the pool and turned the corner and saw Kent standing there with his dog, mumbling something to himself. I watched him before he saw me. He stood in front of his apartment building and bounced back and forth shifting his weight, laughing to himself at some joke in his head, holding a bag of shit, smiling.

"What the fuck is up, man?" Kent said when he saw me standing there. He moved in, bag in hand, to give me a hug. It was good to see Kent, though the bag stank. He had on cut-off shorts, an old T-shirt, and his hair was growing out and was in an awkward stage between long and short. He wore a brace on his right wrist, and when I pointed to it and asked, "You OK, man?" he replied, "Tendinitis, man." Kent had developed a bad case working on *the Kent* in college, and his wrist had never healed.

"I'm married, man," Kent announced as we walked into his apartment, on the first floor, right next to the staircase.

"Married?" I said.

"Common-law marriage. To get a break on this apartment."

How much of a break? No more than a couple of hundred bucks.

It seemed that Kent, though perhaps a little more successful than before, was still living on the edge in Austin. He and his wife, Amanda, had a lifestyle one step up from a college existence, but without the parental money and cultural acceptance. It was a slacker life, aside from the good apartment. Their place had two rooms and measured maybe about four hundred square feet. It was covered with beige carpeting. Kent and Amanda had lived here for a few months, and their furniture and accessories had been collected from various places. On the wall, for example, was a painting of what appeared to be a medieval peasant that they had bought at a thrift store. A sliding-glass door led to a concrete sitting area with an obstructed view of the community pool. If you looked hard enough, you could see a little blue peeking out past the asphalt and moving back and forth in the stiff humid air.

They had two dogs, both disabled, which seemed very fitting for Kent. One, a yellow Lab mix named Hers, had a seizure disorder and was incontinent. According to Kent, "Amanda found her, and she was doing this thing. When she has seizures she starts marching around, and Amanda was like, 'Wow, that's, like, really cute; this dog's been trained to march like this.'"

The other dog was named Luke. He was a mutt with some sort of husky lineage. "One of the first things, he had a hematoma, a blood vessel burst in his ear, and he kept pawing at it," Kent said as he petted Luke. The dog also had allergies and an unbearable skin condition. He had almost scratched himself to death, and Kent and Amanda had created a superlong protective satellite dish for him to wear around his neck to keep him from scratching himself. The animal was in rough shape; most of the hair on his tail had been chewed off, and one of his ears drooped.

As soon as I entered the apartment, I could sense that there was tension between Kent and Amanda. People with ADD can sometimes be a little hard for others ("civilians") to deal with. "Hey" is all Amanda said to me when I came in. "I'm going to walk Hers," she said to Kent as she walked toward the door. About five-foot-eight and pretty, Amanda had loads of self-confidence, which I admired, but there was also a coldness about her. On her way out, she pulled Kent aside in a way that told me to give them space, to just keep walking around and making notes.

I hadn't known Amanda long, but during our short acquaintance, it seemed to me that she kept Kent on a pretty tight leash. Now, as I walked around, I could hear her talking to him in a quiet but stern voice that reminded me of an elementary school teacher's. I didn't blame Amanda, though. Long-term exposure to people as complex as my friend Kent can be difficult.

Later, after Amanda had left, Kent began to tell me about his life. The marriage was not going well. The move had been hard; being in Austin was hard; they had no money. "I mean I might have to get a divorce, dude. She's on my case a lot, man," Kent said. Still walking that line, I thought to myself.

Not long after this, Amanda, Kent, and I settled down in their "living room." I could feel the humidity of Texas seeping in through the cracks of the sliding-glass door. I wanted to jump out of my skin. There was no A/C, and I was sweating profusely through my thrift-store T-shirt. The hot apartment, the sitting still, and Kent's inability to do so, the chaos of life that was palpable here—it all made me nervous. The moment Kent sat down he was back up again. He had never learned the rule that you must sit still. That rule had its nails dug deep into me and affected the way I saw the world. But I hadn't always been able to follow it either.

I wanted to get the day started, but that didn't seem likely to happen anytime soon. Kent had no plan, and neither did I. I was deeply conflicted about Kent. Could he ever "fit in"? Or was Kent, like many people who had lived through typical experiences with ADHD, a perennial outsider? Or were they right? Is there something inherently wrong with Kent?

"You know, I've heard of women who can shoot things out of their vaginas," Amanda said after a few minutes. When she said that, I became desperate to get out of that apartment and do something— *anything.* "Dude, what do you want to do today?" I asked Kent, but he was not listening. He got up and walked to the sliding-glass door. Illuminated by the daylight breaking through the clouds, he paced back and forth as the sun moved in and out of the clouds. "Dude, what should we do this afternoon?" I said again, covering my eyes. But Kent didn't hear me, or maybe he didn't care, or maybe he heard me, he did care, and his honest response to that question was "Dude, women shooting Ping-Pong balls out of their vaginas should be on ESPN."

Now to the big question: is Kent *labeled* ADHD or does Kent *have* ADHD? This may seem like a small rhetorical difference, but it gets to the heart of not only Kent's experience but the social function of ADHD in our culture. Before we get there, though, a quick definition of ADHD, some statistics, and a brief history lesson.

Let's start with the easy stuff. According to the National Institute of Mental Health, ADHD is a condition that becomes apparent in some children in the preschool and early school years. It is hard for these children to control their behavior and/or pay attention. The principal characteristics of ADHD are inattention, hyperactivity, and impulsivity. Some facts: ADHD is one of the fastest growing diagnoses or "diseases" in America. Some professionals estimate that well over 15 million individuals in the United States are diagnosed ADHD. But in the 1950s ADHD did not exist in our vernacular.

What we now call ADHD started life as the sophisticated diagnosis of a kid who was a pain in the ass. The vast majority of individuals like Kent labeled ADHD today in the past would have simply been considered morally deficient. In the 1950s, however, a more humane (or cruel depending on your perspective) diagnostic category was born: minimal brain dysfunction. This is pretty much what it sounds like. Kids like Kent were thought to have a form of subtle brain damage that impacted their ability to control themselves. Over time, minimal brain dysfunction morphed into the clinical diagnosis of hyperactivity, and, finally, in the 1980s, to attention deficit disorder. But what hasn't changed is the fundamental idea that people like Kent have a neurological pathology or deficit.

Now to that splitting of diagnostic hairs I alluded to earlier. Why does all this history matter when it comes to understanding Kent and resolving the question of whether Kent has ADHD or is labeled ADHD? A lot of people have complicated disagreements about the nature of ADHD. There are basically two opposing camps. One believes that ADHD doesn't exist at all and that the ADHD label is an excuse for lazy "bad kids." The other camp sees ADHD as a brain disorder caused by a defect somewhere in the frontal lobes. Under this theory, people like Kent *suffer* from ADHD and can and should take steps to treat their disorder. ADHD would never "exist" in our culture if two historical shifts hadn't taken place in the way that we conceptualize the human experience of health and sickness.

The first shift was a change in the focus of medicine. During the nineteenth century new sicknesses of both body and mind were "discovered" and the discipline of medicine—specifically the emerging discipline of psychiatry—became concerned with, in Michel Foucault's words, the dual poles of the normal and the pathological. It is only as a result of this shift that ADHD can exist as an illness. By no traditional medical standard concerned with mere physical health could Kent, or anyone else with ADHD, be considered "sick." Kent is in every way healthy; there is no physiological problem that he presents, but our culture is no longer concerned only with physical health. Normality of behavior is now the focus. Because of this shift, Kent's identity is filtered through the language of pathology.

The second shift was a change in society's view of abnormal, unconventional, or deviant behavior. Deviants, in the literal definition of the term, were no longer considered immoral but sick. In tandem with this new attitude, psychiatry's dominion spread from the most blatantly troubled individuals to an expanding horizon of human experiences. The categories of pathological sickness multiplied. The poor were sick. The prostitute was sick. The homosexual was sick. The sad were sick. And eventually the child who couldn't sit still was sick.

The search for neurological proof of ADHD has been shaky at best. Mainstream psychiatry maintains that there is universal acceptance that parts of the ADHD brain are impaired. The dominant neurological theory has been and still is that ADHD is a deficit of the frontal lobes that control impulse, inhibition, and behavior. In all the medical literature, this notion has remained fairly stable. No social or cultural conceptualizations of ADHD as just an example of human variance are given credence in medical circles. Nor is the interaction between the environment and the ADHD child considered worthy of much analysis. No credence is given to the emerging research that ADHD can be attributed to a gene that has been positively adaptive over time, connected to creativity, entrepreneurship, and, in some ways, strong individuality.

The other side of the debate is not to think of Kent as someone with a neurological disorder but as someone whose neurological style is *labeled* as a disorder. Under this framework, Kent does not have ADHD, per se. Kent is not sick. On this side, ADHD is entirely a social construct used to control "deviant" behavior. The trouble with this interpretation is that Kent and others actually describe themselves as having some extreme weaknesses that dramatically impact their lives. Kent describes his mind as a TV that keeps flipping channels that he cannot control.

I believe, however, that there is actually a third way to make sense of Kent. It might be helpful to think of ADHD as only a deficit or disorder in particular cultures or environments. During a performance, Kent isn't disabled by ADHD. Sitting at a desk, he is.

All of this, however, does not mean that ADHD, or Kent's struggles, are not real. In fact, I do believe that ADHD is a very real experience, but not a conventional, quantifiable sort of disease. Kent's story is not only a window into the social experience of ADHD but also the question of what kind of selves are acceptable in our society.

"Tell people I don't like to eat at Friday's, OK?" Kent instructed, as we parked in the Austin Arboretum and made our way toward a T.G.I. Friday's for lunch. It's true; Friday's was my idea. After sitting in the apartment for twenty more minutes, listening to Kent and Amanda's back and forths, I decided that action had to be taken. At the very least, we should have lunch, but since neither Kent nor I had any ideas, I picked the first thing that I had seen on the Austin map, the Arboretum.

Walking to Friday's, I realized that the Arboretum wasn't what I thought it was. Because it was listed on all the Austin maps, I figured that it was probably one of those new malls that tries to be some replica of an authentic walking community—the kind that has a fountain at the center and buildings made to look old. I was wrong; the Arboretum is simply a series of large concrete buildings built in the 1960s and connected by a walkway with an overhead awning. Along this walkway are some of America's finest retail outlets and, as we walked along, I could hear the sound of doors opening and closing, and I could feel the air-conditioning rushing out of these grand places, and I could hear the distorted sound of music playing out of invisible speakers. And then I looked at Kent, who did not seem part of this world at all.

"This place makes me want to puke," Kent said to me as we entered the restaurant. It felt like a corporate clone with uniforms, menu, everything all trying to make the point that whether it's Friday or Monday or Tuesday morning, it's still Friday here. Always.

Kent comes from a bizarre midwestern family. He was born and raised in Huron, Ohio, not far from Sandusky, the self-proclaimed roller-coaster capital of the world. He has fragmented memories of his childhood but remembers going to Sandusky to ride the coaster. "I used to take my seat belt off on the Blue Streak, an old wooden roller coaster, and feel like I was gonna fly out."

In between seventh and eighth grade, Kent's family moved to Hanover, Indiana—a town, according to Kent, that flew the Confederate battle flag in its high school gym. Among the many other things that happened to him in Indiana, he twice won a clogging competition at the Indiana State Fair: "[I have] video of one time and pictures of my ridiculous attire from both times as well as some action shots, e.g., one of me doing a—and I don't want to brag—but fucking impressive 'toe touch.'"

It is also fair to say that Kent comes from a family of eccentrics. One of his great-great-grandfathers was a traveling preacher, the kind that got on his horse and went from town to town preaching the word of God. Another great-great-grandfather, Kent said, "invented the seat belt, and his nephew patented it—basically the guy was like using it to strap his wife in. He created the fifteenth car, so they had a lot of money, and then the rest of the family all decided to become ministers and professors." What creating the "fifteenth car" meant, or entailed, Kent could not say. One of Kent's great-grandfathers was also an unruly old man. When he was eighty he got pulled over by a cop, who asked, "Do you need any help, old-timer?" The old man got out of the car, threw his leg up over the police car onto the hood like a gymnast, and smiled through his dentures. He said, "Now can you do this, sonny?"

As we ate our lunch in Friday's, I listened to Kent talk about his family history. He stood up, sat down, digressed, his thoughts spiraling like a saxophone solo riffing around an unruly rhythm: Bush's war,

Amanda, drugs, TV, refined sugar. I thought about how attractive the medical model must be for understanding someone like Kent. The medical model would see in Kent's family tree obvious examples of ADHD. Russell Barkley, the reigning purveyor of pathology, would take one look at Kent and write him a prescription for Ritalin. But this way of seeing Kent has so many limitations and contradictions. Barkley is fond of saying that there is no ADHD when the student plays Nintendo. What other objective sickness exists only when one isn't playing video games? (A boy with diabetes has diabetes whether he is playing Nintendo or not.) In a *New York Times* article, Barkley implied that the set of traits defined as ADHD officially become *ADHD* when these traits begin to cause significant problems in the person's life.

Clearly we are attempting to describe a very complex phenomenon with tenuous circular logic. When Kent performed twenty-four straight hours of comedy, a task that required more focus, attention, and self-control than most regular folks could possibly sustain, this set of traits labeled ADHD was not impacting Kent's life negatively. In fact, these traits were facilitating his success. So for those twenty-four hours Kent was no longer ADHD. Would some say he was cured? What other objective disease, sickness, pathology that you know of can be cured by twenty-four hours of stand-up comedy?

What is clear, however, is that the type of environment he was in played a significant role in Kent's success or failure. Kent's ADHD caused problems for him as soon as he started elementary school. About halfway through lunch, Kent looked at me, his arms moving in all directions like a Calder mobile, and said very clearly, "You can't expect a kid to sit in school for six hours."

He didn't remember much from first grade. He recalled his first-grade teacher, Mrs. W. She was nice enough. And he couldn't forget her classroom, or how his hands started to sweat the first time he walked in. His eyes went to the phonics chart, the blue beanbag in the back, and then to the wall of windows that looked out onto the playground. He recalled the rows of desks all lined up, straight and ordered in a way that made no sense to him. All lined up. That's not how he would have done it; he remembered thinking that. But he found his desk and started talking about his breakfast and Mrs. Sanders, who yelled at him when he rode his bike in the church parking lot. He had none of the usual self-censoring sort of inhibitions. He launched into further descriptions of a guy with crazy eyeballs who lived on South Street. "Now, Kent. Good boys sit still," he was told. "Control yourself."

In second grade, his teacher was "the devil creature, Mrs. M.," who he was sure had "a good heart inside her, solidly locked up, so it wouldn't distract her when she needed to scream her lungs out at the eight-year-olds." He remembered that he had to ask repeatedly to sharpen his pencil in her class. When he wrote, he put too much pressure on the thin lead tip, which would break. Then he would raise his hand.

"Kent, what is it?"

"Mrs. M., I broke my pencil." The class looked at him with pity and contempt, the same way she did.

"Kent, what have I told you about writing so hard?"

"I get excited when I write, Mrs. M." You had to call her by her last name; using her first name wasn't "respectful," he said. He had to learn respect, or at least the behavior people associated with it.

"Fine, Kent." She always said those words in a way that made him feel sick to his stomach. As he walked to sharpen his pencil, he felt the kids looking at him.

Five minutes later, he had to raise his hand again. "Mrs. M., I've broken my pencil. Can I . . ."

"Kent, what is your problem?" she said. As she said this, he felt something just completely drain out of him. It might never come back. At times like these, he told me, "I felt so anxious that I'd feel sick and go to see my mom, who worked in the school, to eat a few pretzels with her and calm my stomach."

"Another emotional-terrorist teacher," he recalled, was named Mrs. C. "One day she told the class that everyone thought they were so special, but everyone in there was just like some other student she'd had before. What a great thing to tell a kid: 'Hey, you're NOT special! Happy Low-Self-Esteem Day!'"

Another thing about Mrs. C.: "She made me wear a dunce cap in class when I did something wrong." And he was always doing something wrong; he never understood the instructions: *You number your paper by putting the numbers and then a dot after each one, not by circling the numbers. If you circle the numbers one more time, I'm going to mark all the answers wrong.*

As he told me of his experiences, Kent kept moving in his chair. The people next to us stared. This wasn't the kind of behavior they wanted to see in Friday's. "What a sad, sad place a school can be," he said.

After twenty minutes or so, Kent got up to go to the bathroom. When Kent came back, he grabbed my arm and looked at me very seriously. "Dude, you have to see this," he said. "I fucking forgot." I followed him toward the bathroom, and we stopped about fifty feet from a row of pay phones. Then Kent pointed to the phones and said, "Dude, I put them there, walked right in here in the middle of the day, and bam." I had no idea what the hell he was talking about.

"Check it out," he said, and so I walked over to the phones. On each handle was a sticker that Kent had bought off the Internet and that read, *This phone is tapped by the Department of Homeland Security.* I looked back at Kent; he was bent over with laughter. I gave him the thumbs-up, somewhat halfheartedly I have to admit. His prank was sophomoric, and not particularly funny, as is often the case with Kent.

"We are all being watched," Kent said. This made me think of something I had read. I told Kent that I believed there are two fundamental paradigms for controlling deviance in our culture. In the model of the leper, the deviant is exiled from the community. But the second, the truly defining model for our culture, is the model of the plague. In the plague model the sick are constantly being watched. "That is my story," Kent said.

It was raining when we walked outside, and as we ran to the bus I could hear the music from each store drift out into the promenade. I could see the dust swirl with the trash and the first drops of rain evaporate on the hot pavement. We got in the bus, and Kent was quiet and so was I. Talking to Kent had made me feel like maybe I had lost more than I realized trying to fit in. But Kent, he didn't lose that kid he had been. Something he had said earlier in the day echoed in my head like a disembodied voice: "I'm going to be a freak," Kent had said. "I've got freedom here. This will keep me free."

By the time we got to Kent and Amanda's apartment, the rain was coming down in sheets, though some of the sky was still blue and sunny. I always loved that kind of rain when I was kid; I used to walk out of my house on Nelson in Manhattan Beach toward the blue sky, hoping to find the exact place where the rain stopped so I could stand on one of the seams in the world, where one foot was wet and the other dry. But I never found it.

"Dude, do you ever not quite feel like yourself?" Kent asked me after we shook off the rain and sat down in the living room. "I mean, man, sometimes, you know, I just don't feel like myself. I think this is true," he continued, "my way of fitting in was being the freak. It is not just a way of saying *fuck you*. It's saying *I want to be known*."

His sense of feeling unknown, invisible, started in first grade, when one of his classmates, who often brought Fruit Roll-Ups to class, brought them for all the other kids but not for him. He still remembers the color of the wrapper and the red of the artificial coloring and how it rubbed off on the rest of the kids' hands but not his. Hurt by this slight, Kent went to his desk and wrote the names of the friends he had, but he could only come up with a few people. Then one day he decided to eat the cover of his phonics book. Ripped it up, chewed each piece, and swallowed it like a good kid at the dinner table, sitting still and eating all his food. And then it happened. The kids laughed. At him, with him—it did not matter—they laughed.

So began Kent's paradoxical relationship to performance. When I asked about the day he ate his phonics book he said, "I realized from the ensuing wave of attention the power of a silly gesture." But, at the same time, Kent's performance was a brilliant turning of the tables on his ADHD. He took what he had no control over—his impulsivity, his rambling mind—and made it something funny, engaging, even beautiful. And all this started early—the phonics book was a beginning, but Kent really transformed his deficits in seventh grade.

In seventh grade, Kent walked into the first day of his English class and sat down in the middle of the classroom. He watched Mrs. K. pace back and forth, he watched the girl next to him, and then he saw the dust on the floor. Suddenly, he thought of a yo mama joke and heard his own voice play out the joke in all kinds of variations, turning it upside down, sideways, and backwards. He watched the clock tick. It was only 9:55 a.m. and he had thirty-five more minutes to sit in this class. He felt his hands burn and his insides twist like origami, and he tried to slow his mind down as the teacher talked about *To Kill a Mockingbird*. He tried not to blurt out answers before she actually asked the questions. Suddenly at 10:00 a.m. he found himself standing up in the middle of his class and yelling, "Surprise!" repeatedly for exactly one minute and then he sat down.

The next day, Kent found his seat again and watched the clock, and ten minutes into the class he yelled "Surprise!" again for one minute and then sat down. The day after that, Kent found his seat again and watched the clock, and ten minutes into the class he yelled "Surprise!" for one minute and then sat down. The day after that, Kent found his seat again and watched the clock and ten minutes into the class he yelled "Surprise!" for one minute and then sat down.

He did it every day that year. If he couldn't be the kid who could sit still, he would be the one who yelled "Surprise!"

After he finished telling this story, Kent disappeared into the other room and I sat and listened to the thunder out over the hills of Austin and felt the humidity. I thought about how hard Kent had fought to be noticed, how he had been willing to risk being misunderstood, humiliated, and rejected to be recognized for who he was. And Kent was still taking huge risks with his creative pursuits—from performing stand-up to writing books and songs. But I can't divorce Kent and his art from what causes pain in Kent's life. This is true in the lives of many individuals labeled ADHD. Their greatest gifts are interwoven with their greatest weaknesses. This might be true for all of us. But we can make something beautiful from this paradox. Our lives can sometimes be a sort of poem—part genetics, part individual adaptation.

When Kent came back in the room, he seemed different. It was as if he had hit the right groove and the music of his self was playing loud and clear. He ran around the room humming a tune, "Surprise." Then he launched into a song he had composed, "Gone Country." As he sang it, he almost disappeared into a character he had created, a character appropriate to the lyrics.

great

I gone country, with my big ol' hat,

Long black boots, and a big ol' hat.

I gone country, with that big ol' hat,

Did I mention my hat? I got a big ol' hat.

Got a tattoo o' Texas in my left armpit.

Book learnin' types can rub their face in dog shit.

Rub yer four eyes in that shit.

Ya better take yer evolutionaryism 'n' split.

I gone country.

Takin' muh belt to muh wife.

Molestin muh children gives meanin' to muh life.

I gone Proverbs, Chapter 19, Verse 18: Discipline your children while
    they are young enough to learn, but don't punish them so hard that
    you kill them.

I watched Kent singing and dancing. He moved his arms up and down, close to his body, his teeth biting down on his lower lip, in time to a silent rhythm. He was dancing through this world of his past, his present, and his creation. He had invented a unique sort of survival technique and was claiming his place in the world. Maybe the more conventional among us cling deeply to the idea of a fixed self, stable and controlled. Kent actively violates this notion with his very presence. But at what cost? At what point does the revolt become its own trap?

"Yeah, he just likes to dance, man," Kent sang, shimmying along the carpet. "That's what he does, man, he dances."

Kent and Amanda later suggested that we all go to the river and take a walk, and then swim. "Sure," I said. Kent and I got in Bob Henry to follow Amanda and Luke down to a tributary of the Colorado River. As we drove, I wondered if Kent would ever outgrow his need to perform. After all, he did get a perfect score on his SATs, go to Brown, and manage to graduate. Kent crept up to the front of the bus, kneeled behind the driver's seat, sat down, and said, "In high school, I tried to be perfect, man, and it freaked me out."

Back in high school, despite his often unconventional demeanor, Kent still felt the pressure to conform, or, as he put it, the pressure to get his shit together. He was a bright kid, gifted intellectually, but by ninth grade he was struggling intensely on the academic front. In tenth grade, after a pep talk from one of his friends, Kent decided that he would get a 4.0 that year and that he would get a 1600 on his SATs. He prepped for the tests by locking himself in his room for hours on end and succeeded. He got a 1600 that year. He also got close to a perfect G.P.A. Another performance? I think his effort reflected something that we all feel deeply, no matter whether or not we admit it. That is the very real desire for social recognition and prestige. Regardless of his motive, he was a success. But at what cost? He told me that his SAT score convinced him that he could be normal, or "perfect," as he put it, all the time. But the effort involved was too grueling for him to keep it up. He started to hate himself.

We parked at the river, found a trail, and walked in single file. Amanda led the way, with Kent in the middle, and me bringing up the rear. It was still hot and humid, and it must have rained for longer than I thought, because the trail was flooded at certain points. The plan was to head to a swimming hole.

Amanda seemed to have softened for a moment. I saw her smile as the wave of energy that Kent brings in his moments of high spirits lifted her up. But later, she went on ahead with Luke and her face turned hard. Amanda, I learned, had attention problems in school as well. She spent most of her time at the University of Texas sleeping late and going to clubs. But she stopped that and learned how to fit into the world.

As we walked, I thought about Kent in high school, pursuing that 1600 score with all the energy he had. The thought of this bummed me out a little, to be honest. This quest for success made me wonder what Kent would do if his upcoming book wasn't successful or was ignored, as so many are. What if Kent's outsider act put him too far outside?

"Here's the fucking swimming hole, man," Kent said, laughing in his corny way. But it was really not much of a swimming hole; the water was polluted and slime green. Kent immediately stripped down and jumped in.

We've come here, all this way, to swim in this shit? I thought to myself. *No, not me.*

"I'm going to hit the rope swing, man. Got to love the rope swing."

After Kent got a perfect score on the SAT he was granted an interview at Harvard. The day of the interview, he dressed nicely, very conventionally: in khakis, a button-down shirt, and a tie purchased from a thrift shop. He was a snappy dresser, he thought. He walked into the admissions office, shook hands with the admissions officer. His foot didn't bounce, this time; he made it stay down on the floor like a good dog. He made eye contact with the interviewer, listened intently, nodded his head, and when it was his turn to speak began with something like "I really feel Harvard is the right place for me pedagogically." He continued, expounding theories of knowledge and pedagogy and curriculum, for approximately ten minutes, until Kent was asked about the "stand-up comedy" on his application. Kent's response to this question was to act like his body had caught fire.

He screamed and began to move frenetically around the room. He grabbed the admission officer's coffee cup and doused himself with it. All of this culminated in Kent screaming, "Somebody help me! I'm on fire!" Needless to say, he did not get into Harvard. And he didn't give a damn.

Back in Indiana, Kent took to wearing a self-imposed uniform. It consisted of a white T-shirt (he always wrote the day of the week on it) and black cut-off shorts. He wore this particular ensemble every day during his senior year in high school. That year, Kent was valedictorian. He was forced to give his graduation speech under the Confederate flag that his high school flew in the auditorium. Kent was strongly discouraged by friends and family from doing anything Kent-like—whatever that meant—while delivering his speech. He did (and did not) follow their advice. At graduation, Kent stood up in front of his peers, family, and community and gave a scathing critique of racism in his school community and American culture. It was not Kent-like—there was no screaming—but he had never felt more like himself on any day of his life.

I didn't swim that day in Austin, but Kent did. He climbed to the highest part of the hill and grabbed onto a shoddy swing. Running full force, he leaped into the air and swung himself back and forth, singing a song about a steamroller. He swung back and forth. The faster he moved, the clearer the picture I got of the real Kent—always in perpetual motion. Then Kent let go and yelled something again about the steamroller and cannonballed into the filthy water. When he stood up, Amanda and I both laughed, not at him, at something—I don't know what. All I know is that we were laughing and Kent was standing in the water, smiling like a fool.

It was almost 10:00 p.m., and the day was over. I had picked up Becky from our hotel so she could have dinner with us. We were sitting in Don's Depot, a bar made out of an old train, having a drink and getting ready to say good-bye. It was still hot out but cool in the Depot. It was oldies night. On the dance floor, old people moved to the music of their youth. Kent was sitting across from me, and I looked at him and I saw him, really took him in, for the first time that day: hazel eyes and straight reddish blond hair, pale, and skinny like a bone. He wasn't moving at all, wasn't performing or trying not to disappear. We were all tired from our day. I thought I had learned something about Kent that I hadn't quite gotten before.

When Kent moved to Hanover, Indiana, he knew no one and was scared to start eighth grade as a new student. People always made him a little nervous; he didn't really know how to play their games or at least not the type of tough games that adolescents play. So Kent came up with a plan for the first day of school—a way to make friends. He decided that he would show anyone who would look something special that he had spent his entire life assembling: his sticker collection.

Kent was a sight to see the first day of eighth grade. He had on hot-pink pants and a purple lycra shirt (the kind his obviously gay piano teacher wore) and a green argyle sweater that he had gotten from his grandfather. He liked that shirt and those pants, and he wanted to look nice the first day of school. That day, Kent went from kid to kid, showing each one his sticker collection. The thing was, Kent's stickers were all collected off fruit from the grocery store and other random objects: Chiquita banana stickers, stickers from tomatoes and honeydew melons, stickers from dental floss. He had about two hundred. This is Kent to me: in eighth grade wearing hot-pink pants and a lycra purple shirt and showing everyone, in a very serious way, his book of stickers. This is Kent showing us the beauty in something we see, and yet don't see, every day.

"Growing up," Kent told me later, "I was this thing that I clung to as the real thing, and then there was the outside world. *Why aren't people fitting into our society we set up?* Maybe it is the society that is wrong and not that kid."

At the Depot, we sat and watched the old people dance. Kent launched into a monologue about being a streamroller: "I'm a steamroller, I'm rolling down the street." When he stopped, it was the first time any of us were quiet all day. I just sat and thought about Kent and who he is. Kent is caught, like most of us, between the desire to fit in and the desire for individual freedom. Some people resolve this struggle, or give up, but Kent is still engaged and taken up by it. I watched the candle on our table burn, the trail of its flame twisting in the air, and I thought of a new way to describe Kent. He is like that moment when water is boiling and it ceases to be water but isn't steam yet; it's something and nothing, its essence shifting and changing, always becoming. Kent, unlike many of us, lives in that state of of creation, of coming and going.

"When I was a kid," he said to me later, "I had the perspective that I would never allow my mind not to have a thought. I would never stop it by saying, 'No that is a bad thought.' I don't know what it was. I just thought that that was right, that is what human beings should do, allow their minds to expand in different directions." In other words, Kent gave full rein to his true self, without judgment. I envied that.

I looked over at Amanda. I could understand why she was so conflicted about her common-law husband. He can be hard to take at times, given his eccentric behavior, but he seems to be experiencing life at a faster speed or greater intensity than most people. And his embodiment of the unsettled self, the shifting self, and uncontrolled self is something we can all relate to. I remembered a poem that Amanda had written for *the Kent* before the two of them started dating. It was meant as a joke—but then again, maybe it wasn't. It may be a lot more: "You ask why . . . Because I ache with a lack . . . of sensibility . . . I could get lost . . . for hours, with you . . . alone . . . oh Kent— this is why I hung you . . . on the office door . . . because I want to know . . . only the things Kent can show me . . . Because I want to feel." Not only Amanda but all of us need people like Kent. They set us free in a way.

I didn't want to leave the Depot. I sat back, watching the old people dance like kids. Then the dancing was over. The band packed up and the old people went back to their chairs, to their cigarettes, to their drinks and dates, and there was nothing more to watch. It was time to go. I looked over and thought I saw Kent clapping with one hand back and forth, back and forth. I was washed over with the sound of old people going home and the sound of Kent's one hand clapping, and I felt grateful to Kent. I admire him. What I realized in the Depot is that I was actually rooting for Kent, and maybe even for myself, in a way I never have before. With Kent, I felt OK, as I was—my leg bouncing, my mind racing, not sitting still in the Depot.

I wish, though, I could say that I know Kent will be OK or successful, but I can't. Sometime after our visit, Kent and Amanda broke up. Kent's *Yo Mama* came out and got some great reviews but sold poorly. He never finished a second book. For a while Kent moved back home with his parents in Indiana, "to heal his wrists," he said mysteriously. But I think it was much more. I think there is a very real chance that Kent could end up living with his parents for good or working at Blockbuster for the rest of his life. Or he could be famous. I don't know if there is a middle ground where he could exist.

"I know I'll be a great artist," Kent told me. When I asked him what he meant by that, he said, "I'll stay true to my vision. There are so many things trying to steamroll you. That is the hardest thing, to stay true to your self. You know, when your head is going crazy, man, it is the hardest thing to love your self." But then Kent laughed. "You know," he continued, "I might be dying tomorrow and lying there cursing God because I died and all I did was write a goddamn yo mama book. But you know, I might be dying and have enough of a sense of humor to see the fact that I did not become a great artist, that all I did was write a few yo mama jokes, as the ending to a damn good joke."

Kent stands on a line between fool and sage, between fame and alienation. He doesn't flinch, doesn't run. He stands on that line and smiles.

6

Welcome Pest Controllers Association

It rained the day we left Austin. The air was humid. The humidity would follow us all the way to Richmond. There I would spend time with a little girl named Ashley and her family. Becky was scheduled to leave the bus at Richmond and head home to New York to start graduate school. For the next ten days I would have to get used to feeling inside out. I was already missing her.

The morning we left Austin, though, it hadn't started to rain yet and I got up before Becky and headed down to Congress Avenue for a cup of coffee and some breakfast. I found a decent, little, hip-around-the-edges coffee shop and drank black coffee, watching the traffic and eavesdropping on Austinites. They were starting their day with gossip and talk of the pending rain.

As I sipped my coffee, I saw across the street a man who appeared to be in drag, pushing a shopping cart. His fishnet stockings ever so gracefully covered the crack of his ass, which was thrown into relief by what appeared to be a pink thong. I had actually seen this man when we first arrived in Austin. He had frightened me, as stupid as that sounds. The streets were empty then, and everyone knows—or should know—that men pushing shopping carts wearing pink thongs are dangerous. Fear of the other is a powerful thing.

"That is Leslie," said the woman next to me. "Excuse me?" I said. "The man that you are staring at, his name is Leslie. If you care." I was caught off guard. I was without question staring. "You would think being from New York I would be used to sights like that," I said. My neighbors laughed and introduced themselves. One was an artist, who told me, "You know, they once ran him for mayor. People wrote him in on the ballot."

Leslie had been and still is a fixture of the south Congress neighborhood. After the Austin police decided to remove the homeless population from respectable neighborhoods, they detained Leslie for a while, confiscating his cart. Angered by this action, a group called Keep Austin Weird (known here for its ubiquitous bumper stickers) mobilized a write-in mayoral run for Leslie. During his campaign, a young, affluent family asked the unlikely candidate to house-sit while they vacationed, but there was one stipulation: Leslie had to mow the lawn. That was no problem; keys were exchanged, and Leslie mowed, in his pink thong, waving to the neighbors. A moment of peculiar triumph.

Becky and I had decided to stop in Gibsonton, Florida, on our way to Virginia, the only stop we had planned. Now Gibsonton is not much of a town. But it had become my new obsession because it was known as a freak-show retirement community. I mean this in the most literal sense: Circus performers from the time of genuine freak shows retired to Gibsonton. I was fascinated by the idea of the freak and the cultural history of freak shows. While the phrase *freak show* has entered into our language in the form of slang, many of us don't realize how popular this form of entertainment was in the early twentieth century. Freak shows were everywhere and they were hardly considered sleazy, fringe operations. They were exploitative, sure, but also transformative. They were a place where the exceptional body, the body of someone with a disability often, was not sick but wondrous.

Beyond this cultural history, I was fascinated with Gibsonton because I often felt like a freak. Through much of high school, when my family moved from Los Angles to Denver, I was the "freak" soccer player. I couldn't read, but I sure as hell could play ball. Even now, because I

had overcome my disability and spoke of this in public, I still felt like
a freak on display. I made my living speaking about my struggles, my
difference, my so-called oddity.

All I knew for sure was that somewhere in the south of Florida
there was a community of people who got sick of being stared at, sick
of the show, and found some other sense of themselves. When I had
told Kent about them, he said, "Shit, those are some proud motherfucking freaks!"

It took us all day and well into the night to get to Lake Charles,
Louisiana. It rained most of the way, and Bob Henry leaked through
every one of his joints like an old creaking man. Between Austin and
Houston were small, segregated, and petrified historic towns. We slipped
through these time warps, passing rows of crumbling historic houses and
small abandoned mom-and-pop stores that Wal-Mart had driven out of
business. We got lost a few times, once crossing the imaginary line between
the historic district and the black district in a small town that seemed to
have no name. The black families stared at the bus, mostly, I suspect,
because it was driven by a white man, a rare sight in this part of town.

After a few hours of driving, we were orbiting Houston, a sprawl-
ing American city of rattlesnakes, oil barons, and high modern art. By
then it was dark. We drove on I-10 through and out of the underbelly
of Texas into Louisiana. *Welcome to Cajun Country*, a sign said. We figured we would spend the night in Lake Charles, a place I knew only
from a Lucinda Williams song about a man who was born in Texas but
believed his soul was in Lake Charles.

We found a Holiday Inn off the main drag. When I got out of the bus,
I was struck by the sound of frogs. I had never really been in the South,
in swamp country, before. I had read somewhere that environmentalists
believe we can tell the health of the planet by the diversity and number
of frogs. These sounded beautiful, like the chorus of a Greek tragedy. I
stood in the white light of the parking lot and just listened for a
moment. Are freaks like frogs? Can we measure the health of our society by the number of freaks walking the street? I liked that idea. I turned
to go in and peered up at the Holiday Inn billboard, which read, in big,
bold, illuminated letters, glowing in the same chemical white hue as the
refineries lining the coast, *Welcome Pest Controllers Association*.

After our night in Lake Charles, we drove to New Orleans, where we stayed
for two days. We walked the city, feeling our way on the cobblestones
past old garden-district homes. New Orleans is drifting horizontally
every year. We felt this drift and were pulled off course by it. On the
second day, we sat in the French Quarter and drank mint juleps, ate
po' boys, and talked about whether we should stay here forever. Becky
wanted to move on, saying that our journey wouldn't be complete
without a trip to Graceland. I thought that was a great idea. This part
of the trip was about feeling like a freak; a stop in Graceland fit
with the theme. Our route had changed. Memphis, Tennessee, was our
next stop.

It would take us two days to get to Graceland on the blues highway,
which follows the corners of the Mississippi River valley through what
used to be, and in some corners still is, the topography of the blues. I
can't say I love the blues. But I love music, and I loved the idea of following the Mississippi into the heart of the country to see Elvis's
home. Along the way, we stopped at Margaret's Grocery off Highway
61 north of Vicksburg. The grocery was built by the Reverend Herman
Dennis and is what one might call an outsider art environment. That's
a fancy name for something pretty simple. Reverend Herman lost his
wife and turned his trailer home into a shrine to her and to God. Later
on it became Margaret's Grocery, two buildings completely covered
with handwritten red and white quotes from the Bible. "Hear no evil,
see no evil" was there, along with "God punishes sinners." We walked
around the buildings and then stopped by the main house, where the
artist in residence still lived. Supposedly he was deaf and a bit out of
it, but if you stopped in he would tell you how to save your soul. We
knocked, waited, knocked again. He wasn't home.

Margaret's Grocery made me nervous. I felt out of control there. It
was too close to home—spectacle as a way to heal—and it reminded
me of my own experience in some vague way. I could feel my chest
tightening. It felt like I had a small bottle in my chest, and in this
bottle I'd stored all this black sludge for many years. If I kept the dark
stuff—the emotions from the past, I guess—all bottled up, it felt under

control. But from time to time, some of the sludge spills out, as it did at Margaret's Grocery.

When I was a child, my world was always out of control. The essence of a learning disability is that so much is called into question, a child's ability to learn, for example, which is considered basic human nature. My dyslexia was a long struggle to use language to make sense of the world. All of that is on shaky ground when the first words you see on the page mean nothing; when you sit in first grade and stare at a page that shakes like a heat line in a mirage; when the nausea of confusion and the fear of explosion overwhelmed your five-year-old frame. My fear always was that someone would come and point at me and say, "You're out. Sorry, man." By *out*, I guess I mean out of the real world, a freak out all alone.

I dealt with this feeling of being out of control with a subtle form of violence—toward myself, toward others. When I was in middle school, I decided I would not eat anything that had more than five grams of fat in it. I remember standing in a clothing store next to the Ice Box, a candy shop in Manhattan Beach, as Sue, who worked there, measured my waist. I'd gone up a size and I brought my hands to my collar bones to make sure I still felt them protruding because that's how I knew I was thin enough.

This need to control, this form of violence against myself was played out in some of my relationships as well. Growing up, only one kid knew about my learning disability: Steve. He was on my soccer team, and we looked like we could have been brothers. In seventh grade we both cut our hair the same way, short, almost shaved bangs and long mullets. Neither of us could read, but I was cruel to him and gave him the nickname Stupid Steve. It stuck at school. In this world of hierarchies, I guess we all need something beneath us.

Ultimately my self-loathing led to loneliness and hopelessness. I had a plan for suicide by the time I was twelve. I wrote it out longhand in my best handwriting. I remember feeling ashamed that I hadn't mastered cursive. Even in my note, which I wrote and rewrote, the curved lines were either too short or too tall. My dad saved me, told me after a baseball game that he loved me and it didn't matter how I did in school.

Soccer also saved me and trapped me. It was a way to be seen. I wasn't fucked up there. And I loved it, in a way that I don't really remember anymore, in a way that I used to feel in my hands and my arms. But a game can't totally support a self, and that is what soccer was asked to do, by me, my mom, my dad. It was supposed to make it all better. The outcome of a game—a win or a loss—determined whether I was good or bad, whether I was OK or defective. By the time I was in high school, my mom wouldn't talk to me if my team didn't win. I could play well, but the weight of the other ten men was on me; the weight of any game was on me. I felt like a freak again.

After an hour of driving, Becky came up behind the driver's seat and put her hand on the back of my neck. I was feeling as dark as the Mississippi. I asked her, "You want to marry a freak like me?" "Are you kidding?" she said. I was still feeling dark and anxious. "No," I said. "What if we have a kid like me? You know, this shit is genetic." Becky was quiet and then she kneeled down at the side of the driver's seat. She looked solid and sure of herself like she did in that photo of her that I so love. "You need to really hear this and really understand this. I hope to God we have a kid just like you."

It was still light out when we pulled into Vicksburg for the night. We stayed that night at the Battlefield Inn, which is what its name implies: a hotel that was across the street from an old Civil War battlefield with an adjacent Confederate-minded museum. It was packed. As I checked in, I was told there was a pool with "a lounge serving drinks for the next hour and live music." I peered out in the direction the man was pointing and saw a little pool, crowded with people, and a makeshift bar. I could hear the faint sound of a Casio piano, programmed to a rumba beat, and a high-pitched voice singing. "You also have a chance to win big," the man behind the counter said to me, pointing toward a roulette wheel. "Spin it," he said. I did, and I lost. What I lost, I didn't know.

The next morning, I felt better. At checkout I saw in the lobby two caged African parrots, who reminded me of a bird named Charley that I had as a kid. We found him on the street one day and took him home. He was a part of a rogue group of small birds that had escaped from a pet store during a fire in the 1970s and roamed the South Bay. When we found him, he was just a baby and was hurt. But he recovered and soon started talking. He said three things: *Charley is a pretty bird. Hi, Jon. Fuck you.* I think he'd absorbed many of my feelings about the world. When I was in high school, I couldn't wait to come home and have him say hello to me. On bad days, I felt invisible, but at least Charley said hello to me.

The drive that afternoon took us through some of the poorest parts of Mississippi. Our only stop that day, Clarksdale, didn't have that worn feel of deadened poverty. At least not the white parts of town. Clarksdale is a famous stop on the juke-joint circuit. It's the town where bluesmen sold their souls to the devil to play guitar.

I had read about an art gallery in town called the Cat Head that sold outsider art, so we parked and quickly found it. The Cat Head was filled with work pulsating with the raw aesthetic of the South. Many of the artists were local bluesmen and their kids. I made small talk with the owner. He had come to Clarksdale from St. Louis to listen to the blues and decided to quit his marketing job and stay. I browsed the store and bought a few things and then prepared to leave until something on the other side of the store caught my eye. Across the room was a giant hand-painted freak show banner.

I walked over to the banner. It was a pitch-perfect send-up of an old-time freak show advertisement. In the center was a picture of what was advertised as the world's smallest pygmy, and up top it read *The Museum of Wonder.* The banner was painted by a reclusive artist named Butch Anthony. Next to the banner was a short biography of Butch. According to this bio, in Seale, Alabama, Butch ran the Museum of Wonder, where, and I quote, he lived with "Bob Ross, the telepathic chicken." Butch couldn't read well as a kid but went on a full ride to Auburn University to study zoology. I was fascinated by Butch. Here was a man who couldn't read, who had created his own museum of wonder, his own place in the world where he wasn't a freak. There was something there I thought that I needed. In that moment our route changed. After Graceland and before Gibsonton, would be Butch Anthony, a telepathic chicken, and the Museum of Wonder.

Memphis is a shell of a city. Beale Street is a blues theme park dominated by big names such as B. B. King. The road to Graceland, however, shows you more of the city than I'm sure the city planners and city council would like. Large houses quickly give way to segregated black neighborhoods. Of course, as Graceland Avenue gets closer to the show, it is filled with signs of the Elvis industry: "Love Me Tender" hotels, coffee shops, and souvenir shops. Just past the Graceland gates is one of Elvis's planes, poised to take off.

It was hot that day, a soul-crushing heat. I felt raw and hungry. The line for tickets roared with every different accent from every corner of the country and the world, swirling around and mixing with the hum of the air conditioner. The man next to us said, as his overweight kids fought over a candy bar, "Elvis, Elvis, Elvis, Elvis," over and over again. I wondered what pulled people here. People lined up to see Stalin's tomb in Red Square, Mao's in Tiananmen Square, but in the United States, we went to Graceland. Every culture has these places where we stand in line to stare at a body.

The gate in front of Elvis's house seemed to be a wailing wall of sorts. People had left flowers, notes, and gifts. As we drove through the gate, a man dressed like Michael Jackson danced out front. He had it down: one glove, a white sequined shirt with tight black pants, and a perfect moonwalk down the street and into the heat. At Graceland, the script starts the moment you get off the bus, every word written by Elvis worshippers. The tour begins with the formal dining room, the archetypal room of an American family. We're supposed to imagine him there, perhaps during the fat period, wearing an outrageous outfit and carving a Christmas goose. The next stop is a room with carpet on the walls, and walking through it is like descending into the bowels of the Elvis myth. But the script ignores the drugs and other darker features of the life. But maybe that is why people have come, because they know most of that and they want the myth.

The freak show as a cultural institution may have died in the early twentieth century, but it was alive and well at Graceland. The last stop on the tour was a room filled with stuffed Elvis outfits that hovered in the air behind a glass wall. I'll always remember Elvis as twenty head-less costumes. Maybe those costumes were part of what made him real. I watched people look at the costumes as they sang his songs to themselves. Elvis served the same purpose of an old-school freak show, giving people something to stare at, something that affirms both their normality and their superiority and just maybe frees them from both. Elvis was not really about Elvis; he was about us. Elvis, like other freaks, was a body that would dream for us and have our nightmares.

As we piled back into the bus, Elvis said good-bye over the loud-speakers. The Michael Jackson impersonator was still outside the gates, slowly making his way down Graceland Avenue doing the moonwalk. I put on an Elvis shirt for the ride to Alabama. It pictured fat Elvis in a white jumper, and it said *Love Me Tender* on the front. Was there a difference between a freak show and a museum of wonder? We would soon find out. Butch's Museum of Wonder was our next stop.

It took Becky and me two days to get to Seale, Alabama. When I had called for directions, Butch had told me that he lived on Poor House Road. This had to be a joke. I mean what are the odds that a man who ran a Museum of Wonder, in rural Alabama, with a telepathic chicken lived on Poor House Road? My instincts seemed to be correct, at least at first, as we drove around in circles, past Confederate flags and abandoned farms, with no such address to be found. Then again, the directions Butch Anthony left on my voice mail had hardly been precise. For example: "Turn right at the tree that looks like a dead man." After about twenty minutes of driving, I pulled over at what appeared to be Seale's town center, which was essentially the junction of two one-lane state roads with a feed shop in the middle.

"Excuse me," I said to the man behind the counter in the feed shop. "Do you know where the Museum of Wonder is?" I felt foolish the moment this came out of my mouth. "The Museum of *what?*" the man said. Butch must have been playing with me; it all must have been a joke. I gave it one more try. "The Museum of Wonder." "You mean this," the man said as he gestured widely like an actor taking a bow. "This isn't it?"

Onward, I thought to myself, back to the bus, to Gibsonton. Before

I could drive away, a truck pulled up in front of us with a sticker on the back that said *Normal People Scare Me*, and a man over six feet tall, with surfer-blond hair, wearing overalls and no shirt, walked up to the side of the bus and said, "How you all doing? I'm Butch." I got off the bus, shook his hand, and introduced myself. Becky did the same. We all stood for a moment, not talking, wrapped in the kind of silence that surrounds strangers once they're no longer strangers but not friends yet. After a few awkward seconds I said, "Well, shall we?"

"Sure," Butch said in his low drawl. "Follow me." We followed his truck down a winding dirt road to his home, and we were greeted by a floppy-eared hound dog, which promptly rolled over to be petted. "She has fleas," Butch said. The overalls, the drawl, and the hound—this was almost too much. Was it all just some elaborate joke? A great marketing plan for faux outsider art? "Well," Butch said as he pointed toward the woods, "let's see the museum."

The Museum of Wonder was a *shed*. Literally. Up above the shed was a sign that read, *If you smoke, put your butt here*, pointing down toward a bedpan. The shed had dirt floors covered with hay and a pungent smell of must and rotting wood. My first thought was *What the hell did I just travel two days for?* I looked over at Becky, and her face held a slightly different expression, more in the vein of *We traveled for days to be killed by this man in this shed*. "You ready for the tour?" Butch said as he proceeded to walk us through the five-by-five shed like a docent at the Metropolitan Museum of Art.

"These," Butch said, "are the bones of an old race of pygmies." He laughed and then pulled himself back together and went on to use technical jargon to tell us about the lives of the Alabama pygmy. He played the role of learned guide, a staple of any freak show. What's next, I wondered, the world's smallest man and then the conjoined twins? Was this guy for real? He didn't seem to be a killer, but was he some kind of fraud?

Then my eyes stopped at what appeared to be an article about Butch in a local newspaper. I read the article and then reread it. It featured a picture of him, when he was a teenager, standing next to what looked like a dinosaur bone. "Is this real?" I asked him. "Is this true?"

He nodded. Butch, at the age of fourteen, when walking in the woods, found one of the first dinosaur bones in the state of Alabama.

It was no big deal to him. He struggled with reading, but he knew how to read the land—its curves, its secrets. He thought of the bone as a gift, he said. Though he did not graduate from high school, he was offered, on the basis of this discovery, a full-ride zoology scholarship to Auburn University. He still struggled with reading and writing, but he went anyway. During his college years he went around the world on digs. Yet he dropped out. I asked him why, but he didn't answer me. (On his Web site—yes, he has a Web site—it says that he failed to earn his degree because he did not want to take public speaking or calculus. "I don't need no degree to do what I'm doing: art," he wrote.) "Do you want to see some more of the museum?" he asked us.

The Museum of Wonder now seemed different to me. Not a fraud at all. Mixed with the museum's real bones were beautiful found objects, fake displays, and Butch's own art. Most of the latter were masks welded onto boards plastered with 1950s-style men and women. But there were also banners painted in an old freak folk art vernacular. Butch had created a modern Victorian cabinet of curiosities. It was a place where you could look at the unusual items with awe and curiosity. Nietzsche said that the capacity for awe of spectacle existed in every ancient culture, as an experience that sustains life. Butch's Museum of Wonder walked the line between spectacle and freakdom.

After we left the museum, Butch invited us to his house for lunch. We walked through the woods about a hundred yards to what appeared to be a three-story log cabin. The first stop was the kitchen, where Butch served us tomato and pepper sandwiches on white bread. Butch's home was decorated with his art, the art of his friends, and found objects: frozen animals, beetles on spikes, baby mice in jars. When he took us on a tour of the house, I felt compelled to ask, "Did you build this?"

He nodded his head. "I sawed every log and pounded every nail," he said.

"Did you study architecture?"

"Nope."

"Did you ever work construction?"

"No," he said and then added, "I just like to build things. I learned by building tree houses as a kid."

Though self-taught, Butch told us that he had been a part of the Rural Studio, an off-campus program of the Auburn University School of Architecture, founded in 1992 by the late Samuel Mockbee and D. K. Ruth. The founders won a MacArthur "genius grant" for their work. I don't think I've ever been affected as much by a building as by Butch's house. *All of its parts fit together.* These are the best words I can find to describe it. The rooms fit; they fit the eye, they fit the space and purpose. I don't know if Butch used traditional measurements, but it seemed like the house flowed intuitively, the way inches and feet never could. Butch started building his house in 1988 using large timbers salvaged from an old local factory. It took him twelve years to finish it. He had even designed his own pulley system and had to hang from trees to build the upper part of his house. It seemed that Butch's house, like all the items in his Museum of Wonder, was organic.

During the house tour I came across a child's chalkboard that had *the Seale's Philosophers' Club* written on it in rough block letters, like a child's. I thought it was a work of art, like a Duchamp ready-made.

"What is that?" I asked, thinking it might be for sale.

"Oh, you know, that is just what we call ourselves. We get together every week and, you know, just talk." Seale's Philosophers' Club had just three members, all artists: Butch, a man named John Henry who lived in a trailer, and a man called "the Mayor" who held no elected office but ran a small gallery in town.

I'm sure that many people had thought that Butch was stupid throughout his life. But underneath his quiet and slow manner was a brilliant, creative, and original mind. Butch refused to define his life using anyone else's terms. He created his own measure of worth and intelligence, inventing his life in an original way. It would be patronizing to say that Butch was like everyone else. Butch wasn't normal, and he wasn't a freak. He was wondrous. And in that assessment I found something that gave me hope—for me, for Kent, for all of us outsiders.

Before we left, Butch took Becky and me back to the Museum of Wonder to see Bob Ross, his telepathic chicken. "He's blind," Butch said with a laugh. Butch explained that Bob Ross wasn't, in fact, telepathic. Butch had rigged a contraption for Bob Ross to sit on and lay plastic eggs with bizarre fortunes inside of them. Butch once made two hundred dollars at a county fair from Bob Ross's prophecies. Standing with this blind prophet that clucked, Butch looked at me and said, "I saw on the Internet that you didn't read well." I told him that was true. "Me too," he said and then continued, "My dad and I didn't quite get along with that." I smiled. "Yeah," I said. "Me too."

At that point, Bob Ross got loose and started flapping around the Museum of Wonder. I watched Butch surrounded by all these petrified artifacts he had found in the earth. These were the earth's scars, its history, buried for so long, and Butch made them beautiful. Butch wasn't angry. He wasn't anxious like I was. Butch had found a way to transform not only the earth's scar tissue but also his own in his Museum of Wonder. I thought in that moment that maybe the short bus trip was my museum of wonder. Just maybe I could come out on the other end healed, transformed.

Butch got Bob Ross under control. "You all want Bob to tell your fortune?" Butch asked. I thought about it. "No thanks," I said. I didn't need to know the future just quite yet. I was OK in the Museum of Wonder.

Becky and I set out for Gibsonton, Florida, heading down through the spine of Georgia and into its populous neighbor state. This past week had been a journey through the American landscape of freaks, and Gibsonton was the last stop. After a full day of driving through Georgia, the highway shot us into the panhandle of Florida. It took us one more full day of driving to get to Gibsonton, which we found by accident. I stopped the bus, walked into a bar, and asked a woman for directions. "You're already there," she told me. Gibsonton was a polluted town dumped out of the highway intestines of Tampa. We had come all this way for this? There was nothing to do, so we sat in the bar and had some bad chili. I struck up a conversation with the waitress about Gibsonton's history as a freak show retirement community. She told me that the "performers" (i.e., the freaks) had a social club (the Showman's Club) not far away. She gave me directions. She wasn't hopeful, though, that anyone would be there.

Buried in a subdivision of small Florida ranch houses was a huge building in the style of an old European union hall or social club. The parking lot was empty, and I pulled in and walked toward the building. It was closed for the season, or for good, I didn't know which. The air was heavy with humidity, and the space felt like a carnival had recently vacated the premises. I sat down. The pavement was hot and steamed in the sun. In a way it was appropriate that there were no more freaks to be found in Gibsonton.

The old-fashioned freak show had died by the beginning of the First World War. Sure, there were still vestiges here and there, but its golden age had passed. People with strange differences were no longer considered magical or transcendent, but sick and defective. It would be wrong not to be grateful that the exploitative part of the freak show is gone. But don't be fooled by the shiny veneer of progress. The exceptional body is still exploited, though our language has changed. We are bound more than ever to the tyranny of our dreams of the perfect body.

Sitting on that hot concrete, I thought about our next stop, Richmond, Virginia. The state itself is a historic site when it comes to the story of freaks. It is the home state of a woman named Carrie Buck, who grew up in the Virginia epileptic colony and was involuntarily sterilized by the state in the 1920s. The U.S. Supreme Court deemed Carrie's sterilization, and thus involuntary sterilization all over the country, constitutional.

Richmond was also the location of my next interview, with Ashley, an eight-year-old deaf-blind girl, and her mom, Deborah.

It was also Becky's last stop on her short-bus ride. Fittingly, we were late for her train to New York. I didn't want her to leave. I would miss her deeply. With Becky I didn't feel like a freak. When we finally arrived at the Richmond train station, we had no time for a long, drawn-out good-bye. I pulled BH over, opened the door, and Becky jumped out. She sprinted and got on the train just in time. She disappeared into the compartment and my stomach sank, my throat tightened. I was alone.

But then Becky turned around and stepped out of the train. She didn't wave good-bye. She extended her arm like a warning, tightened her fist like a boxer, and sent me on my way in a manner only she could.

7

How to Curse in Sign Language

Ashley and Deborah

I have to be honest. As I drove from my hotel to a Starbucks in a non-descript strip mall on the outskirts of Richmond, Virginia, to meet Deborah, I was tempted to just keep driving and blow off this stop. Let me explain. I had traveled to Richmond in part because of an impassioned letter that Deborah had written me describing how she was fighting for her daughter Ashley's educational rights in a local public school. I was drawn to Deborah's description of Ashley as a resilient kid who was fighting right alongside her mom. I imagined Ashley as an eight-year-old Helen Keller.

This image quickly changed, however, when I spoke to Deborah on the phone before our rendezvous. In the background, I heard a high-pitched noise that unnerved me. This was Ashley. On the phone, Deborah told me that our day would consist of coffee at Starbucks, then a visit to the child-care center Ashley was attending for the summer, where I'd have the opportunity to observe Ashley's intensive speech therapy.

This all made me very worried. Thus far, the people I had spent time with—like Brent and Kent—were wrongly labeled as disabled, at least in my opinion. They were people who had been screwed by our culture, by our limited idea of what is considered normal. But it seemed to me that Ashley really was not normal. She was broken, and missing two of the five senses, which hampered her ability to make sense of, and navigate through, the world around her. In my mind, Ashley was *abnormal.*

It would take me all day to learn how wrong I really was.

When I arrived at Starbucks, I saw Deborah, sitting alone, not drinking any coffee. She appeared to be in her midforties and was wearing tapered jeans and white shoes. She looked like a nurse who was exhausted after working the night shift. Raising a child like Ashley, I thought, she must feel fatigued all the time. She sat in her chair like someone who had been standing for years.

I sat down and introduced myself. There was no small talk. Deborah started right in with her story. She had grown up in a rural setting, in Virginia Beach, in a middle-class Catholic home. The household income was just enough to meet the family's needs. Deborah had a twin brother, and their extended family was large. Family gatherings often included more than seventy-five people, "nudging and talking over each other," she told me. "I loved it."

She took a job at the Norfolk Police Department when she was sixteen years old. Nothing fancy, a keypunch operator, but she was hooked, and went on to become a member of the Norfolk Police Department. Her class at the police academy was the first to include female cadets. During training, she met the man who later became her husband; he was her supervisor, and, according to Deborah, "he was adamant that women had no place in the force." She wanted to prove him wrong.

Despite Deborah's commitment to police work, it took an emotional toll. As she put it, "Cops have to grow calluses over their personalities so they can deal with the many horrible things they see on a daily basis." Eventually, she left the police force, but by then her marriage had deteriorated. "I was the typical codependent wife," she says. "I cleaned up all his messes. . . . It was not until I got pregnant that I started to realize my life had to change."

The problems continued even after the birth of their son, Chip.

Finally, after months of drama and upheaval, Deborah—with the support of an Episcopal minister—filed for divorce, went to court, and eventually got custody of her son.

Ashley came into Deborah's life through an announcement posted at a local United Methodist church not long after she and her young son had moved to Richmond. Deborah was trying to rebuild her life. She was working in computers, a career she had set in motion when she was still a cop, and completed her bachelor's degree in computer science while working full-time. She was also taking an exercise class at the aforementioned church. One day, she arrived early, thirty minutes before her class began. To kill time, she stood around reading various postings on the church bulletin board. The tip of a yellow piece of paper, buried under the rest, caught her eye, and she uncovered an announcement from the United Methodist Family Services. This organization was holding an adoption information program for people who might consider "challenging" adoptions. She decided to attend the session just to "see what the group had to say."

The meeting was held in a community center with fluorescent lights and bad coffee. This wasn't a slick adoption center. There were few women in attendance. (None of them had come because they had failed to conceive a child through in vitro fertilization. And no one was here because the process of adopting a baby from overseas was too time-consuming.) These women sat in folding chairs and listened to a two-hour session about babies who were brain damaged, young children with emotional problems, and infants who might not live to see their tenth birthday. Deborah just listened. All she said about that meeting was, "I felt I was being led."

After the meeting, Deborah signed up for a nine-week training session followed by what is known as a "home study." This training was a prerequisite for going any further in the adoption process. According to Deborah, "the leaders of the training didn't pull any punches and shared the very difficult things involved in the adoption of special-needs or older children." Many of these children would need lifelong care. Many would require advanced medical supervision at home. Many would have emotional problems. But after each session, Deborah "felt even more strongly about adoption as an option." Most people who have gone through the adoption process consider the home study to be the most difficult. It requires the prospective parent to undergo multiple background checks, physical exams, and a financial audit; to obtain three letters of recommendation; to write an autobiography; and to submit to three unannounced home inspections by a social worker. Deborah passed the home study with an almost perfect score, and then, in her words, "the search began."

It lasted over a year and a half. Deborah was looking for a child with physical disabilities, not a child with emotional challenges. Here and there were children who could be a good match, but they always went to another family. "I began to wonder," Deborah said, "if I had read my 'leading' incorrectly." She was on the verge of giving up when she got a call from her social worker about Ashley. Deborah was one of two finalists vetted from a field of eighty-five. "Don't expect much," the social worker said. "Ashley looks different. She is not the cutest baby around."

Ashley had been born to an alcoholic, anorexic mother fourteen weeks prematurely. She weighed just over one and a half pounds, and her medical birth records state that she smelled of alcohol when she was delivered. A liver biopsy was performed right after her birth, and it showed that a tumor was present. She also had a "brain bleed." Even more threatening to Ashley's health was a rare condition she had, called Juvenile Xanthogranulomas, which causes tumors to form all over the body. These tumors, according to Deborah, "formed on Ashley's skin, under her skin, on her eyes and ears, on other vital organs, and on her brain."

Deborah and her social worker drove to Ashley's foster mother's apartment. Deborah was warned again about Ashley's condition. At that point, Ashley was about eighteen months old and had just been through surgery to have her first brain tumor removed. She was a "failure to thrive" baby, which meant she ate nothing and only drank a little milk. The apartment was nice enough, Deborah remembers, but had a hushed feeling.

After the introduction and pleasantries, the foster mother pointed to a crib. The three women walked over together, and Deborah peered down at the baby she was told was not quite normal. But that is not what she saw. "I thought she was beautiful," Deborah recalled. "Her left eye, because of glaucoma, was about twice the size of her right eye. And although that skewed the symmetry of her face, she had a smile that lit up the room! She was not the least bit intimidated by having three extra people in her small space and was quite friendly with everyone. She let everyone hold her, and as we all talked and cooed to her, she explored everyone's face with her hands."

Deborah walked away from the crib and pulled the social worker aside. "I love that baby," she said. "I would very much like her to be a part of my family." The social worker had the same questions that I did. Why would she want to adopt a child with so many needs? "I struggled with the answer," she told me. "Perhaps it is my belief in God, or some other manifestation of my faith, but I just felt that choosing to adopt Ashley was the correct path to follow at that time in my life. I knew that the challenges would be many and lifelong. But, at the same time, I felt that whatever strength I needed would be found, that help would be available, and that my life, Chip's life, and, most especially, Ashley's life would benefit from the adoption. I know my answers are not very clear and concrete, but as soon as I made the decision to adopt, I felt a peace come into my heart."

Ashley's early struggle for life was far from over. She had a second brain tumor removed just before she turned two years old. Soon, she also had her gallbladder removed because of a tumor, and there was another one forming between her ears and brain. Ashley also had a seizure disorder. On top of all that, she was deaf and blind. Most of us would have seen Ashley's life as either not worth living or pitiful. Deborah saw something different. Deborah saw her as nothing exceptional, as just a little baby.

Back at Starbucks, though I had finished two cups of black coffee, I was exhausted by the time Deborah finished this part of her story. While I admired her and the courage with which she faced this struggle, I had trouble listening. This was not the story that I had imagined. I couldn't see beyond the tragedy of her story. Deborah looked at me and said, "Well, should we go? I mean you want to see Ashley, don't you?" I wanted to say no, but I nodded my head yes. I was already planning where I would get drunk that night.

After coffee, I followed Deborah to her house in the burbs. It was a typical suburban house with a slight difference. Out front was a large street sign that said *deaf-blind child area*. Once inside, Deborah gave me the obligatory tour, the dining room, the kids' rooms, and the kitchen, with its linoleum floor and faux wood cabinets. I noted that Deborah had a peaceful, quiet way about her when she wasn't talking about Ashley's struggles. Anger did not have a place in her world. Faith played a huge role in Deborah's life. As we walked through her house she told me that finding a church that was welcoming to Ashley had been nearly impossible. The world—even churches, it seemed—shared my fear of people like Ashley and all of its subtle manifestations.

"When I have tried to take her into the service with me," Deborah said, "I am constantly asked to take her out because of the noises she makes and her overall restless nature. It is always the same old story—Ashley appears and acts different from others in the church. It really saddens me." This actually wasn't surprising. Most of the major religions of the world have a long history of associating disability with sin, evil, or the devil. The Church has often been one of the leading institutions to dehumanize people on the wrong side of normal.

My time in Deborah's home was brief, a pit stop for her to refuel before we headed to Ashley's summer school. It was a good thing that Deborah's job allowed her to make her own schedule. Without this flexibility, which most people do not have, I don't know what kind of life Ashley would lead.

Ashley had had terrible experiences at her regular public school. Referring to Ashley's school trouble, Deborah said, "You know, they are often afraid of Ashley, some of the kids and the teachers. They treat her sometimes as if she is contagious." I nodded my head, feeling ashamed for understanding their feelings. "They *stare*."

These gazes, according to Deborah, were some of the most painful things that she and her daughter endured together. "Surgeries or any medical procedures are things that hurt, but only for a short while," Deborah continued. "The pain of rejection, the pain of being thought of as somehow a 'broken' or inferior person, the pain of ridicule or derision doesn't go away." These experiences "were ten times as painful as her surgeries."

At the time of my visit, Ashley was attending a wonderful school called the Starling Child Care and Learning Complex. "Starling is mostly a poor minority school," Deborah told me as she drove us there. "And for some reason the staff love Ashley. Maybe it's because they can understand her experiences better than most." When we pulled up to the school, located in a strip mall in a black neighborhood, Deborah parked the car, and I prepared to get out. But then Deborah stopped me. She grabbed my arm, looked me directly in the eye, and said, "You have to know that Ashley is not one hundred percent deaf or blind. No one is ever one hundred percent anything. It is important that you know that, Jon."

The school itself was rough around the edges, but it was obvious that the staff cared about their work. This institution was also committed to a policy of inclusion. As we walked through the halls, I saw many students with disabilities. Ashley was in a fully inclusive, mixed-age classroom. When Deborah and I arrived, the class was having lunch. "There is my little girl," Deborah said, pointing across the small kids' desks, her face illuminated with the first smile I saw all day. I followed the trajectory of Deborah's outstretched hand and saw a little girl who struck me as strong, not sickly at all. She had a body that looked at least twelve years old. "She's a good eater," Deborah said. "Isn't she beautiful?"

I didn't answer the question. Not because I disagreed with Deborah, but because I really had no way to make sense out of Ashley. I didn't see Ashley as a whole. It was as if all I could take in were parts of her. She was wearing a red dress, and her hair was short and black. Her right eye was smaller than its counterpart and was glassy and colorless. She walked around the lunch table like a spinning top that had lost its centrifugal force. She made strange noises, which ranged in pitch from a low hum to an ear-piercing scream. Ashley heard nothing but felt vibrations.

I hoped Deborah didn't notice, but I was staring at Ashley. Not a genial get-to-know-you kind of glance, but a deeply dehumanizing stare, the kind of look that Deborah had talked about earlier. This is the type of stare that people with physical disabilities are very familiar with. But I didn't know how to stop. I didn't know how to make sense out of Ashley. I am ashamed to write this, but a part of me wondered if Ashley and I belonged to the same species.

Ashley confronted me with my own deep prejudices about what it means to be a valuable human being. I didn't know if I could truly value a body that was so damaged. Ashley also challenged some of my ideas about intelligence. If Ashley couldn't hear, speak, or see, how could she learn? And if Ashley couldn't learn, was she a fully functioning member of the human race?

Unfortunately, my reaction to Ashley is not without historical precedent. The history of the deaf, blind, and the deaf/blind is a story of being seen as less than human. It begins in Western thought with Aristotle, who believed that "if one of the faculties is lost, some knowledge must also inevitably be lost." Of the senses, Aristotle noted that sight was the most valuable as far as the necessities of life were concerned. Historically, the blind have fared better socially and economically than many others with disabilities. A somewhat positive mythology developed around the blind: the archetype of the blind prophet and the blind poet. Like any myth, however, this archetype was a dehumanizing fallacy.

In modern times, according to Kay Alicyn Ferrell, a professor of education, "The rise of monotheistic religions led to a belief that blind individuals needed to be cared for and sheltered by society." During this time, the blind were infantilized. In the nineteenth century, many within the blind community fought for access to education. Professor Ferrell describes the shift from charity for the blind to empowerment as a fight against "visual imperialism."

Now to the history of the deaf. It was Aristotle's contention that, of all the senses, hearing contributed most to intelligence and knowledge. This led Aristotle to characterize deaf individuals as senseless and incapable of reason. Much of the early marginalization of the deaf had to do with religious mythology. The ability to speak was considered a gift from the breath of God. Without speech, the deaf were denied moral status. Even during the Enlightenment, a period defined by questioning religious beliefs, the deaf were denied full humanity. In this period, man became defined by language and was considered as separate from animals by his spoken and written word.

Lastly, a short history of individuals considered deaf/blind, and I mean really short: Throughout most of history, the deaf/blind were considered subhuman.

This dismissal of the deaf/blind as human beings, however, changed in the nineteenth century. Most people wrongly assume that the first deaf/blind individual to question these limited notions was Helen Keller. In a fact, almost half a century before Keller, a deaf and blind woman named Laura Bridgman was the first deaf/blind individual to learn language. Bridgman became an international sensation. She was taught by Samuel Howe, was the subject of numerous scientific treatises, and was said to be the most famous woman in the world after Queen Victoria at the time.

What is interesting about this history, and specifically about the history surrounding Bridgman, is what deaf/blindness meant to the culture of the time. Deaf/blindness was a window into complicated cultural debates about the nature of being human. Central to these debates was the question of language. Is there an innate human capacity for language, what Howe called "the Organ of Language" that we all share, whether the language is spoken or signed?

As we waited for Ashley, Deborah talked about how her daughter was treated. "My experience has been that people will try to avoid that which they do not understand. So many people look at Ashley, see the physical differences in her, and assume that everything else about her is different, *and inferior.* What they don't see is the warmth and compassion inside her, her ability to forgive and forget all the slights from other people, her drive to experience everything she possibly can, her love of nature, and her gentleness around babies and young children."

I wanted to take in all those things, too. But I didn't know how to yet. This was the sort of understanding and respect that could never come from staring at someone. "I have to apologize," I said to Deborah. "I've been staring at your daughter." I waited for her outrage. To my surprise, Deborah didn't look angry, or sad, but hopeful. "It's OK. You've already taken the first step. You've been *honest*."

At this point in our day, it was time for Ashley's language instruction, a mix of American Sign Language (ASL), touch sign, and speech therapy. Later, I asked Deborah about sign language and about whether Ashley's blindness prevented her from using it. Deborah reminded me that while Ashley has no vision at all in her left eye, the vision in her right eye is 20/2000. This means she can focus at about one to two inches from her face. Deborah elaborated: "She does her signing directly in front of her body, and if she perceives the person to whom she is signing is not paying attention, she will gently put her hands on both sides of their face and move their face to look at her."

Ashley's language instructor came right up to me and introduced herself. "I'm Theresa," she said as she shook my hand. Theresa was in her late thirties and was a large, joyful woman. She seemed like a natural educator, and had a son with a learning disability who struggled with learning to read and write.

"I think that helps me when I work with Ashley," she said. "You know, a struggle with language is a struggle with language whether you're deaf-blind or not." Theresa then turned her attention to her student, signing something to Ashley who signed back. But because I don't know ASL, I had no idea what was being communicated. "I asked her if she was ready to work," Theresa translated. "What did she say?" I asked. "What would any kid say? No, of course," Theresa reported.

I spent the next twenty minutes watching Theresa, trying to understand what she could see, but I could not. Deborah pointed out that the first thing Theresa did when she saw Ashley was smile. I didn't smile when I first saw Ashley, thinking that Ashley couldn't see my expression. Deborah laughed when I mentioned this to her. "To Ashley, your body can't lie." Ashley could feel a smile even if she couldn't see it. After Theresa smiled at Ashley, she touched her on her arm and then got down close to Ashley's stronger eye. She spoke and signed, "Good afternoon." Then she asked, "How are you?"

Theresa was vigilant about letting Ashley know what was going on in her environment. She signed and told Ashley what was on the floor, what chairs had been moved, what time the bell would ring. According to Deborah, this is essential. "One of the biggest potential sources for stress and frustration for Ashley is not being aware of something, especially something that would impact her. She needs access to the environment."

It seemed to me, though, that the essence of Ashley's learning was stimulation. Theresa was constantly bombarding Ashley with touch, signs, and her voice. She handed Ashley a stuffed bear, signed the creature's name, said the name, and then let Ashley take it all in. Ashley reached up and put her hands on Theresa's mouth and felt the curvature of her lips. She waved her hands in front of the air expelled from Theresa's mouth. She moved her hands down to Theresa's jawbone and felt the structure of her face. She then moved her hands down to Theresa's throat, and her face broke out in a smile, and her steady rocking picked up pace. When Theresa said "bear," the vibration of human communication rippled through Ashley's hands.

All of this was pretty simple, but important. Theresa respected Ashley as she would any other child and allowed Ashley to express herself in her own language.

But like many deaf children, Ashley has had, at best, limited access to signing classrooms. When Ashley started school at the age of two and a half, she was in a classroom led by a teacher who signed with the other signing children. According to Deborah, after one year the school district abolished all signing classes and reassigned the teachers to classes for children with cochlear implants, which are a huge issue in the deaf community. The National Institutes of Health describes a cochlear implant as "a small electronic device that can help to provide a sense of sound to a person who is profoundly deaf or severely hard-of-hearing. The implant consists of an external portion that sits behind the ear and a second portion that is surgically placed under the skin." Many in the deaf community believe, however, that cochlear implants are a nefarious form of cultural genocide for the deaf. The essence of deaf culture is its language—sign language. Implants threaten to suck the life out of ASL.

Teachers are now told to emphasize speech and not to sign. Lipreading was also actively discouraged or prevented. "Classroom teachers were instructed to cover their mouths when they spoke so the children would not be able to read their lips," Deborah said. "The entire emphasis was on getting the children to adjust to their implants and learn to 'hear' and speak." Children without implants, which are initially painful and not always effective, were moved into segregated classrooms with children who had a myriad of other disabilities. Without signing support, according to Deborah, "the education of those children like Ashley suffered greatly. Many formative years were lost, and I'm not sure they will ever be made up."

Even a sign advocate like Deborah, who believes ASL is a natural and valid language, still has Ashley attend extensive and expensive speech therapy at a local hospital. Ashley's therapist uses a new technique called Tadoma, in which the person with deaf-blindness places a thumb on the speaker's mouth and then spreads the fingers across the speaker's cheek to feel the vibrations, the positions of the lips, the air expelled, and other physical cues. Does Tadoma work? Is it worth the effort? (It is very time consuming.) Research so far has not been promising. "A great deal of time and money has been spent on trying to get Ashley to speak," Deborah told me, "but there has not been much success."

It seemed to me that Ashley, like many deaf children, was caught in bad institutional policies that have systemically undermined ASL as an option. "Even if Ashley were a candidate for a cochlear implant," Deborah said, "I don't think I would make that choice for her. She has demonstrated a definite preference for sign, and I don't feel the need to put her through more surgery just so she has the potential for speech."

But implants are in vogue in her community. "Many, if not most, children in my area with hearing impairments have been getting cochlear implants," Deborah says. "It seems to be almost as common and expected as getting braces for a child's teeth," Deborah said, "and it has indeed had an impact on services, especially in my school district."

As a result of the trend toward implants, Ashley has spent most of her life without a natural language. Nor has she really been educated. She has had only two trained ASL teachers. What is the cost of teaching speech versus developing Ashley's mind and communication skills through ASL? Research is unequivocal: Deaf and deaf-blind children who acquire signing early have the best educational outcomes. Without signing, education becomes limited. "The school would like to pigeonhole Ashley as incapable of doing academic work," Deborah said. "Rather, they do things like learning to cook, community trips, and learning to clean up." A policy of emphasizing speech for these children is really a policy of forced assimilation of a unique minority group.

"It has been my experience," said Deborah, "that the school staff expects the children to change and is determined to help 'fix' them. The sad thing in my mind is that these children are not 'broken' and do not need fixing." Deborah could have been talking about Brent, Kent, or me.

Before the end of the language lesson Deborah tapped my shoulder and pointed to Ashley. "Do you see that?" she asked me. I didn't know what she was talking about, so I just shrugged my shoulders. "She's laughing. Take a close look."

I looked to the other side of the room. I watched Ashley's face, not her awkward gait or her colorless eye, but her whole face. Her face looked like a Picasso, a face held together with its own inherently savage beauty. Deborah was right; Ashley was laughing. And so was Theresa. I looked back at Deborah, and she was laughing too. Everyone was in on the joke except me. "What's so funny," I asked. "Oh nothing," Deborah said. I pressed her again. "Well, I don't want you to think less of Ashley, but Ashley just cursed us all out in sign language," said her mother. "She has a problem with that; we're working on it." Ashley knows more curse words than the average eight-year-old. I was down with that. I was one of the most foul-mouthed children in the history of California. Her defiance, her will to communicate made me finally able to feel closer to her. In that moment I saw Ashley not as a collection of problems, but as a little girl who loved more than anything to curse out her teachers in a language many did not understand.

I ended my day with Deborah and Ashley back at their home. The plan was to have dinner with the family: Ashley; her brother, Chip; and Deborah. Deborah had invited me to dinner at the beginning of the day,

when we sat talking at Starbucks, and I had lied, saying I had somewhere I needed to be. But now I wouldn't have missed a dinner with
this family for the world. Deborah and I had some time to kill before
the rest of the family got home. So before dinner we sat around and
talked about Ashley's experiences, the power of language, and the
importance of inclusion. When we got onto the latter topic, Deborah
told me a story that she had already shared with me over e-mail and in
a phone conversation. In fact, she had already shared this story with
me during our day together. It was as if this story was somehow the
essence of her and Ashley's struggle.

It was the Christmas season, December 2002. That night, Deborah
and the kids piled into their car and headed to the elementary school
for the big holiday show. Ashley had been given a part. This was huge.
Ashley was educated in a fully segregated special educational room,
but on this night she would be on the stage with the rest of the kids.
She was given a tiny baby rattle that she was supposed to shake at various times during the performance with the prompting of her aide.
That's all the teachers thought she was capable of, but Deborah went
along with the plan. At least Ashley would be on the stage.

Deborah and Chip sat in the makeshift auditorium, on steel-blue
chairs. She had her camera in hand, just like all the other parents.
When the lights went out, Ashley walked on the stage with the rest of
the kids. She wobbled a little, but she found her spot. These things
matter, Deborah thought. These small moments of inclusion. Sure, it's
just a first-grade holiday program. But if Ashley can't be here, what's
next? Who gets to draw these lines, and where would they stop? No,
this night, this act of inclusion mattered, Deborah thought. She poised
her camera and sat on the edge of her seat.

Then it happened. Before the program began, Ashley was placed
three feet to the side of the group. Her aide stood next to her, holding her hand. The aide did not know touch sign or American Sign
Language, Ashley's primary forms of communication. The only way
Ashley would have to communicate would be to grip the aide's hand
harder.

The first song was "Frosty the Snowman." Ashley waited for her
cue, a slight touch on the hand, to shake the rattle. As the kids sang, she

swayed. The aide seemed nervous, but when the time for Ashley's part came, she shook the rattle with force. Deborah was filled with a sense of pride. When the first song was over, there were more songs to come, but not for Ashley. The aide led her off the stage. Deborah wondered why. What was going on? Why was she leaving? Ashley was supposed to stay on stage for the whole night. That had been the plan all along, but someone didn't want Ashley on the stage for the whole perfor-mance. As they escorted Ashley off the stage and out of the audito-rium, a parent in a fancy coat stopped the aide and, looking right past Ashley, said, "Good job." To the aide.

Before dinner on the day of my visit, Deborah spent an hour or so with Ashley on the porch swing. Deborah held Ashley close to her, like a baby wrapped in her arms. Ashley's healthy limbs were spilling out in every direction. Ashley held her hand up in front of her face like she was looking through a prism of light. Deborah holds Ashley a few hours every day. When it rains, they walk down the middle of their street together, holding hands, mouths open to the sky, tasting the rain.

After their time on the porch, Ashley came in the house and grabbed an electric toothbrush and stuck it in her mouth. She rolled on the floor, lost in her world of vibrations. "She needs that for stimu-lation," Deborah said to me as I watched Ashley. "You know, I used to be freaked out about it," she said, referring to the self-stimulation. "But the human instinct is to engage," she said. "Ashley is no different." Deb-orah was right. Ashley lived in a world without sight or sound, but she had heightened senses of smell, of taste, of touch. As Deborah explained to me, "If Ashley doesn't recognize a particular food on her plate, she smells it first. If she is looking for new clothes, she runs her hands down the fabric first to see if it is something that feels like she wants it to feel." We should not underestimate the power of touch. The philosopher Jean-Jacques Rousseau believed that touch was the essence of an ethical life; touch defined our humanity.

We had take-out pizza for dinner, washed down with a few sodas, and Ashley had Top Ramen noodles. I sat next to Chip. It is common to think that the siblings of people with disabilities are damaged by this experience. This may be true for some, but it wasn't true for Chip. He was an honor student. In fact, he wanted his mother to adopt another child with disabilities. "I want another family member," he told me at dinner. "I love my family."

Dinner was uneventful—until Ashley slurped up soupy water from her Top Ramen bowl, held it in her mouth, and then tilted her head from side to side like a wobbly baseball souvenir. Conversation stopped. "No!" Deborah screamed and signed. All eyes were on Ashley. I watched her as she balanced herself on the side of the chair and turned her "good eye" toward Chip. "Ashley, don't you dare spit that at me!" Chip said and signed. Her lips curved into a half smile, and she rolled her head around, just as Ray Charles used to do while playing the piano. "Don't," Chip said again as he tried not to laugh. But he couldn't help it. Ashley tilted her head back and then made a swallowing motion with her throat. "Thank you," Chip signed. Ashley nodded and signed back "You're welcome" and then spit a mouthful of soupy water in Chip's lap.

Everyone laughed. Even me. I was no longer staring at Ashley; I was in on the joke.

Before I said my good-byes I asked Deborah if she had anything she could give me to help me remember our day. She left the room and came back holding a photograph of Ashley sitting on the beach. "I just love this picture," she said as she handed it to me. "This is my beautiful little girl. Feeling everything."

That picture was taken in the late summer of 2002 at Virginia Beach. It was a few days before school started. Deborah, who had fond memories of the beach, had saved a little money for a vacation. She got her family a hotel room right on the ocean, so the kids could see the sun rise. On the last day of their holiday, they went out on the beach at sunset. Deborah's twin brother, a photographer, was there. Ashley had been to other bodies of water before—lakes, rivers—but she had never been to the ocean. She stepped onto the sand, wobbled a little, as everyone does on the beach, and started walking toward the ocean. But fifty feet or so from the water, she stopped and put her hands out. Other kids were running around in the sand, whining about the cold, asking to go home and eat ice cream, but not Ashley. She stood there in a world of vibration and taste and touch, "relishing every sensory experience."

After a while, Ashley walked up to the line where the ocean meets the sand and sat down. The reaching palms of the surf touched the tips of her toes and she lifted her hands to feel the wind and salt spray. She sat like that for five minutes on the edge of the world, the sea, a shifting line, its edges never anywhere for long. Ashley pressed her hands out like she was feeling someone's face. When a wave washed up on shore, the spray lifted off the water and the ocean came to her toes and then her shins. She laughed in a pitch somewhere between a scream and a song.

8

I Don't Know, I Don't Remember, It Doesn't Seem to Matter Anymore

RICHMOND, VA—NEW YORK, NY

After my dinner with Deborah and her kids, I was feeling guilty about how long it had taken me to see Ashley's humanity. So I decided to follow through with my plan to get good and drunk. I found a Chili's knockoff, walked inside, and took a seat at the bar. Sitting across from me were two men wearing white hats and white polo shirts, with the collars uplifted. "Hey, dude," one said to the other, who was drinking an Amstel Light. That would be my night—guys in white polo shirts drinking light beer and speaking a dialect of grunts and slang, the language of many American men. I knew their world and their expressions well, from my own days of grunting and Amstel drinking.

Throughout high school I tried to be one of those white hats. I went to high school at a place called Green Mountain in Lakewood. This was a place just being built on the first rise of the Rocky Mountains, and the trees were held up with wire and string. It was a middle-class utopia shaking in the altitude like a mirage. My first semester at Green Mountain was physically painful. I hadn't started soccer yet, and I hid in the bathroom during lunchtime and in the library during my free period, just shuffling around to appear busy.

High school was a constant battle between the white hat side of myself and another side that tenuously believed I had a valuable mind.

That first semester at Green Mountain, I read *East of Eden* cover to cover twice, though I almost failed my classes. This side was nurtured here and there by gifted teachers like Mr. Starkey. He was my sophomore-year English teacher and he told me that if I wanted to be a writer, all I had to do was write. That year I also became best friends with another soccer player named Mike, who was from the other side of Green Mountain's invisible class lines. With Mike, I tried to carve out a self that wasn't just about fitting in.

But when soccer season began, I was one of the first sophomores in the school's history to be in the starting lineup. I hung out with kids like Niles and Corey who embodied American normal. I dated a blond-haired, blue-eyed cheerleader. By the end of high school, the side of myself that Mr. Starkey had encouraged was pushed aside, to the other side of the line that I had drawn on myself in sixth grade, that marked my identity as a dumb soccer player. By the end of high school, the plan I had outlined years ago was coming true; I was given a scholarship to play Division One soccer at Loyola Marymount University.

In spite of my athletic success, I didn't have a hopeful vision of my future. I started to drink self-destructively. Sometimes I'd sleep fifteen hours straight only to wake up exhausted. I was arrested when I was eighteen for underage drinking and spent the night in a detox center, wearing a white paper gown and a hair net. My mom picked me up, which was a good thing because I had planned to drive the car up into the mountains and off the road.

At the bar in Richmond, I watched the white hats drinking. I realized something I never could have imagined in high school: not only was I not like them anymore, maybe I had never been like them. Maybe I had misunderstood who I was for a very long time.

I was hungover the next day. To make matters worse, I had slept in an oddly shaped hotel room whose curves made me feel like a rat at the dead end of a maze. The room didn't get much sun, and it reeked of industrial cleaning fluid, smelling like a bad mix between a school and a hospital. I felt raw, depressed, as if some machine had sucked everything out of me except blackness. I had come to the end of the first real leg of this journey. In two days I would pull into New York, where I would pick up my sister Kelly. Between Richmond and New York, I had only one stop, in Charlottesville, Virginia, less than an hour from my hotel.

As I pulled out of Richmond, I put Ashley's picture up above the driver's seat. A large part of the road to Charlottesville was a speed trap. Police lined the sides of the road and hid behind trees. Luckily, I didn't go all that fast. Bob Henry just wasn't capable of that sort of effort.

I had never been to Charlottesville before, and I was traveling there to see a roadside memorial to Carrie Buck, who had been really kind of a big deal. She was the most famous casualty of the American eugenics movement, which had dehumanized people with disabilities.

The eugenics movement dominated international thought about difference and disability for a span of about twenty years, beginning in the early 1900s. The pioneers of eugenics took it upon themselves to measure which lives had value and which did not. The movement began in England, with the work of Charles Darwin's cousin Sir Francis Galton. From the very beginning, eugenics sought to eliminate people considered "defective" and their gene plasma from the population through a variety of public policies. The set of ideas that came to be known as eugenics resulted from the crossbreeding of emerging genetic theory and the disciplines of public health and public policy. The category "defectives" was broadly defined. According to one handbook on eugenics, defectives were "epileptics, drunks, morons, imbeciles, deaf, dumb, blind, women of loose morals, and vagrants." In reality, defectives were the poor, racial minorities, and people with disabilities.

Eugenics was hardly a fringe operation. Men of all political stripes supported it. Nor was it a pseudoscience that existed on the margins of mainstream intellectual life. At the height of the eugenics movement there were many eugenics departments at major universities such as Princeton, Brown, and Stanford. Eugenics-oriented scientists sat on major boards and comprised the leadership of professional scientific organizations. But eugenics was not just academic theory. It was put into practice. In the United States, eugenics theory supported a growing nationalism and age-old racism and influenced the country's

immigration policy. Eugenicists argued that eastern Europeans, specifically Jewish and Catholic immigrants, carried defective "gene-plasma"
that would debase the national stock. In the United States, rural communities held fittest-family contests at local state fairs, where families
were judged like livestock on their fitness to breed.

The most famous and devastating eugenics policy was involuntary
sterilization. By the middle of the twentieth century, more than twenty-
eight states had involuntary sterilization laws on the books for those
deemed defective. These were often individuals living in state-run
facilities for the insane, epileptic, and *feebleminded*—a catchall word
and antiquated term for people with developmental disabilities. As a
result of these policies, over forty thousand U.S. citizens were forcibly
sterilized. Which brings us to the case of Carrie Buck.

Carrie Buck grew up in the Virginia epileptic colony. It is still a
matter of debate whether Carrie was actually a person with a disability. What is clear, though, is that she was considered "feebleminded" by
the state of Virginia. She was also poor. Carrie's mother was from a
rural community in the Blue Ridge Mountains, and the family was sent
there after requesting financial assistance from the state. Often institutions like the Virginia epileptic colony were simply holding pens for
poor people. Carrie was promiscuous and became pregnant. The
epileptic colony lobbied to have her sterilized. Her case was appealed
and ultimately sent to the U.S. Supreme Court in 1927. Evidence was
presented that not only Carrie and her mother were feebleminded,
but also her one-year-old daughter. Chief Justice Oliver Wendell
Holmes wrote the majority decision that Carrie's sterilization was
constitutional because, according to Holmes, "three generations of
imbeciles are enough." It was later shown that Carrie's daughter had
an average or above-average IQ. To this day, fifteen states still have laws
permitting the involuntary sterilization of "defectives," although they
are rarely put into practice.

When I finally got to downtown Charlottesville, there was no sign
for the memorial to Carrie Buck. I pulled over to the side of the road
and looked through one of my U.S. tourist guides. I flipped through to
Charlottesville but found nothing. This must be a mistake, I thought. I

decided to head into downtown; surely one of the many tourist offices in this historical city would know what I was talking about. Once downtown, I parked and walked around aimlessly.

I finally called the main tourist information line on my cell phone from the University of Virginia's main green. It was a beautiful day, and I watched the co-eds sun themselves as I was put on hold. After a few minutes, I got an operator and asked about the Carrie Buck memorial. "What?" the operator said. "Never heard of it, but this is not the best place for information on historical monuments." She proceeded to give me the address of a state-run agency that was in charge of things of a historical nature. "But," she added at the end, "I ain't ever heard of what you are looking for."

I figured the memorial wasn't exactly Disneyland, but I thought someone at least would have heard of its existence. It was a big deal in 2002 when Virginia's governor, Mark Warner, publicly apologized for the state's actions against Carrie and dedicated the roadside memorial to her. I wondered what would be the reaction if this were a monument to a different minority group? What if this was a monument to the Holocaust? Granted, the Holocaust was an event of a totally different magnitude, but there is a direct line between the sterilization of Carrie Buck and the Holocaust. The first group to be targeted for systemic extermination in Nazi Germany was people with disabilities in a little-known program called Operation T4. Nazi "scientists" traveled to the United States to model their "mercy" killings after the eugenic practices of American scientists.

It was midafternoon by the time I found the historical information center on the outskirts of Charlottesville. The center was closing soon, and the woman behind the counter seemed to have had a long day. I waited in line, and in front of me were shelves lined with copies of a guide to various monuments to the founding fathers that dot the area. Surely, I said to myself, this woman would know the location of the monument. "I was wondering if you could point me toward the monument to Carrie Buck," I said to her.

She didn't look up and replied in a monotone, "All the information on monuments is in the guide." Then she handed me a copy.

No need to argue, I thought, as I stepped back and flipped through the flimsy pages only to find what I had come to expect: nothing. I got back in line.

"Can I help you?" the woman asked me.

"What I'm looking for isn't in this guide," I said.

"What are you looking for?"

I could feel the frustrations of the day. I began calmly, "A monument to a woman who was sterilized," but my calm lasted all of two seconds. I told her all about eugenics. Forced sterilization. The Supreme Court. Oliver Wendell Holmes!

Things took a turn for the worse. Filled with anger, I looked at the clerk and yelled, "And he said three generation of imbeciles is enough! Do you realize he said that? A chief justice of the Supreme Court of the United States of America. He actually said that. Can you fucking believe that?" I had stepped over the line.

"Excuse me, sir," she said, "but you are yelling. I'm going to have to ask you to leave."

I gave it one last shot. I calmed down and said, "I mean, are you telling me you have no idea where this memorial to a woman who was sterilized by the state is?"

"I have no idea. I've never heard of it," she said. "Now please leave."

I walked outside and sat on the steps in front of the building. I thought about the trip to find this invisible testimony to what was an invisible past. Eugenics was an ambitious attempt to normalize the population, to dehumanize the other: the defective, the abnormal, the person with a disability.

In the disability rights movement there is a concept called ableism—the idea that our culture's treatment of people with different cognitive and physical experiences is a form of discrimination. Inherent in the idea of ableism is that the marginalization of people who are different is a civil rights issue. Eugenics embodies one of the greatest assaults on the civil rights of people with disabilities. Ableism draws a line between acceptable and unacceptable human experience. Ableism is normalcy's enforcer.

As I left the office, I thought about what the first lobotomy patient had said after her frontal lobes were cut. This woman was hardly insane; she was reported to be moody and difficult. After the procedure, the lobotomist, Walter Freeman, looked at her and asked if she remembered what had bothered her before the operation. "I don't know," she replied. "I don't remember. It doesn't seem to matter anymore." The operation was considered an unequivocal success.

I drove through the last of the collegiate sprawl trying to find the highway I would take to New York, which was only a day away. Before I got on the highway, I pulled into a parking lot and turned the bus off and sat in the heat in front of what looked like a frat house. This was the perfect place to end the first part of my journey. So much of what I had seen and heard over the past few months had been about how our quest for frat-boy normalcy keeps everyone in their right place. I watched the pretty girls wearing short shorts that said *UVA* on the rear. I used to want to be normal like them. But not anymore. What did I want to be? I wasn't sure, but I had time and, more important, I had more short-bus stories to hear to help me answer that question.

PART TWO

Burning Man

New York, NY–Seattle, WA

9

I Can't Remember to Forget You

NEW YORK, NY—KENNEBUNKPORT, ME

On August 5 the short bus rolled out of New York City with a new passenger: my sister Kelly. She quickly settled into the copilot seat and bravely tackled the first and most important responsibility of any copilot: reading the map. With confidence, she shouted out directions to help me find I-95 north and promptly got us lost. It turned out that Kelly had a significant map-reading disability. A perfect copilot for a short bus.

When we finally found the highway, the traffic on I-95 was horrible, as it always is. Large trucks were speeding to or from New England. There were potholes and narrow lanes. This was a road I knew well from my many travels to and from Brown. Our plan was to spend the night in Providence with a friend of mine from college and then head up to Maine the next day. The stop in Providence wasn't a necessity; we very easily could have kept driving all the way to Maine. But I hadn't really been back since I graduated, and it seemed fitting to stop. Brown was the place where I both metaphorically got off the short bus and, paradoxically, got back on. I went to Brown with no understanding of myself as part of a community of outsiders. I went to Brown lost between the dumb kid who could only play soccer and a new identity, which I had to create from the space left over from the person I used to be.

It was nice to be traveling with Kelly. Kelly was born in San Francisco and lived there until she was almost twelve. I've come to have an ambiguous sense of Kelly's early life. It is not something that's been talked about directly, but it was a time of chaos. This fact has been filtered through years of family amnesia, lies, and denials. I was never told directly about what happened, by Kelly or anyone else. I guess, like most of my family history, I came to know this fact through years of osmosis, of body language, of someone yelling at someone else over Christmas dinner.

But even in the middle of this chaos, Kelly always came through as a strong individual, even from an early age. She never really babbled as a kid, just went right to talking. When Kelly was two years old, she often refused to walk even though she physically could. She was famous for her sit-down strikes. Whenever she felt like it, Kelly would sit down, wherever she was, and refuse to move for however long she pleased.

She always seemed to be around during important moments in my life. Kelly is ten years older than I am, but she is closer to my age than my other two siblings. She is much like me when it comes to our school experiences. Long after she left for college, I found what I thought was, because of the handwriting, one of my notebooks, buried in a box. I pulled it out and took it to school, and it turned out to be Kelly's from years before. The irony, though, is that Kelly was never labeled learning disabled but gifted. It's common family knowledge that out of all of us, Kelly is the most intelligent.

I'm asked all the time how I could ever have gotten into, let alone graduated from, an Ivy League college like Brown, and I have all sorts of academic answers. But I couldn't have done it without Kelly. Her support and her presence in my life helped me survive my negative experiences in school. Kelly provided me with a place to go to make sense out of the pain of my life. I still remember the day I realized this.

It was Christmastime. I was in fourth grade, sitting with Kelly in the living room in our house on Nelson Street. Kelly was in high school and was depressed. She ditched school most days and went to therapy and ate ice cream right out of the container. I know she felt like she had no place—no place at school, no place at home. Kelly, along with my other two siblings, Billy and Michelle, were the only kids on assisted lunch in school, and they talked like kids who grew up in a housing project. Kelly was emerging into herself as an artist, a creative thinker who did not fit into upper-middle-class Manhattan Beach.

Within this world, Kelly had created her own space. She lived in a wild, beautiful room. She decorated her space with a huge mural with pink pigs using a pig stencil she bought at the fabric store. She had five stuffed pigs as well and each had its own name. There were Mmmm-bubba, Ahhbaaba, arribaribaribabahbumba, Louielouielooay, and, my favorite, Stan the Man.

Kelly slept through most of Christmas break. We had the house to ourselves, and we sat in the living room talking. I had no words for what was going on in school. I just felt numb. We sat on our plaid sofa, passing a container of ice cream back and forth. "I'm depressed," she said to me. I had no idea what that word meant, but I knew what she was talking about. "I am too," I said, handing the carton over to her. We sat like that for an hour, eating ice cream, talking about music and how much school hurt us, though neither of us actually went to school much that year. When the ice cream carton was empty, she said to me, "Good can come from bad. I just haven't found the good yet."

That idea made a huge difference in my life. Kelly would repeat almost the exact same thing to me years later—on the night I was arrested for a DUI. This breakdown had been a long time coming. Winter break, my freshman year at Loyola Marymount, I slept on Kelly's floor and felt like I couldn't move. I didn't eat ice cream, but I read a lot of Virginia Woolf and James Joyce and slept until three in the afternoon. It had been a pretty terrible year. Soccer was fucked. I had injured my ankle the first day of training camp, and recovered about four games into the season, only to play with tendinitis in my knee for the rest of the year. I was getting my ass kicked in school. It felt like the fabric of myself was ripped, and I didn't know how to stitch it back together.

It would take a year for things to change. The next semester I got chickenpox and was in bed for a month and stopped playing soccer. I began taking classes in literature and poetry. The next year, in the fourth soccer game of the season, I broke my leg and tore ligaments in my ankle in the final seconds. I lay on the field in tears, filled with relief.

The day of my DUI I had gone to San Pedro with my roommate Ivai to celebrate a birthday with his family. They were first-generation Croatian-Americans, and that day we ate Croatian food and talked Baltic politics. After the party, Ivai and I drove back to L.A. and it started to rain; it poured like the sky had broken. The car felt like it was floating, and the Talking Heads song "Once in a Lifetime" came on the radio. That night was the end-of-the-year soccer banquet; because of my injury I felt like a fraud even attending. By dinner I was drunk. The rest of the night, pretty much unconscious, I drove a group of friends from party to party. With a car full of people, I ran a red light and there was a cop car behind me. I was arrested. Kelly was the first and only person I called. I slept that night on her floor and begged her to run me over with her car. That night she told me, "Good can come from bad. You just haven't found the good yet."

It would take a long time for the good to come from my experiences. Shortly after the DUI, I got it in my head that I would transfer from LMU. Transferring was an idea that Kelly gave me. She had transferred from the University of California at San Diego to UCLA. I have to admit the first time she mentioned it to me, I laughed out loud. Without playing soccer, I thought schools would take one look at my high school transcripts, light my application on fire, piss on it, and send the whole package back to me with a nice pink bow. Kelly knew better. She told me that often for transfers, high school grades are devalued, as are SAT scores.

I made a list of schools myself and booked a ticket to the East Coast for my winter break. Some schools agreed to interview me; some didn't. At those schools that opted not to interview me, I sat outside the admissions office until someone would meet with me. I guess from the experiences that I had been through, something, a determination, a resilience, had come from, not in spite of, the bad. Kelly was right again.

It took us four hours to get to Providence. As we rounded the curve of the interstate into downtown, it felt like I was going back in time. It was a landscape that I knew well, and driving into Providence felt like coming home. This was a strange feeling, because if there was any place where I felt like an utter outsider it was at Brown, a world of kids who could name all the Ivy League schools by the time they were ten. I had no idea what an Ivy League school was until I was nineteen. But Providence felt like the place where I became the person I am today. Transferring to Brown was the most important decision that I had made, and Kelly was a part of that. I looked at Kelly in the rearview mirror. Her belief that we can transform the pain of our experiences was passed on to me and remains essential to my life.

Before we found a parking place, I turned around and said, "Dude, I know we have never talked about this, but would you do away with the struggles you had as a kid?"

She did not hesitate, answering, "No way. Sometimes these painful things make you who you are."

We spent a day in Providence before heading to Maine. The next morning, I got up early, before the students. I took a cup of coffee to the main green and sat where I had sat years before, almost to the day, for transfer orientation. And I thought about that first trip to Brown.

In early August 1997, my mom and I drove up together from New York City. We were quiet most of the ride. My life was packed into the trunk of my brother's Honda Accord, and I wore soccer shoes, old Sambas with white stripes. (I wore these shoes every day at Brown until the soles fell off during my senior year.) Things were changing between my mom and me. Soccer had something to do with it, I'm sure.

The entire summer before I transferred, I told myself, and my mom, that I would play soccer at Brown. All my good feelings about myself came from that game; without it, I was the stupid kid. But I was sick of playing. Literally. I woke up before games and felt like I had the flu.

Ironically, it was actually my mom of all people who gave me the courage not to play soccer at Brown. I had ditched a lot of school when I was younger with my mom's blessing. We usually went to the zoo—

mental health days, my mom called them. But we ditched the first day
of school only *once*.

We didn't go to the zoo that day. We rented shitty bikes somewhere
in Marina del Rey and rode them all the way to Santa Monica. The
chain on my bike kept falling off, but I didn't care. I wanted to get
stranded at sea and never come back. When we got to Santa Monica,
we walked to the edge of the pier and I played skeet ball and watched
the men from south L.A. fish. I looked down inside each of their bas-
kets to see what they had caught. I ate a few fries, and we walked to
the edge of the water, and my mom held my hand. We walked to the
swing set and I got on one of the big swings. My mom told me the
same story she always told about the day she fell off a slide and broke
her arm. She lifted that arm and ran her hand down the length of the
scar that formed from the break. I launched myself forward into the
sky. When I was done swinging, I said to my mom, "I don't want to go."
And she said, "You don't have to."

What a gift from my mom—you don't have to do what they tell
you to do. Make your own life. The question for me was, while my
mom could tell me that about school, could she say that same thing
about soccer? Soccer was always the place where I was better than the
rich kids in Manhattan Beach, and that was really important to her. I
was terrified to tell my mom that I had decided not to play at Brown.
But when I finally did, as we drove to Brown to see the school, she
looked at me and said clearly and strongly, "You don't have to do anything if you don't want to."

I was greeted at the Brown transfer registration by a bald man wearing horn-rimmed glasses who spoke in a dialect of artist-intellectual
that was unfamiliar to me. He was a nice man, though. "I'm Steve," he
said. Then after five minutes of registration formalities he said to me,
"I need a wacky fact, man."

"What?" I asked.

"It is just a stupid ice breaker for later," he said. "You know, something wacky about yourself. You speak German or spent a year traveling the world, something like that."

German was out. I looked down at my old Sambas. Then I looked at Steve and pulled from deep inside myself something I had never said to anyone. I don't know where it came from—from Kelly, from the outings at the zoo with my mom, maybe, from the space between the past and the present.

"Well," I said to Steve, "my wacky fact is that I did not learn to read until I was twelve and I'm dyslexic."

That night, at orientation, all the transfer students sat around in a circle. "OK," the transfer counselor said. "Let's each introduce ourselves, tell us where you have transferred from, and maybe what you did this summer." So it began: "I transferred from Yale, and I worked for the NIH this summer." "I transferred from Princeton and worked on a cure for cancer." "I transferred from Harvard, and I'm on the short list for the Nobel Prize." *What was I doing here? Who was I to think that I had a place here?* Then someone stood up, a guy with purple hair, bicycle chains around his wrists, paint-smeared jeans, and said, "My name is Dave. I transferred from a two-year college for kids with learning disabilities and attention—ah, let's say attention issues—a tard school, and I worked in construction last summer." I thought to myself, *That's my boy.*

I went right up to Dave. "What's your fact, man?" he asked me. I told him. "Dyslexic?" he said to me. I nodded my head because I couldn't get the words out. Dave nodded back like we spoke the same dialect of tard-ese. "My fact," he said, unprompted, "is that I learned to weld when I was eleven years old." He paused and raised his eyebrows and then laughed. "So it seems that I learned to weld before you learned to read."

I thought I could feel the world shifting. I looked at him like I might cry for joy. "That," I said, "is fucking hysterical."

We stood in the hollowed-out old school building for an hour and talked about hiding in the bathroom and feeling defective. In less than two months we started writing a book together that would later be published. In that space my relationship to disability and to normalcy changed. I was still a little ashamed of being dyslexic and still striving for normalcy. But right then we were two Brown students, standing in the yellow light of an old school building, two outsiders not knowing what was in front of them, but knowing, at least, we were not alone.

———

The day Kelly and I left Providence, I had lunch with a friend of mine named Matt. He was seventeen years old and had been diagnosed ADHD and bipolar. A few years earlier, he had attended one of my talks. After it ended he e-mailed me and told me a little bit about his life. At one point, when Matt should have been attending high school, he didn't leave his room for most of the year. In that room he thought about killing himself, not in some dramatic or violent way, but in a clinical way. I wondered, as I drove to meet him: Did Matt come out of that room more or less himself? Was Kelly right—does good come from bad? Can we create anything from these experiences? At the very least, Matt had a great sense of humor. He ended his first e-mail to me by telling me that I had left twenty cents on the stage after my talk. If I was ever in Providence again, I could collect my twenty cents, plus any interest owed.

Matt and I had lunch together on the east side of Providence. When I picked him up at his home, he had come down the stairs wearing baggy jeans and no shirt. His hair was shorter than the last time I saw him, and he looked different, older and bigger in some way. But he also seemed withdrawn, his personality sucked inside of himself like a kid sucking in his cheeks. But between Matt's quiet moments were bursts of his self that wove everything together or forced everything apart.

At lunch we talked about school and his plans for the future. He seemed scared that the deep depression, which had almost cost him his life, might come back. But at least now he knew what had brought it on: bipolar disorder. "You know, man, that really fucking helped me." For Matt's whole life, his mood swings were written off as him being a pain in the ass. Now he had a name for them. Sometimes this makes all the difference. Matt also had a plan. "Fuck school," he said. "I'm going to City Year."

After lunch we went back to his house to say good-bye. Matt lived with his folks in an old and worn but beautiful place that felt as comfortable as broken-in jeans. The home had no air conditioners, so all the windows were open and the breeze fluttered into the rooms. Before I left, I asked Matt if he wanted to write something on the bus.

The entire wall of Matt's bedroom was filled with quotes from books in a black Sharpie pen. He told me that he writes on his wall like we write to each other.

"Sure," he said as he grabbed his Sharpie. It took a while for Matt to figure out what he wanted to make permanent. After a few minutes, he wrote, *Yesterday love was such an easy game to play.*

"That's it?" I said.

"No," he said, and he started to pace. I watched him and thought about my old self who used to live in this city. I thought I could feel him shedding his skin again, turning inside out, trying to remember who he once was, so he could know who he could be. I watched Matt trying to create that self that fits him best. Finally, Matt stretched out his arm and, in black, on white, turning gray, he wrote a line from the movie *Memento, I can't remember to forget you.*

Back at the hotel, I found Kelly dancing to a Madonna song emanating from her newly acquired iPod via a small white beat box. She looked at me very seriously. "Tunes!" she shouted. Kelly has a passion for music. Some of my first memories of her are driving in one of her messy cars filled with cigarette smoke and blaring music.

"Now we can go to Maine!" she said, pointing to the white beat box.

It was in her cars, in her messy apartments, always filled with music, where I learned that my past did not determine my future. That I could change. I laughed at her and said, "You know, you give me courage." She did. Her presence convinced me that, somehow, something worth knowing would come from this journey.

She walked over and gave me a hug and then said, "Dude, I have to say, if a woman with no job, no money, two cats, who lives with her parents gives you courage, you have some serious fucking problems."

Kelly spent most of the drive rocking out in the back, and I watched her dance like a little kid at a wedding. I always loved music as a child, but I was ashamed of this passion. My mom, a radical philistine, denounced any music, or art, that wasn't for the revolution. But even this was a pose. Mom was passionate about Bob Dylan, U2, and Bruce Springsteen, of course, any band that sang about the working man or politics. But she also fell in love with Paul Simon's *Rhythm of the Saints*. I caught her one day playing this album. She was standing near the sink, her sleeves rolled up from washing dishes, the scar on her arm white on white skin, staring out the window watching the snow fall. She moved her lips without making a sound. When she saw me, she turned the music off and looked to the floor as if I'd seen her naked.

Music can do that: take us out of our skin and help us become someone new. Billy Joel's *Greatest Hits* was the first album that truly changed me. Of course, I had a few songs I loved before that. I was obsessed with "Turning Japanese" and used to stand on our kitchen table and, quite offensively, modify the shape of my eyes while singing that fine ode to the fear of foreigners. Then, of course, there was "Whip It." (The less said about that the better.) But Billy's *Greatest Hits* was the only tape my dad had in his car. He never played it when I was in the car, so I waited for the times after school or soccer practice when he left me alone to run an errand. When he was out of sight, I climbed into the front seat and opened the cassette case. I was only eight or nine, but when that album came on I was no longer in a world of malls and cold hallways. When I saw my dad coming, I ejected the tape and stared out the window like nothing had happened. Something as good as Billy had to be hidden.

After Billy, nothing could touch Miles Davis's *Kind of Blue*. Kelly, as it happened, had this classic on her iPod, and I asked her to play it as we drove out of Providence toward Maine. *Kind of Blue* was the soundtrack to my first semester at Brown. I had never heard anything like Miles's horn, the controlled and beautiful chaos of the structured improvisation. I listened to that album every day of that semester. It was fall on the East Coast, with its diminishing light and humid cold air sticking to my skin like cellophane. Miles was the sound of me not playing soccer, the sound of old buildings and prep school cadences, the sound of not knowing who I was or what I was doing. It was the sound of change.

Kelly and I spent the night in Bedford, New Hampshire, at a Holiday Inn, and I had dinner with an acquaintance of mine named John and his parents. John had had a traumatic brain injury from an illness when he was a kid. He was nineteen or so, and we had met briefly after a conference. He introduced himself by saying to me that his face was swollen because he ate too much. He rambled for a long time, moving between coherency and its opposite until I excused myself. When I told John that I might stop in to see him on my travels, he started leaving me messages on my cell phone such as "Dude, 12:45" and "Take a right left right." Things along those lines.

Over dinner, John's parents told me the story of what had happened to their son. As they talked, John shut up for the first time all night and sat perfectly still and listened.

John's sight had been blurry when he woke up one morning in elementary school. He thought he was tired but got on the bus and rode to school as usual. It was after first period when the sides of his eyes started feeling funny and he felt hot, like he was under a heater. He didn't want to miss the project that his class was working on, but he wanted his mom. He walked up to the teacher and asked to go to the nurse. The long hallway to the nurse's office shook, and his ears rang. His throat closed up. The sounds of the other classes broke over him. He never made it to the nurse.

A janitor found him and carried his hot body to the office and someone called an ambulance. John was unconscious, and the EMT thought he would die before they reached the hospital. He was in a coma for the next week in a hermetically sealed room, with researchers from the U.S. Centers for Disease Control and Prevention in spacesuits testing him. He had encephalitis; his brain had swelled and had pushed against his skull, causing massive bleeding and damage. He would never be the same.

"I'm almost the same John again," he said after the story was over. It had been almost ten years since the incident. His parents nodded their heads, but I knew it just wasn't so. For a long time I wanted to hope that finally things were okay, we had recovered from our troubles. I wanted that for John, for me, for Kelly, for all of us carrying around painful things that have happened. I wanted to believe that there is some essential self, that we're not just these sets of injuries and responses to injuries. I hoped that something about ourselves is transcendent, that we're not just this brain matter and these electrons, not just a collection of dents and holes. But it seemed to me that John came out of that hospital room different, changed. He came out of that hospital room with a broken head and a different life and future.

John's mom drove me back to the Holiday Inn that night after dinner. We didn't talk much, but as we got closer to the hotel I asked her if what happened to John had changed *her*. "I'm a completely different person," she said. "I was going to live one of those lives, fancy car, big house in the suburbs, those lives. John's injury changed all of that. And you know, I'm grateful for it. I have different values now." When something breaks, we can choose how we make sense of it, and John's mom chose to see change in a positive light. Maybe the human experience is like a split tree trunk, the tree incorporating a moment of violence and trauma and growing around it. We all have damaged selves in some way, and the question is: Do you put your self back together holding on to that flickering image of the ideal self, or do you let that go, and see yourself for what you are—damaged, with other parts of you stronger for it? I don't think we can ever be anything other than imperfect shadows of some impossible ideal.

Standing in front of the Holiday Inn, I thought about this time with John and the rest of the journey. After Maine, Kelly and I would head back into the middle of the country and I would start the long journey back home. But first, Kelly and I would ride together into the Nevada desert, to Black Rock City and Burning Man, where the freaks of this country were gathering to create something new. Can, as Kelly said, good come from bad if we have the courage to find and create the good? In the stories to come, I hoped to find out.

It took three hours, traveling in suffocating summer traffic, to get to Kennebunkport. Kelly and I didn't really talk; we were still settling into the trip. Yet we couldn't get too comfortable; more change was on the way. In two days, our friend Christopher, who had helped modify the bus, would join us to help make a documentary of our journey. But he would become a little more than just a cameraman. Kelly, it seems, had already developed a huge crush on him.

Once in Kennebunkport, we stayed for three nights with John and Miriam Whitehouse and their family. Miriam was one of those moms

I had met while doing a presentation. Her family was made up of working-class Mainers trying to hold on to their community as it changed from a small town, to a suburb of Portland, to a land of summer homes filled with Massachusetts license plates.

I had traveled to Maine not to see the Whitehouses but to spend time with a man named Cookie. Miriam had introduced me to Cookie when I was staying in their home for a week during a previous trip. One night, we all got drunk, and over the howling wind of a March snowstorm Miriam told me about a man who was considered the town eccentric. He lived in Cape Porpoise, the working-class fishing village that lies between Kennebunk and Kennebunkport, which are predominantly wealthy communities. Cookie was an old-school Mainer who had made a living working on the piers. Most people, and some who have known Cookie his entire life, considered him to have a developmental disability—though Cookie did not see himself as disabled in any way. I remember the way Miriam's voice changed as she supplied further details: "Cookie, who is well over six feet tall, *also* walks around town in a dress, high heels, fake tits, and a blond wig," she told me. In addition, she said, Cookie was a painter, mostly of primitive Maine landscapes.

I remember asking Miriam how she and the rest of the town made sense of Cookie. Was he crazy? A transvestite? Mentally delayed? She looked at me like *I* was crazy. "We just think of him as Cookie."

10

The Turnaround Dance

Cookie Davis

CAPE PORPOISE, ME

He was born Coleman Davis, in 1951, in the local hospital not far from where he has lived his entire life. He grew up with the nickname Cookie, though no one really knew why people called him that. During the time that I spent with him, actually there was some confusion as to what I was to call him. It all began with Miriam and me in front of his house waiting for him to answer the doorbell. As we stood there in the August humidity, Miriam complicated matters. "I still call him Cookie," she said, "and he hasn't complained yet, but he might want 'new' people to use his new name. He said something to me recently about changing his name to Dominique . . . and then he went on to list, like, five middle names."

This profusion of names did not strike Miriam as odd, just part of the package. "I mean his cat has, like, ten names," she said. Ten, I would learn later, was a slight overstatement. The feline in question was, in fact, named Wolfgang Amadeus Gauguin London.

That day I spent with Cookie was clear and blue like a nineteenth-century landscape painting of coastal Maine. That morning, I had followed Miriam to Cookie's house in Cape Porpoise. The tourists and summer residents were out like locusts escaping the August heat. The roads were crowded with Volvos, sunburns, and New York and Boston accents.

Miriam had described Cookie's house to me as "a shack with no running water." Cookie, age fifty-two at the time of our interview, had lived in this house for his entire life. Cookie's father had died of a heart attack when Cookie was a kid, and his mom, Viola, passed away in 1998 of an aggressive breast cancer. According to local legend, Cookie had been strangled by his umbilical cord during delivery; this had resulted in some sort of brain "damage." But this may have been a local myth, perpetuated to explain Cookie's behavior. The story of his birth was never actually confirmed by Cookie. Miriam doesn't buy the idea that he is developmentally delayed or has had any type of brain damage. But she does acknowledge that Cookie, who often dresses in women's clothes, marches to the beat of a different drummer. "I'm not sure if we do understand Cookie," she wrote to me later. "He is very contradictory in many ways. He doesn't really seem mentally delayed to me, but it's more like he's in a parallel state of consciousness."

Cookie's mom had left him the deed to her house, ensuring him a place to live for the rest of his life. The town has always rallied to support Cookie. The managers of the Cape Porpoise Pier hired him to work in the bait shed for the lobstermen. Over the years, Cookie came up with many interesting enterprises (one year he created homemade Christmas wreaths), and friends and neighbors have always bought whatever he's selling. Miriam told me that beyond this, Cookie lived "on state aid and handouts, as well as on money from collecting returnables, running errands for local restaurants, and income from his paintings." The town of Kennebunkport does not collect taxes on Cookie's property, and many assume it is planning to lay claim to this land once he's dead. "The official Kennebunkport town government still holds to old-fashioned Maine values, which include protecting the underdog," Miriam said.

Through most of the years of Cookie's life, Kennebunk has remained the type of small town that used to constitute American life—a place that took care of its own.

But Miriam, and others I spoke with, said things are changing.

Kennebunkport is now an outer-edge bedroom community for Boston; it's also close to Portland and has become a popular retirement destination. Kennebunkport's population has increased dramatically in the past decade. According to Miriam and others, the entire area has become "yuppified." Real estate prices have soared, and expensive homes now outnumber the older cottages. "Out of the thirty or so homes on Langsford Road where my husband's parents live," Miriam said to me, "almost all of them have been bought by out-of-state new residents."

These changes have affected the town's sense of community. According to Miriam, "Whereas you used to recognize and speak to almost everyone you saw, wherever you went in town, now more people are strangers to you than friends. Because the town has grown so rapidly, the sense of community has eroded. There is a clear sense of the little guy being pushed out of the way by the rich." Especially, I assume, if the little guy is not particularly prosperous and is a little bit different.

The erosion of community is, in fact, an epidemic in the United States. Robert Putnam, a Harvard professor and the author of *Bowling Alone*, a popular academic book, has documented this sad phenomenon. Americans, he writes, are in general less engaged in such activities as civic organizations, social clubs, and local institutions of every stripe. The decline has many roots—from suburban sprawl to individual financial pressures, changing workforce dynamics, and the advent of modern entertainment, including the Internet. Putnam, like many others, argues that this transformation is one of the most significant challenges facing the United States. The decline in community has significant consequences for both the public and for individuals. According to Putnam, an "impressive and growing body of research suggests that the civic connection helps make us healthy, wealthy, and wise." Individuals engaged in the concerns and activities of a community "become more tolerant, less cynical, and more empathic to the misfortunes of others."

I wondered, standing in front of Cookie's home, if a less community-minded America will still have a place for people like Cookie.

"Hey, Cookie!" Miriam yelled as she banged on his door (she'd given up on the bell). "Just a minute," came a response, finally, from deep in the shack. It was almost impossible for me to understand what this voice was saying. (Cookie's speech, I would learn later, reflected the colorful, indigenous accent of rural Maine, one of the last, strong regional accents in the country.) His appearance, however, didn't quite jibe with what I'd heard. Cookie finally answered the door, wearing a pink bathrobe and a wig. He didn't greet me but just pointed out toward his barn, which he had painted, and said, "I'll give you that one for one hundred dollars."

I really didn't register what Cookie was saying. I was trying to get my mind around his appearance. His head almost touched the roof of his house. He was tall—huge—maybe over six-foot-five. He was one of those people who go through life walking into rooms that were too small for them and trying on shirts with cuffs that were too short, ending in the middle of their forearms. He had blue eyes with a speck of black and his face was deeply lined. He had the hands and arms of someone who had worked on the docks for years, and the veins on his forearms bulged like a bodybuilder's. But these strong hardworking hands were clutching that lovely bathrobe; he appeared to have makeup on as well. Cookie, it seemed, was beyond any of the stereotypes that I would have used to categorize him. Was Cookie an old-time Mainer? Was he a cross-dresser? A drag queen? Was he the town eccentric? Or was he just a man who had a fondness for pastels? And how did a town that was all about overalls, jeans, and chinos accept a giant ex-fisherman who habitually dressed in a pink bathrobe?

The place to start with all these questions was with a tour of Cookie's house. So after a few pleasantries and a quick good-bye to Miriam, whose hair, Cookie said, "looked a little frizzy," we got started. I had been given countless house tours on this trip thus far but, needless to say, Cookie's was a little different from the others. "It is not a nice house," Cookie said as we walked in. "But I love it. I keep it clean." That much was true, within reason. "I shake the rugs out every day," he said with a proud smile.

The layout of Cookie's home was such that with one pivot of his large feet, he could point to the kitchen, bathroom, bedroom, and the living room. As Cookie talked, his words punctuated by the sound of his shifting feet and sand on linoleum, I became intrigued by his manner of speech. Deep and beautiful, it sounded like the linguistic equivalent of a shore with jagged rocks, still pools, and rocky beaches. Cookie's cadence was as erratic as a twisting shoreline, and his voice rose from a whisper to a rant with nothing in between. All in all, though, he had an amazing verbal confidence for someone who had rarely ventured far from his shack.

Cookie's sense of decor was also a study in extremes. On one hand, his house was filled with images of local landmarks and points of interest, like a grandmother's house. There were watercolors, oil paintings, and pastoral calendars depicting a local church, an island off the coast of Portland, and a lighthouse in the fog. On the other hand, juxtaposed against these pastoral paintings was what many might consider a respectable amount of pornography of a European persuasion. Now, don't get me wrong; none of this was in any way grotesque or illegal, and the amount was nothing more than a married man might stash in the basement of his home in an American suburb. What was of note about Cookie's taste in porno was that all the pictures depicted some form of gender bending.

"I'm writing a book," Cookie told me in the middle of his house tour, briefly turning my attention from his decorations. "Great," I said. "Can you show it to me?"

Cookie did not need to be asked twice. He disappeared into the other room and then came back carrying a book of colored paper. He smiled broadly. "I've just started. This book is about my struggles and my transition," he said. (I knew that "transition" was a word used by those considering sex reassignment.) Cookie had not made much progress beyond the title page of his opus, but that was all I needed to see. Here was the remarkable appellation that Miriam had alluded to early in the day. The author of the book was Dominique Helene Louise Emmanuelle Victoria Heather Renee Dejaneario London.

"All of these?" I asked. "These are all your names?" He nodded. "How did you come up with this?" I asked. "Just fooling around," he said. "It's a mouthful," I said, in a rare restrained moment. I started to say the names and he joined in, and we said in unison, "Dominique Helene Louise Emmanuelle Victoria Heather Renee Dejaneario London." Then he repeated, "This book is about my struggles and my transition."

Perhaps there was just a *tad* more to Cookie's story than I originally thought.

"So," I said, "what should I call you throughout the day?" He didn't answer right then. Later when I asked him the same question he gazed at me and responded, in a tone somewhere between a joke and a confession, "Dominique, Cookie . . . you can call me anything you want." Then he added, "Just don't call me late for dinner."

Any attempt to try to understand Cookie's life must start with an exploration of how he was treated in his earliest years. Like many of the interesting people I've gotten to know, Cookie was still affected by old memories and hurts. The past was still very much with him. Throughout our day together he would mention a teacher who demeaned him, a group of kids who tormented him, and his experience of being labeled "slow." Gradually he confessed that he was often called "stupid," and ultimately "mentally retarded."

Cookie grew up in the 1950s, a time of massive cultural optimism, social change, and institutional conformity. From what I can gather, he was never able to fit in or conform to our culture's cognitive norms. I asked him what it was like growing up in his conservative small town given who he was. "Not that good," he said. "I had troubles. The kids made fun of me. The way I speak. The way I act." The harassment Cookie suffered was actually more than making fun, more than what we commonly write off as teasing. For Cookie, it was a kind of violence, attacks with lasting psychological repercussions.

One day after school, Cookie was chased and attacked by a group of kids whom he described as a faceless mob. Being chased was nothing new for Cookie. This group of kids would often walk a few steps behind him, shouting taunts like "retard" and "fag." Some days they would just eventually stop; on others they would pick up the pace and start coming after him. Cookie, who was terrified, would run faster and faster, filled with terror, the kind of awful fear that only people who have been chased really understand. On the day (or days) of the attack, his pursuers caught Cookie and pelted him with rocks.

Also omnipresent in Cookie's memory was a teacher named Nails. "I called her Nails because she had long fingernails," Cookie said, "which looked like claws." Cookie was plagued by a very specific memory of Nails dating back to when Cookie was six. That day, Nails went too far. One of the students was doing work on the blackboard that Cookie just couldn't master. To remove himself from the situation, Cookie was watching the light outside the window filter its way through the bare trees. It was the dead of winter, and I imagined the light was the color of tarnished silver.

"I wasn't doing anything, and she just put her claws into me," Cookie told me. "You got to get it right," Nails screamed at Cookie. He said, "*I am* trying!" Then, according to Cookie, the teacher called him "stupid." This label came as no surprise to him. He knew people called him that "around his back," as he put it. If they said it to him directly, he always responded. He certainly responded to Nails. "I said, 'No, I'm not stupid!' And then I was out of control. 'I'll show you, bitch!'" he screamed at her. "And that's when she dug her claws right in." Cookie pointed to his shoulder. According to him, Nails had dug her fingernails deep into his shoulder until she drew blood. "I just turned around and drew back," Cookie said. He punched her. "I nailed her right on the jaw."

It is still unclear to what extent Cookie was labeled, at this point in his life, as mentally retarded. But according to Carl Pipen, who went to school with Cookie and has known him his entire life, Cookie was always enrolled in some form of special education. His academic experience, specifically during high school, seemed to have been one of warehousing and social promotion. According to Cookie, when he was seventeen years old he was officially told he was "retarded."

"They thought I was stupid," Cookie told me. "I walked out—I told the doctors to fuck themselves."

It is at this point that Cookie's story and my attempt to understand his experience merge with the social history of what used to be known as *mental retardation*, but is currently referred to as a *developmental disability*. Before both of these terms came into use, however, such cognitive states were grouped under the heading *feeblemindedness*.

The history of these terms is not stable. Rather, their use provides a sort of loose history of how culture and society—to use a phrase coined by James Trent, a professor of sociology—"invented the feeble mind." Most of us tend to think that what we call mental retardation is an objective phenomenon. In 1973, however, in one of the latest reshufflings of language, the American Association on Mental Deficiency "changed the criterion for mental retardation from one to two standard deviations" of "normal IQ." In plain English, thousands of people earlier classified as mentally retarded woke up one day and were no longer retarded.

According to Trent, the cognitive state that we've come to know as mental retardation or developmental disability was originally regarded as "an expected part of rural and small town life." "Simpletons" and fools were kindly regarded, even romanticized by the likes of William Wordsworth, and cared for by family members and the community. Trent convincingly argues that this rather accepting conception of cognitive minorities—while still at least a bit evident in some small towns around the United States today—changed in the nineteenth century when feeblemindedness was invented and pathologized.

In the nineteenth century, feeblemindedness became a clinical category, with individuals who were previously integrated into the community now considered to be patients in need of rehabilitation. Influenced by pedagogical advances by French educators of the deaf and blind, a new class of training schools emerged. Their goal was to rehabilitate these lost souls and return them to the community. By the beginning of the twentieth century, however, the goal of community integration had been nearly abandoned. In the mid-1900s it was common for people of all political stripes to talk about "menace of the feeble mind." Cognitive minorities were no longer gentle fools. They were dangerous and in need of "total institutionalization."

Coinciding with the rise in total institutionalization was an expanded clinical definition of mental deficiency. As a result of widespread intelligence testing in the army during World War I, a new clinical taxonomy emerged that delineated discrete diagnoses such as "idiots," "imbeciles," and "morons." The latter were of special concern to eugenicists because they looked and acted "normal" but were degrading the country's gene pool. At one point, the army's IQ testing suggested that almost 40 percent of the entire U.S. population were morons.

In the 1950s, this elaborate system was abandoned, at least clinically. (Yet think how often people who are ignorant of their original meanings use words like *idiot* and *moron* in casual conversation.) That decade, however, was a paradoxical time to be someone outside of our cognitive norms. A new lobby for middle-class parents advocated for those diagnosed as mentally retarded. This new lobby created the American Association on Mental Deficiency and moved the discourse away from inherited traits. Such people were not considered dangerous, per se, but were thought to be trapped in a perpetual childhood. Ironically, however, at a time when the social stigma of having a "slow" child was somewhat lifted, institutionalization continued at a brisk pace.

Institutionalization is no longer the dominant social paradigm for people with developmental disabilities. What has replaced it is the rhetoric of community care, which emerged in the 1970s. Community care was a philosophy arguing that people with developmental disabilities were best served within their communities, not by large state-run institutions. Without question, empowering individuals to stay within their communities should be the ultimate goal of any public policy that concerns the lives of people like Cookie. But this notion has been co-opted by anti-big-government politicians determined to decimate federal and state social service funding. Not surprisingly, community-care initiatives have remained woefully underfunded.

So what did we learn from our short history of the feebleminded? If the social history of mental retardation is a story of shifting realities, one thing has not changed at all: Cognitive minorities are still one of the most socially and economically marginalized groups in the United States.

Eighty degrees and 90 percent humidity be dammed; Cookie was determined to look good for the rest of our day together. "Oh yeah . . . you'll see. I'm gonna wear my six-inch heels," he said as we left his house and made our way to the bus. "And they're white."

I was drawn to Cookie in large part because he was an artist. He was a painter. Our plan to pass the time was for him to paint a mural on the inside of the bus. He decided that he was going to render Goat Island and the surrounding bay. Goat Island sat in the bay outside of Cape Porpoise Harbor. The island was uninhabited and had only one structure: an historic lighthouse built in 1822. Cookie had seen this island almost every day of his life since he was a child. The way its rocky shore sat against the shallow bay was beautiful, he recalled. He said it was a part of the body of Maine, a special place, and it was important that I had this image of it to take with me as I traveled.

As Cookie began priming the white surface of the bus, I thought about his connection to and knowledge of the landscape of Maine. All of Cookie's paintings were grounded in a deep feeling that suggests the importance of place to the artist. Cookie knew the coast and the way it curved and dipped like he knew his own body. Cookie's paintings were a form of realism done with a flat, top-down perspective like an aerial map.

Each of his Maine paintings had a story within it, an implied narrative. In 2001, though I had never met Cookie in person, I hired him, through my friend Miriam, to paint an old door. When the painting was finished, Miriam explained that according to Cookie his scene on the door showed boats returning to port after an unsuccessful day at sea. Each boat had a name. Cookie knew the captain of each boat; he knew the exact catch for the day for each, the local gossip about the boats and crews, and all sorts of stories about the fishermen's families. To use a term from the writer William Least Heat-Moon, Cookie's paintings were *deep maps* of Cookie's world.

These deep maps, and Cookie's creativity, provided a different way to make sense of Cookie, a way quite different from labeling him retarded. Within the tradition of folk art, there is what is now called visionary, self-taught, or outsider art. Outsider or visionary art (the two terms are used interchangeably) is defined as art by individuals who live on the margins of society—minorities, people who are poor, or those with disabilities. Actually, most outsider artists fit into more than one of these groups. These artists are individuals, like Cookie, whose frame of mind and reference is radical, completely removed from the expectations and standards of others.

Grandma Moses is perhaps one of the most famous of the outsider artists, but I knew that Cookie resented and resisted being compared to her. Someone in town once compared his painting to the work of Grandma Moses. Upon hearing this, Cookie stopped in his tracks, put down what he was carrying, and said, "I ain't no fucking Grandma Moses."

It took a while for Cookie to emerge as the town's full-blown outsider artist. This is common in the stories of visionary artists; very often there is a considerable gestation period involved. Many do not paint or make any art until later in their adult lives, and most never make art professionally as a means of income. After graduating from high school, Cookie went to college. Where Cookie went to college or if he ever finished was never made clear to me. After college, he came home to live with his mom, and he, like many locals, worked odd jobs in the fishing community. Cookie worked the Chum Shack on the pier—a shit job, he said. It meant basically a life of scooping out fish intestines and other dismembered fish parts used as lobster bait.

Surprisingly, during this time Cookie got married. His wife, Lisa, was a local woman who, according to townspeople, was "gorgeous" and "looked like a model." Cookie was willing to share very little with me about his marriage. What I know is that Cookie and Lisa tied the knot in the early nineties in Australia and lived there together for two years. Lisa came from a wealthy family. As Cookie recalled, "She was good; she was an artist; she loved to drink—she got herself smashed." The marriage did not last long. Cookie went mum again when I raised the subject of their divorce, though, according to him, they were still friends.

At about the same time as the divorce, Cookie's mom, Viola, became very ill. She was sick for a few years. Cookie loved his mom deeply and by 1998 her body was ravaged by an aggressive cancer that metastasized pretty much everywhere it could. Cookie's mom was his life; he had never lived for long with anyone else. It was during this time of change, his mother's illness and his divorce, that Cookie started to paint.

Cookie did not draw a direct line between what was happening during this time in his life and his painting. I don't know if he really knew why he started to paint or why he continued. He described painting in the language of compulsion, a very common way for artists to verbalize their feelings about their work. His style appeared almost fully formed from the beginning. The first things he painted were the storage sheds on the pier and then the shed outside his house. From the beginning, Cookie's paintings portrayed his hometown and told stories. I wonder, though I never asked him, if his *deep maps* were a way to honor his mom. It is interesting to see them as testaments, testimonials or memorials to a way of life that is slowly dying.

Cookie's art was soon picked up by a local gallery in Kennebunkport run by an entrepreneurial New Yorker. This man may have thought of Cookie's paintings in the outsider genre. Or perhaps as pastoral Maine landscapes perfect for the tourist trade. Regardless, Cookie's work was suddenly hanging in a genuine art gallery, although it was a tough sell to the tourist market. Along with his landscapes, Cookie had developed an artistic fascination with rocks and naked women. His preference was to paint both at the same time. At one point, I was told, Cookie approached the gallery owner and asked if he could paint his pregnant wife naked, on some rocks of course. Needless to say, Cookie's gallery representation was short-lived.

Back in the bus, I asked Cookie what he thought about the comparison of his work to that of Grandma Moses. This time, he had a different, more refined response: "I follow Monet and Gauguin and Rembrandt." He paused and motioned with his brush toward the mural he was painting. "This is not folk art. It is retemperance," he said. "Retemperance?" I replied, suggesting the need for clarification. He pointed at his picture of Goat Island and then gestured beyond, toward the small town center, past the Chum Shack, toward the Maine coast. He started to talk again about his art. "It means thinking of a place and doing it," Cookie said, looking a little sad, and then added, "So that's the whole thing, you know."

In his own way, Cookie demanded to be seen as an artist without any qualifying labels. In many communities, people like Cookie are seen only through the lens of labels. They are considered "sick." After World War II, American society began its economic shift from an industrial economy to a service economy. This brought an unprecedented rise in the social service economy: more shrinks, medical doctors, social workers, and educators. As John McKnight, a community activist and professor of public policy, wrote in his book *The Careless Society*, this social service economy needs people like Cookie as its raw material. It needs a sick client.

After painting for a few hours, Cookie took a break to have lunch with me. We sat in the humidity and ate deli sandwiches and talked about music and life in Kennebunkport.

I mentioned to Cookie that I had some music. "Classical?" he asked. "Oh, you like classical?" I guessed. "Medium rock, as they say," Cookie clarified. "Like, uh, Metallica."

I did not have any medium rock. I had few genres. "All I have is pretty much just eighties music," I told him. "Eighties music," Cookie said and put down his turkey sandwich. His eyes enlarged. "I *love* the eighties' music," he said emphatically. Cookie loved Duran Duran, Flock of Seagulls, Men at Work, Billy Ocean, and some band I had never heard of that he called ELO (Electric Light Orchestra). "I just love the way they sing," he said. Then he looked at me very seriously and confessed, "It's great having people here to keep me company."

Cookie's life had been lonely, but there had always been a core group of people who looked after him. Many of these folks were still around, but I was told that, recently, Cookie had begun to recede from his community. According to Miriam, Cookie had started to display what she called "erratic behavior" beginning a few years earlier, around 2001. As we ate lunch and talked about music, Cookie addressed this change that people perceived in him, attributing it, at least partially, to the presence of so many new people around. "They don't understand," he said about the newcomers to his town. "Because of this stuff or that stuff. Because when I have to go somewhere I wear a dress. I really don't give a rat's ass. I don't care about the rat's ass. If I wear a dress, it's none of their business."

The dress wasn't news to me. Miriam had told me that Cookie had an interesting style before I had met him. His ensemble included a blond wig that he never washed but did cut and refashion into many interesting new hairdos. When Miriam asked him about it, he told her that it was a disguise, that he was hiding out from a repo man who wanted to take his truck for late payments. The wig, I would learn from Cookie, actually had nothing to do with the repo man. It was the first step in resolving what Cookie called his "situation." "This is true . . . the situation," he began, looking me directly in the eye. "The situation is the reason I want to change completely. The situation is the reason I want to become a woman."

It seemed that the community of Kennebunkport was now being asked to empathize with someone a little more complex than the eccentric artist in drag. It was being asked to accommodate someone who challenged a basic norm of our society: the stability of gender. Cookie had been hinting all day that he wanted to actually become a woman surgically. He was now starting to self-identify as transgendered.

A transgender individual is someone with a pervasive desire to change gender, often through surgical means. This is very different from someone who conceptualizes him- or herself as, or has been labeled, a homosexual or engages in cross-dressing behaviors. A transgender person has a continuing desire to be a different gender. Questions about the causes of this intense feeling have no clear answers. Two broad explanations have been proposed: biological and psychological. Some psychologists assert that transgender behavior has a Freudian, psychosexual basis—i.e., the bad mother messed up her kid. On the other hand, medical professionals assert a vague biological origin for transgender identities. Though certainly contentious in medical circles, many doctors' preferred treatment for transgendered people is sexual reassignment surgery.

Two interesting questions, for me at least, are *how* society has constructed transgender desire over time and whether it is considered a "real" identity. The modern history of transgender begins in late-nineteenth-century Germany, where a group of doctors, influenced by a dominant European belief in a continuum of human sexualities and gender, applied a theory of natural human bisexuality to individuals who reported being trapped in bodies they considered incorrect.

The more popular and widely disseminated history of transgender experience began in the United States when an ex-marine named George Jorgensen traveled to Europe in the 1950s and had sexual reassignment surgery. George became Christine, and she captured the public imagination and was obsessively covered by the press. Through this coverage, Jorgensen's story set the terms for the way that our culture understands transgender individuals, as well as the way that many "trans" individuals understand themselves. Jorgensen's story is filled with pervasive suffering and a vague realization that something was "always wrong."

Cookie told me a very similar story, describing his childhood as a time of gender confusion. He was a boy who thought of himself as "Daddy's little girl." "I always loved to play with girls," he said. "Even at five years old, it was just the way it was. I'm not ashamed of saying it." But it wasn't until later, when he was grown, that he (like many individuals in this situation) found the language to describe to himself his sense of suffering. "I was watching the television documentary about where this guy turned into a woman, and the hell of it all is, here I had the same feeling for the past fifty years. That's how I found the proverbial needle in the haystack."

Of course, most of society sees Cookie's desire to change gender through the lens of sickness. According to the *Diagnostic and Statistical Manual of Mental Disorders* (*DSM*), Cookie has gender dysmorphic disorder, or GDD. Like many diagnoses in the *DSM*, from ADD to depression, GDD has a social history that has little to do with people's actual lives. Judith Butler, a gender theorist, asserts that GDD is just a politically correct way for shrinks to pathologize homosexuality, which was not fully demedicalized by the American Psychological Association until 1983. Many individuals who want to transform are forced to use the official diagnosis to get treatment from doctors. Surgeons, for the most part, help people who are sick and have a "disorder," not people who assert a fundamental right to determine their gender.

Despite all the different ways to judge Cookie's gender-bending, his goals are pretty simple and universal. After we finished lunch, Cookie looked at me and said, "My real dream is, after the whole situation is over, I want a nice generous guy, to just, you know, just help me out and take good care of me and to love me." He then added, "And I would do three things. First, I would work somewhere. The second is have fun. And the rest of it," and here he paused and smiled. "The rest of it is I would find a nude beach where I could sunbathe naked. And believe me, I LOVE sunbathing nude."

"OK, almost done," Cookie said as he put the final touches on his mural of Goat Island. He had re-created the entire scene from memory. I saw a picture of this island later, and Cookie did justice to the way the rock sat in the bay, alone, surrounded by shallow water.

At that moment, a song by the Gap Band started playing on my stereo. "I *love* this!" Cookie screamed. It seemed that I had stumbled upon one of the few similarities between Cookie and Becky, my wife-to-be: They both had a passion for the Gap Band's "You Dropped a Bomb on Me." "I love that group," Cookie said. "I love that Gap Band because the Gap Band is really, to me . . . down to earth. They have the right beat."

I looked at Cookie's mural, and I saw off on the rocky shore one flower growing out of the rock close to the waterline. What would happen if the tide came in too far? Earlier, as Cookie started to paint that flower, I asked him why he chose to put it there, so close to the water-line. "Oh, yeah," Cookie said. "I like flowers. Just the way they are, the way they are. The way they project themselves as gorgeous wild things."

Cookie pointed at the mural ecstatically. "I'm gonna add one more thing you're going to love," he said. "Black buoy. Tells you where the rocks are. I love the rocks," he added. I sat in the heat, in the back of the bus, and I admired Cookie's vision of the coast. "I like the little windmill on top of the lighthouse too," I said. "Northerly wind coming in," he said as he pointed to a small shack, somewhat like the place where he was born and made his life and remade his life. "Little lop-sided . . . little house." "You think they use it anymore?" I asked him. Cookie nodded his head. "Oh, yeah!"

It was almost six at night when Cookie finished painting Goat Island. Our day was almost over. All that was left were a few errands and a trip to the beach to watch the sun set. I had not gotten an answer to the question that had haunted me all day: Did Cookie still have a place in his community?

Before we left, Cookie went back into the house to touch up his makeup, and I drove Bob Henry up the block and turned around in a cul-de-sac that led to the new condos near Cookie's house. The condos weren't done yet, and the ground was torn up; its black underbelly was exposed to the sky. What would the people who lived there think of Cookie? They most likely would not be from the old Kennebunkport. They wouldn't have any memories or experiences that tie Cookie to their sense of self and sense of home. Cookie, for them, might not even be Cookie; they might never learn his name. In a place where old-fashioned ties have broken down, Cookie might just be the crazy guy down the street; he might be considered dangerous.

Later, Cookie told me about the time when a man from what he called "the committee" came over to his house. According to Cookie, the committee came over sometime in 2001. He heard a knock on the door. When he answered it, he didn't recognize his caller. "You don't know me," the person said. "I am on a committee; I'm asking you to leave town; we don't like your type."

"What do you mean, you don't like my type?" Cookie said.

"Genderwise," Cookie recalled the caller as saying. "You have to leave town, or we are going to ruin your house."

The next day, Cookie called a friend of his who was a town select-man. No one had heard about any committee. But according to Cookie, the person who came to his house may have been a developer. Later, Cookie said, the man offered him money to move. Cookie, of course, turned him down. "They thought that I was infected. I'm supposed to be gay and infected."

We made our way downtown in two vehicles, with Cookie's truck leading the way. The sun had opened up the sky, as in one of Cookie's sea paintings. The trees moved in the wind. The road was choked with traffic, and a number of families were walking to the beach. (They had the glow of wealth, like models in a Ralph Lauren ad.) As I followed

Cookie, I thought about how gender and cognitive minorities are faced with violence every day. Small cruel gestures and horrific violent crimes. Why should someone feel the need to police another person's body? Gender identity and sexual desire are multifaceted and varied, perhaps much more so than we realize. Intersexed individuals, for example, previously known as hermaphrodites, are much more common than the medical establishment leads us to believe. Throughout human history, almost every known culture has made space for the divergent human body. At the same time, gender variance has been violently suppressed. Perhaps our greatest acts of violence are reserved not for those experiences that are most foreign to us but for the ones that are closest to the truths about ourselves.

But while I knew all of this intellectually, I was still deeply challenged by Cookie. As I drove, I remembered something Cookie had asked me when I first arrived. Before I went into his house he looked at me and said, "You're not going to make fun of me are you?" At the time I brushed it off, but Cookie had sensed something that I was afraid to admit. There was a time in my life where I would have made fun of Cookie—during my white hat days in high school. Cookie was resisting the idea of a settled fixed self. He was asserting his right to change. Like most of us, though, my identity had been set for me. I might have made fun of Cookie before, but I would never now. I admired him.

As we drove through town, however, I was filled with hopelessness about Cookie's future. A town of tourists, a community of summer residents cannot support people like Cookie. And his new focus on his gender issue may just be the straw that breaks the camel's back. He could end up destitute, in a home; somehow one of these developers may convince enough people that he is "infected."

As I was having these thoughts, Cookie slowed down in front of me, pulling over to the side of the road and rolling down his window. He leaned his body across the passenger seat and ecstatically waved to a man who was walking down the street with his young daughter. The man stopped and faced Cookie and then pulled his daughter closer to his side. He looked somewhat confused, and I braced for some sort of terrible hostile gesture—some sort of confrontation between two worlds. This man put his arms around his daughter, then spread his hand wide like a fan and waved to Cookie. His daughter waved as well. In something quite short of a Mainer accent, he yelled, "How you doing, Cook?" Cookie honked his horn and yelled back, "Just great, just great."

I followed Cookie from there through the other side of town, tracking his blond wig like a flashlight on a dark trail as it wove between European sports cars and T-shirt shops, lobster shacks, and old fishing piers melting into the ocean. Soon, we found a place to sit on a point that jutted out into the ocean. The Bush family compound was off to the right and the coast to our left. The Atlantic Ocean was spread out in front of us. Our day was just about over. The sun was still high in the sky, but it was at that point where it was hard to tell whether it was going up or down; it just sat on the horizon as if it could stay there indefinitely. I didn't really know how to end my time with Cookie, so we just sat in silence until Cookie began to talk: "Like I said, just take it easy with that painting. Put it this way, by the time you hit Reno, Nevada, it should be dry." He was referring to the mural of Goat Island he had done in the interior of the bus. This was his gift to me, and it was a chance to see a place through the eyes of someone who knew no other place, whose life was woven into the fabric of his community. "I won't let anyone touch it," I said. I told him I would guard it with my life.

Cookie then pointed to the bus. "I don't think I would wanna do that," he said, referring to the journey I was making.

"Why not?" I asked.

"It would be a long haul," he replied. "Take a lot of gas. And it'd be a long haul in a manner of speaking." Then he pointed out to the coast and the ocean and the town behind him, "and I gotta stay here," he said.

Cookie won't be made to leave anytime soon. According to Miriam, there were still many old-timers left on the town council who would fight for Cookie. Why? Miriam and others looked at me funny when I asked that question. They shrugged their shoulders and just said some version of "that's what people do for other people here."

Carl Pipen, who has known Cookie his whole life, called it good old organic care, the way it should be. It wasn't just the old-timers who fought for Cookie. I'd learn later that a fund had been created in Cookie's name by a group of realtors and an attorney. Many of these people had known Cookie for a long time, but some had not and were new to the community. The money was raised specifically to help pay off Cookie's back taxes in case the town decided to collect them, buy him a new car, and fix his home.

It was August 9 and time for me to head home. From that day forward, I would be heading west again. It was the exact turning point, and it had to be honored in some way. "I got an idea here," I said to Cookie. "Ever heard of the turnaround dance?" There was no reason why he would have. Becky invented the turnaround dance, and it was pretty simple. Anytime Becky and I were walking and we reached our turning point, we honored that turn with a dance. I explained this to Cookie, and he looked nervous. "You don't have to worry about it. I'll do it. The turnaround dance doesn't have to be long or good or graceful or anything at all; it just has to be done."

The soundtrack for our turnaround dance was obvious: It had to be "You Dropped a Bomb on Me." I walked back to the bus with Cookie and hooked up the stereo and rummaged around through my tapes. I looked at Cookie's mural in the bus. His name in the corner was smudged by the humidity of the day and my carelessness. I found the tape and set up the stereo.

I stepped into the middle of a patch of dirt off to the side of the road. I tried to get Cookie's attention. I started to call out "Cookie," but then I stopped. I still didn't know what to call him. Cookie? Dominique? Hey, you? I was just as confused as when I had started. So I just started the tape. "You don't have to do it, only if you wanna do it," I said to Cookie, meaning the dance.

"I'll think about it," Cookie replied. I played the tape, and the Gap Band shouted out toward the Bush compound and beyond. I closed my eyes and I turned my journey around.

When I was finished, Cookie walked up to dance without hesitation. "OK," he said. It was quite a sight: Cookie was framed by the

Atlantic Ocean stretching out behind him, a six-foot-five, fifty-two-year-old ex–lobster man, world traveler, master of the retemperance, transgender individual.

I thought about his gender-bending. Cookie is on the edge, as he has always been. The human form and experience is defined by variance. It seemed to me that it is only within the fabric of a community that this variance can thrive. It is only within the fabric of these relationships where Cookie can be Cookie until he decides she's Dominique.

The Gap Band blared out of the back of BH. Cookie put his arms out like John Travolta in *Saturday Night Fever.* He spun around and traced an invisible circle. Leonardo da Vinci's perfect human? A version of the Tibetan Buddhist conception of divinity as a woman and man fused together, violating all duality? No, just Cookie.

Cookie danced an ungodly dance, fell over, and laughed. "Awww, shit," he said. "Pretty good, huh?"

11

Big Things, Little Things

CAPE PORPOISE, ME—SEAMAN, OH

After dinner that last night in Kennebunkport, the Whitehouses and my crew hung out, talking and drinking. Then, one by one, Miriam, her husband, John, and Kelly went to bed. Christopher and I were the only ones left, facing the time when it isn't really late anymore but early. I felt restless, couldn't get Cookie out of my mind, and so I decided that the best thing to do would be to walk down to the town beach and go swimming. When I'm drunk, I often wander, and I've been known to walk fifty New York City blocks at three in the morning after a night out. Sometimes I think I'm a descendant of nomads and that I'll never be able to feel at home anywhere. But, then again, when I'm drunk I usually end up calling my mom.

My mom has always been a fighter. She is a tough, cursing Irish woman who raised three kids on welfare. You didn't mess with my mom, and I learned to fight from her. But, underneath this, lurking between her bursts of anger and good humor was a latent depression. Despite her resilience, my mom is sad—is, was, and maybe always has been. I have this memory of her, perhaps my first: I'm in an old sky-blue plastic pool, I'm four, and the fog is crawling up Seventeenth Street, gradually embracing our house, backyard, and block. I see my mom there staring off into nothing and I look down and her dress is in the pool where the water has turned different colors of red and magenta. I try to say something but she doesn't hear me until she turns and says, "What?" She looked old and sad. I was filled with a raw primal fear. She might disappear. She had before, or so I would learn later. Before I was born my mom spent a month in a bathtub, hardly getting out, her skin turning white and wrinkled, her eyes watching the white walls and the light move from the morning to the afternoon. Her hands skimmed the surface sending small ripples crashing against the porcelain tub. Clinical depression, sure, but all I knew was she was gone in a way. I had noticed her sadness as a kid when I was in elementary school. Everyone has a unique chemistry. My mother's had always scared me. I worried I had it in me as well.

That last night in Maine was tar black, no sky, and the beach was cold and empty. When I arrived, I put the lantern down in the middle of the sand, and it created a haze of light five feet in every direction. I took my clothes off and ran into the darkness. It was so dark that I couldn't see anything once outside the haze of the lantern. I walked out into the Atlantic Ocean and stood in the dark and thought about what was in front of me. My trip was winding down; I was beginning the final phase of the journey. This scared me. I had spent most of my life moving.

Movement is in my family's DNA, and for a long time I felt like a flip-book character: the faster I moved, the more of me that came to life. I stood in the dark and thought about where I had been and where I was going. I had been moving for so long that I didn't know who I was when I stopped. But I had seen glimpses of what I could be in the past two months. I wasn't fighting myself anymore.

Everyone was hungover the next morning. It felt like even the Whitehouse dogs were pawing their heads. As would be the case for the rest of this trip, Christopher was up before the rest of us, showered and shaved and smelling like peppermint Dr. Bronner's soap. "How you doing?" I said as I rolled out of bed and covered my eyes. "Oh yeah, real nice, really good, ready to roll," Christopher said.

The bus had been cleaned and repaired; all the things that had fallen apart had been put back together again. Our goal that day was to get back to New York—Scarsdale, in fact—and then head into the middle of the country toward Seaman, Ohio, where we would spend a weekend with Katie Basford, a young woman with Down syndrome, and her family. In between New York and Seaman was Allentown, Pennsylvania, and an amusement park called Dorney. Our plan was to ride the roller coasters with a friend named Cully.

"Dude," I said to Kelly, who was sitting behind me as we drove out of Kennebunkport. "You got the copilot now. The map is all yours." She looked terrified. "It is all spiders," she said. We eventually found the highway after twisting through the summer traffic and cutting across southern Maine, through western Massachusetts and parts of Connecticut into the stomach of New York State. As we drove, small town after small town passed by the window.

I wondered how many people like Cookie must be out there in these small towns. Do people know their names, or do they live alone? Have they all been evicted? Do they live in poverty? At least in Kennebunkport, the town eccentric is alive and well, walking the streets in six-inch heels. We need that. We need Cookie as a testament not only to the importance of community but to the power of transformation, a reminder of our ability to create ourselves.

But Cookie also reminded me of something else. As I drove, I was filled with an old memory, one that I had forgotten.

One day, during my junior year in high school, I was killing time with a friend of mine from the soccer team in the hallway at school. I was sixteen and my hair was down around my eyes, I was dating a cheerleader, and everything was supposed to be right but it was wrong. As my friend and I talked in the hallway, this guy that I didn't know at all but who to me looked "faggy" walked by. When he got closer to me, I acted like I was going to punch him in the face. He fell back and into a set of lockers, and I laughed. I called him a fag. He tried not to but he started to cry and walked away.

As I drove, I thought about that person in the hallway who could do something like that to someone else. Sure, I was a hurting kid, and people do cruel things all the time; but that was no excuse for my actions. I know now—and this is something major that I've learned—

that people who are different or those who feel powerless are often the first to humiliate or ostracize those whose situations they should empathize with. What struck me as amazing during the drive to New York was how much I had changed. And my experiences at Brown had a lot to do with that.

My personal and intellectual experience at Brown is best described as an explosion: an explosion of how I thought about myself, an explosion of ideas about disability, an explosion of how others saw me. In two years at Brown I went from the learning disabled closet, from the stupid athlete who was arrested for a DUI and was close to suicide, to becoming a published Ivy League Truman scholar. In two years. In the aftermath of this explosion I felt like pieces of shrapnel sent in different directions. I was still trying to put the pieces together. A part of me thought I was still that stupid kid and I had just fooled everyone. Another part of me thought I had been given the keys to the kingdom, and before I was asked to return them I should keep on striving for more. And then some of me just wanted to get drunk.

"Dude, I swear to God, if this is Scarsdale, they built that building like yesterday," I said as we drove down Highway 9 near White Plains. We were lost, and it was dark, and we were hungry. "What will they have to eat in the dale?" Kelly said, using my slang for Becky's hometown. "Chinese takeout," I said. "Can we get some beers?" she asked. "Dude, you know the rules. No drinking in the Golden household," I reminded her. (Golden is my in-laws' surname.)

Scarsdale makes me feel like shit about myself. It always has and always will. It is one of *those* neighborhoods that are used like adjectives, like Beverly Hills, and which signify wealth and success. When we arrived in town, I felt my stomach sink the same way I always did when I first pulled up in front of Becky's house. Here I was again, caught between two notions of what I was and should be. On one hand, I was part of a ragged short-bus crew, working on some crazy project with my white-trash unemployed freaker sister and all. On the other, there were so many things I had been told I should strive for: success, power, *Scarsdale.*

"It's interesting," I said to Kelly when we finally got out of the bus at Becky's parents' home, "just like Cookie is the resident freak show in his community, I'm the resident freak show in the Golden house. It's just a good example of how arbitrary it all is. When I'm chillin' at Cookie's, I'm the normal dude."

For all my cognitive dissonance, the Goldens have been nothing but generous to me and to the different crews that I've dragged to their home over the years. The next morning, I came downstairs around 10:30. Christopher was already at the breakfast table, showered, shaved, caffeinated, and chatting away with my future mother-in-law, Linda. "Oh yeah, sweet," Christopher replied to something Linda had said, his *e*'s drawn out like someone from the South. Christopher was just enthusiastic, *extremely* enthusiastic.

It is important to note that I had given Christopher a few nick-names, all of which he hated. The etiology of this first nickname, CPK, is pretty straightforward; his real name is Christopher Thomas Klonecke. During our bus renovation, months earlier in L.A., we had dinner every single night at the California Pizza Kitchen. After that, he became CPK. From this pinnacle of originality, my nicknames for my friend have gone way downhill, ranging from the Pizza, for obvious reasons, to Sea Biscuit, and finally Sea Bitch. I'm not sure how the last two evolved.

When I saw CPK sitting with Linda, it was the first time that I really visualized him as a part of this trip, not simply as the guy who was riding along. And suddenly I was happier than ever to have him as a member of our short-bus crew. CPK is brilliant, a graduate of USC film school and the editor of an Academy Award–nominated short film. But beyond that, he is the kind of guy who laughs at jokes. I mean, really laughs. That may sound like a small thing, but it's not. In some way, you can break the world down into people who are quick to laugh with others and those that aren't. CPK finds humor in the world, and he lets you know it. Those are the kind of people you want around.

Over a cup of great Joseph (I also have a number of different names for coffee), CPK and I got down to the business of figuring out what the hell we were going to do about the power situation in the bus. It was an ongoing concern. Since I had left L.A., the bus had essentially no independent power system. And without some sort of power system, we had no way to run the fridge. I thought using coolers was a low-tech sort of solution, but CPK strongly disagreed. "What we need is this," he said, pointing to a diagram he had sketched out, to scale, on a notepad.

The next day, we left Scarsdale with a very expensive power system consisting of two looped marine batteries. For the first time in the trip, our refrigerator was humming, cool, and stocked with food. Our goal that day was to get to Allentown, Pennsylvania. It was well after ten at night when we finally found our destination. We drove the backroads into the city center to locate our hotel. It was late, and the town was empty, and many of the buildings were boarded up. It was so quiet that we decided it was our duty to counter the city's emptiness with Billy Joel's song of the same name. We found it on the iPod and turned up the volume. Did Billy Joel think that if he sang about the town it would come back to life? It was worth a shot but didn't seem to have much impact. But we sang along, filling the yellow light from the street-lamps with an incantation that, for one moment, transformed the white noise of an empty city's bones creaking and settling.

That night, we stayed up drinking wine and eating cheese sand-wiches and talking about how we can transform the forces that shape our lives. By three in the morning, however, we had all settled back into the grooves of ourselves. Kelly, as always, was snoring, and CPK assumed what would be his signature style of sleeping: He lay on his back, the sleeping bag pulled to his neck, and he crossed his hands on his chest like he was entombed. Mummy style, I called it. As usual, I couldn't sleep, so I kept drinking and I called my mom.

The next morning, the power on the bus was dead.

Dorney Park and Wildwater Kingdom, outside of Allentown, was a sea of American bodies. We were looking for two of these torsos in particu-lar: Cully, a middle-aged man, and Chad, a teenager with cerebral palsy who moved through life in an electric wheelchair. As we scanned the scantily clad and sweating crowd, I was amazed that anyone had ever been able to peddle the ubiquitous bullshit about American perfect bodies. Only in the imaginations of advertisers does this fiction exist. In front of us was a sea of singular bodies—fat, skinny, lumpy, tall, short, long, fucking weird bodies. Maybe they were all dreaming of being the same kind of beautiful. I hoped not.

I had struggled with my body image as a kid. Maybe because I was so worried about my internal self ever feeling right, I didn't quite trust the external me, either. I hated my too-white skin and hoped it would be covered by dark hair when I got older; then when that happened I hated the dark hair. Gradually—and I do mean decades—I started feeling a little better. Now, here at this park among all the half-naked people, I wished I had gone to more places with extreme public nudity. Want a cure for body dysmorphic disorder? Look at more naked people. Come to Dorney on an August afternoon with the world in shorts and halter tops. Nobody's perfect.

Cully was late, which was somewhat bothersome because he had yelled at me the night before about the possibility of my perpetrating a similar offense. "If you are one minute late, Jonathan," Cully had threatened over the phone, "we are leaving your ass. We got roller coasters to ride, man. Shit!" I had met Cully, like most people who came into my life after college, during one of my speaking trips. He had picked me up at the Scranton, Pennsylvania, airport, and we drove to my talk. Cully was in his midforties and was one of those guys whose story you know after an hour car ride. I didn't really listen to him the first time we met. I listened around the edges like I was skimming a book.

Skimming was OK with Cully because he was one long-ass story. He is an ex-junkie and onetime adolescent terror, and now a mobile therapist and a strong advocate for kids with disabilities. Cully is my kind of freaker. Cully's job is to support Chad's social development. There was one thing that connected this crew together: Chad, Cully, Kelly, and I were roller-coaster freaks. Hence our rendezvous.

Chad was one of the kids with whom Cully spent time as a social worker. Not only did he have cerebral palsy (CP), he was also considered mildly developmentally delayed. This means that Chad has a below average IQ, as measured by traditional tests. This doesn't, however, mean that Chad is stupid. IQ and authentic intelligence are two very different things. CP is a loss or impairment of motor function caused by an injury to the brain either during fetal development or after birth. There is no cure for CP. Chad will always be in a wheelchair.

As we waited for Cully, Kelly grew agitated. "Dude," she said. "Let's leave those fuckers." I nodded, but added: "If we wait for Chad, we don't have to wait in line." (In amusement parks like Dorney, people in wheelchairs and their guests get to go to the front of the line.) I took my sister's silence as brief submission to my overpowering logic. I don't know where Kelly's love of roller coasters originated or when it began, but I had inherited my love for these crazy, scary experiences from her. When I was a kid, when all the shit started to go wrong in my life, Kelly created something that she called special days. These were days, once a month, when we ditched school and did something together: a movie, a trip to the park or—the ultimate special day—to Disneyland.

We always went to Disneyland on a school day, so there were never any lines. I loved everything about the place. Disneyland was like I walked into the back of someone's mind while they were dreaming. I loved the very beginning of our days the most. When you first walk into Disneyland, you are faced with a great existential choice: Do you go left to Adventureland or do you go right to Fantasyland? All the shit that was happening to me as a kid, all of the fear and all that I couldn't control or transform because I was powerless, was released into this one moment of absolute choice that *I* got to make. Each visit to Disneyland began with Kelly asking me, "So which way should we go? It's your choice. It is your day." I always chose Adventureland.

"You're late," Cully said ironically as he slapped me on the back with his big hands. Although he didn't bother to explain his reason for being late, he wasted no time introducing us to his charge: "Jon, this is Chad," he said, pointing toward a young man, about seventeen years old with dark black hair, folded into his wheelchair. "And this is Sy, Chad's dad," he said, pointing to a man I hadn't been expecting.

I bent down and shook Chad's hand and then extended my hand to Sy, a large guy who wore jeans, work boots, and a denim vest. You have to like a grown man who sports a denim vest.

"Nice to meet you both," I said.

"You ready to ride some roller coasters?" Cully asked.

My mind was soon preoccupied with two pressing concerns. First and less serious was whether or not Kelly would push Chad out of his chair and speed off into the distance. If we walked quickly, I put the odds of this happening at fifty-fifty; if we were slow, I'd revise to sixty-forty in favor of Kelly stealing the chair. The second question, however, was of much graver concern: What would be the first ride of the day?

I recognized that this was not my day to organize. Hoping that they didn't know what the hell they were up to, I gingerly pressed the group on whether or not they had a plan. "So," I said sheepishly, "you know, I don't care or anything, but do you guys have a particular route you like to take through the park?" Chad smiled from ear to ear.

Slowly nodding his head, Chad outlined his plan of attack. First, we would head directly to a ride called the Steel Force. Then we would make our way through the park in a circular manner, stopping in the middle for lunch. We would end our day all the way at the other end of the park on a ride called the Talon.

I had nothing but respect for Chad's particular route through the park. There was even a sort of poetry to it. The day's first ride would be one with a huge drop and the last would be a looping ride. Chad, it seemed, was wise beyond his years; this was the work of a true roller-coaster Zen master obsessive. The brilliance of his route was that he had planned to bookend our day with what I call the two poles of the roller-coaster dichotomy. Let me explain.

I believe that you can sort people into two categories: droppers and loopers. Drop roller coasters and loop roller coasters are two fundamentally different experiences and hence attract two fundamentally different types of riders. The tension between these two is one of the great, unrecognized dichotomies in the world. Tragically, the drop/loop thing has historically taken a backseat to the dichotomies of men/women, white/black, normal/abnormal, able/disabled, mind/body, et cetera. These categories are all well and good, but I believe the difference between drop and loop coasters needs to be elevated to the pantheon of major human dichotomies. Don't even ask about the water-ride folks.

The first stop of the day was Steel Force, which had a respectable

drop-coaster name. (Many are industrial sounding.) Drops—usually—
are rides that force you to look into the abyss, to face fears. Our crew
decided to ride Steel Force in three different cars at different points of
the train. Cully and I would sit up in the very front with Chad and his
dad behind us, then Kelly and CPK more toward the back. Christopher
seemed terrified. "Oh oh God," I heard him scream as we headed up
the first hill, on the other side of which was the huge drop.

For Cully, however, as any seasoned drop rider knows, the trip up
the hill is the most important part of the ride. For my pal it was an
almost religious experience. It was one that Cully, in particular, needed
to narrate. He babbled on and on. I wasn't listening to Cully. I'm all
about drop roller coasters, so I was waiting for the moment when we
could go no higher and hit the point above the park where everybody
looked the same, like dots in a Seurat painting. Cully was still talking.

In the middle of Cully's narration, I heard him say something that
I had never heard before. "Brain tumor," I heard Cully say over the roar
of the roller coaster's machinery. I thought he was talking about Chad.
"Chad has a brain tumor?" Cully shook his head and pointed to the
front of his skull. "Doctors can't do anything about it," he said as he
smacked the side of his head. I was shocked.

"What are you supposed to do?" I asked Cully as we rose, panicked.
Cully didn't respond. We were at the top of the hill. There was nothing left to our ride now but falling. Cully looked out over the park, and
then pointed at Chad in the car behind us. But he didn't say anything.
There was a peaceful calm to Cully that I couldn't understand. The
ride Cully and I were on had come to its tipping point, and in between
our rising and our falling there was a moment of still silence. "What are
you going to do, Cully?" I asked before the momentum of the roller
coaster took us over. "Live," Cully said. "Live."

After Steel Force, the rest of the rides before the loop ride were
bullshit. Spinning rides were for the weak. Tower-of-death rides for
the masochistic. But Chad's story, punctuated by the hum of his
wheelchair and the sound of his slow voice over the roaring machines,
was the attraction for me. His tale wasn't about being oppressed or
screwed over. At no point in the day did he tell me anything about
being discriminated against. He had no anger or anything approaching

ire. He actually loved school (a notion with which I simply cannot empathize). He was fully included in his local high school. His tale, actually, was much more about all the things he truly cared about. And it seemed that Chad, after his family, cared most about his job at Sam's Club.

Chad has a fairly simple but important job at Sam's Club. Every day he rolls up in his chair and parks himself right next to the sliding-glass door out of the range of the sensor. There he waits for the first customer of his day. "Welcome to Sam's Club," Chad says when that customer arrives. What he enjoys most, though, is the moment when the customers look at him and say hello back. "I love that!" he said. What an amazing and important moment. Hundreds of times a day, little boys and girls, men and women, old and young stop for a moment and look at Chad. Really look at him, his bent wrists on the controls of his wheelchair, his small legs, his head tilted sideways, and his words slow and slurred and forced. Chad sits there and says hello to each and every person who walks through that door, and he is proud of that. "I love it," Chad said to me over the mechanical din. "It is my job."

There is a real dignity to the job. But too many people like Chad are denied that opportunity. Chad didn't need more surgery to fix his body; he needed more days at Sam's Club.

Our last ride of the day, the Talon, was a quintessential loop ride. Loop rides are often named after animals or their parts, hence the *talon*. Loop rides are all about speed, movement; they are not about falling but about flying. I knew why Chad liked these rides so much. His body, from the time he was a kid, was grounded. Chad and his twin brother were born months premature. According to his dad, when they were born the doctor said, "Take a good look at them because they'll probably be dead by morning."

Chad's brother died after a year. Chad grew up in hospitals and surgeries marked his life. "I've been through so many operations you wouldn't believe," he said to me. At one point, he had an extremely rare kind of back surgery. "That's where they cut my spinal cord," he said without revealing any reaction whatsoever, as if he were explaining a routine checkup. After the surgeons cut his spinal cord, and replaced his hip, Chad had to learn to be in his body all over again. Most of his life has been about *just*. If he could *just* get off the respirator, if he could *just* survive this operation. If he could *just* eat, if he could *just* talk, if he could *just* be in school like the other kids. "I kept saying to myself," Sy explained, "that there was too much to Chad to think that he could ever *just*."

What Sy said made a lot of sense. Chad refused to let his body *just* be confined to a wheelchair. Chad enjoyed the falling of Steel Force, but what he really loved were the loop rides, which were about flying.

I have to say, though, that while I respect Chad's skills as a coaster rider, I could never *really* be down with a loop man. Don't get me wrong; I like a good fast coaster as much as the next guy. But intellectually, these don't do it for me. Normally, I would sit them out, but that day, I figured I would give it a go and ride with Chad. Maybe I had something to learn. As we waited, I quizzed the boy a little bit about what he thought about loops and drops—and other stuff. Chad looked at me and said that he was proud that he had learned the difference between big things and little things.

As we boarded the ride, I pushed Chad to elaborate. "So Chad," I said over the roar of machinery, "what are the little things?" This wasn't me being patronizing. This was something that I needed to know. So many of the previous days had been for me about thinking through what matters, what doesn't, how we as human beings decide that. "Names," he said. "You know, when, like, my brother calls me names. These are little things. I let them go." I nodded; that seemed wise to me. "And big things?" I asked as we were buckled in. "Blood," he said. "When there is blood, *that* is a big thing."

Before we took off, I looked at Chad's legs, dangling under the force of gravity. He looked to me like an origami crane, the kind that some Chinese people believe escorts them to heaven. Loop rides, I realized sitting next to Chad, are optimistic; they are about imagining and experiencing the impossible. "You ready?" Chad asked me. "Oh, yeah," I said. "Let's fly."

I learned from Chad that my dichotomy was bullshit. I needed to fly as much as I needed to fall. We all do. And you know what? We ended our day on a water ride.

The sun was setting by the time we were done riding our roller coasters. Before we left, Chad told me what he wanted people to know about him. "This is just metal," he said, pointing to his wheelchair. "Just metal. *This*," he said pointing to his body, "is no different from anyone else."

One of the most powerful concepts within the disability rights movement is the idea that we all have temporarily able bodies. This idea had always been an abstract one to me, but not after my day with Chad and Cully. I was still scared of that idea, to be honest, but after Cully and Chad I knew what to do with that fear. If we are always falling apart, all we can do is learn to enjoy whatever looping or falling or twisting ride we are on.

12

Katie's Book of Life

Katie Basford and Family

SEAMAN, OH

It took a leap of faith to get me to the Basford family farm. I was warned in advance by my host, Candee, that to get to her home I had to cross an old bridge. This crossing was described as "a little risky." When we finally arrived at the bridge, which looked well over one hundred years old and none too reliable, our party was faced with an existential dilemma. I called Candee on my cell phone and she proceeded to tell me that the bridge was built in 1890 and was in need of repairs. (Many inspectors had told her that the bridge was unsafe.) I was worried about whether it would hold the weight of our bus, but Candee was confident that it could. After a pause, she added, "And it is worth a try, isn't it?" At this point, I could see the Basford farm, and Candee and her daughter Katie, a young woman with Down syndrome, whom I had come to see, were standing on the other side of the bridge, waving me forward. Worth a *try*? A threesome is worth a try. Raw food is worth a try. But plummeting down a ravine? What the hell.

So I took a deep breath, drove across the bridge, and was greeted, as a reward for my courage, by the sound of Candee and Katie's laughter as well as a pack of what seemed to be wild dogs. Candee shook my hand and said, in an accent not quite southern and not quite midwestern but pure Appalachian, "You can have one or all of them, if you like, sweetheart." Candee was forty-eight years old. She was a native of Seaman where she had been born and raised and which she had never left. She seemed to me as deep, as filled with currents and energy, and as intimidating as the Ohio River.

Katie stood a few feet behind her mom. I waved to her. Katie and I had spoken to each other only once, over the phone, so I reintroduced myself. Katie was twenty-four years old. She had red-brown hair, like an autumn leaf, and was about five feet, two inches tall. Because of her Down syndrome, Katie's bodily proportions were different from those of typical folk, and her coordination was off. She moved like someone in one of those fat suits, all the neurons not quite connecting to the muscle tissue moving in slow motion. Also because of her Down syndrome, Katie's face was a soft oval, as were her eyes. She wore thick glasses that put her eyes into relief like fish eyes in a fishbowl. Despite, or perhaps because of, all this, Katie was quite beautiful. She had the soft elegance of a 1940s movie star shot through a gauzy camera lens. At the time of my visit, Katie had never left Seaman for long, though she hoped this might change. She had a bit of wanderlust, as I was soon to learn.

Before we sat down to lunch, I got a quick tour of the Basford home by Candee's husband, Gary. He had played basketball in high school, and his body still carried memories of plays, passes, and bench presses in his muscles and in his hands. He was seven years older than Candee and had been a carpenter for twenty-five years. In 1982, he began teaching vocational education, then took up part-time cattle farming in the mid-1980s. He had done most of the more recent work on their home, an old farmhouse built in stages. As is the case with most authentic farmhouses, as the family grew the house grew.

"You ready for some lunch?" Gary asked me after the brief tour. "We're serving up our residents here!" he said with a deep laugh. Gary was referring to the fact that we would be enjoying hamburgers made from Basford farm beef. During lunch, we made small talk, chatting about Gary's work as a teacher. But I wasn't really paying attention to Gary. I was watching Katie.

Katie stood up, giggled like a little girl, and made strange faces at Christopher, who was filming. I tried to reconcile the image in front of me with the person I had expected to see. When I had been seeking people to profile, a disability professional had recommended Katie to me. She had described the young woman as a strong and important voice in the disability community. I didn't see that person at lunch in front of me. I saw what appeared to be a fairly immature twenty-four-year-old making faces at the camera. I wondered if I was missing something.

What was obvious was the palpable tension that quickly settled over our meal. I had expected this. The Basfords had some reservations about spending the day with me and being a part of my project. The first time I spoke with Candee, she seemed to hesitate about my visit. She had said, "Well, your story is different from Katie's. Your story, Jonathan, is a hero's journey. That is not Katie's story. Katie's story is something different." Her words implied that I believed that everyone's path should be like my own.

I would learn later, however, that the family's concern wasn't just about me. "We had been burned before," Candee said to me later. "Most people miss the point of Katie's story," Candee said. "They made it either too nice or too mean, but they missed the point."

My most vocal critic was Katie's younger sister, Meghan, who was home from college for the summer. At lunch, Meghan sat across from me and I could feel her distrust like heat radiating off asphalt. "I don't like the title of your book. It is demeaning to people like Katie," Meghan said to me. "Oh, it's just a working title," I said sheepishly. She shrugged.

It was going to be a very long stay.

After lunch, Katie excused herself to get ready for work and promptly returned in her McDonald's uniform. Katie had worked at McDonald's for several years. I would spend most of the day with Candee, because Katie worked until five. I did, however, join Katie on her thirty-minute commute to work with her sister. Katie couldn't drive herself because she couldn't pass the vision test. This is very common for individuals with Down syndrome. About 50 percent have problems with their vision and hearing. Katie depended upon others to take her places, but no one seemed to resent this. Katie gave high fives all around as she departed, and I followed her out to the car, where Meghan waited with her hands on her hips. "Get into this car, girl!" she said.

On the drive to Katie's job, I tried to make small talk, hoping to ease the tension I felt around Meghan. "Is this the new Metallica album?" I asked. "I like Metallica," Katie said. "You know, Jonathan, you can download them on the computer or something." I nodded my head, not knowing what the "or something" meant. The conversation proceeded innocuously as the rolling hills of Seaman passed by. I learned a few things about Katie really quickly. I learned that she was in college, had a boyfriend, had really liked high school. Katie talked in sentences no longer than four or five words in quick bursts, like someone who held her breath all day long.

What became very clear was the paradox that Katie presented to me and perhaps to the world. In some ways Katie was the most "normal" person I spent time with on the trip. She worked at McDonald's, took community college courses, had a healthy interest in boy bands and a keen knowledge of celebrity gossip. (She'd inform me later that Jennifer Lopez was not married but cheating on Ben Affleck.) She read *Vogue* and *In Style* and watched MTV, *JAG*, and Animal Planet. In many ways, Katie was really sort of your average young woman. If such a thing exists.

On the other hand, Katie was the single most "different" individual I spent time with in my three-month journey. I say this for one simple reason. Every person I visited—from Brent, to Kent, and Cookie—had forty-six chromosomes, as do the vast majority of human beings. Katie had forty-seven, which made her a member of one of the few biologically different minority groups in the human race: the Down syndrome crew.

Katie broke my contemplation with a litany of the places she had been in her life. "I've been to Philadelphia to New England to Maine to many other places. . . . With my friends and with my mom to conferences." "Conferences?" I asked. "Yeah," Katie said, "to present." "Present?" I asked with a level of skepticism. Katie wasn't fazed.

"Present on my experiences . . . college life . . . I've been taking classes in college. And my experiences in high school." Katie presented on what many might consider to be an ordinary life.

Meghan turned to me and said, "Katie has a boyfriend. She wants to get married." I had spent only half an hour with Katie, but this did not come as a surprise to me at all. Katie, I suspected, had a very healthy sexuality. From the moment of my arrival, she had been flirting with Christopher.

"Married?" I asked Katie.

"That's what I'm thinking," she replied. "Me and my boyfriend are talkin' about getting married." Katie was referring to Steven, a man whom she had met in college. He was twenty-one years old, three years younger than Katie. According to Candee, Steven may have been in special ed, but he did not have Down syndrome and he never spoke about having a disability.

"You like younger men," I said to Katie

"I sure do." She laughed.

"Congratulations!"

Katie was, in fact, engaged to Steven and was planning a wedding at the farm. Kids might be in the future. "I'm not nervous, just excited," she said.

I wondered what else Katie hoped would come to pass in her future. As we drove, I asked her about her job at McDonald's, which she had held for the past four years. It was getting, in her words, boring. "Oh, I just clean. And add ketchup to the machines," she said, referring to the most basic entry-level job in the Mickey D's purgatory, one step up from janitorial services. It was also unclear if this billion-dollar corporation actually paid Katie the minimum wage. Because Katie had never received a raise, she could not have been earning any more than the minimum wage. And, of course, McDonald's provided no medical insurance or other benefits. She worked only four hours a week, though she had been asking for more work and more responsibility. "I told someone about it, one of my managers," she reported. "He said yes, but he hasn't done it."

"Tell him what you would really like to do," Meghan prompted.

"Instead of McDonald's," Katie said, "I would like to work in a laboratory. Maybe with DNA. Watch how they do it." Katie was enrolled at a local community college and had just completed a course in biology.

"Have you found any laboratories where you might be able to work?" I asked.

"Maybe Cincinnati," Katie said, then she added, "I like cities. I like the buildings. To eat. To go shopping." As she flashed a shy smile, she confessed, "I like to go shopping a LOT!"

I wondered what I had to learn from a woman who wanted to live what many would consider to be an ordinary life. Was this *all* she wanted? To be ordinary, not exceptional? Before we dropped Katie off for work I repeated her dream to her out loud to see if she wanted to clarify or change anything. "So you and your husband would live outside of Cincinnati and you would work at a lab. That's your dream?" I asked Katie, somewhat flippantly.

Katie looked right at me, not caring what I thought her life should be, her pupils magnified by her thick correctives lenses, and said, "Yeah!"

Most of us know that Down syndrome is an anomalous chromosome condition that results in an individual having forty-seven, rather than forty-six, chromosomes. But what most of us don't know is how common Down syndrome is or how complicated its biological origins and social history are. Let's start with the easy stuff, the facts. Down syndrome occurs in one out of every 600 to 800 live births. That means that there are around 500,000 individuals with Down syndrome in the United States alone, roughly the population of Wyoming. However, 80 percent of embryos with Down syndrome are not carried to term, leading some to hypothesize that the condition occurs in one out of every 100 to 200 fertilizations. Moreover, Down syndrome has been with us for all of human history and has also been reported in gorillas and chimps, our closest genetic relatives.

Like most cognitive differences, the history of Down syndrome is marked by shifting labels and rhetoric. There is very little written on the early history of Down syndrome, but we do know in some cultures and communities these individuals were considered just a part of the human continuum, while in others while they were thought of as sub-human. Though the biological origin of the condition was not discovered until 1959, Down syndrome as we know it today began with John Langdon Down in late-nineteenth-century London. John Down's understanding and theory about this experience ruled the field for almost seventy-five years.

John Down was a prominent English doctor who focused on the Siberia of the medical world: the field of "idiocy." As you can imagine, during Down's day this diagnostic category had a wide breadth, including, to quote the journalist Mitchell Zuckoff, "idiots on the bottom, imbeciles on the next higher rung, and the feebleminded on what passed for a top rung."

John Down was, by all accounts, a complicated and paradoxical figure. To paraphrase Zuckoff, Down was horrified by the conditions of English asylums for the feebleminded and dedicated much of his life to reforming them. But Down was also a racist and an unabashed social Darwinist. The title of his breakthrough paper on what would become known as Down syndrome was "Mongolian Type of Idiocy." His theory can be paraphrased as follows: Mental deficiency in white kids is a form of arrested evolutionary development. Down had all sorts of classification systems based on a hierarchical evolutionary ladder, but the one that made him famous was "Mongolism idiocy," a diagnosis that was used for people like Katie through the 1970s.

Embodied in Down's theory and his subsequent work is a conceptual trap that I believe is still present in our culture's understanding of Down syndrome. Beyond Down's racism, which is distasteful but also consistent with mainstream thought of the time, Down's description of individuals like Katie is infantilizing. Down had great empathy for the individuals he studied and worked with. He described them in glowing terms as angels, perpetual children, and as almost impossibly kind. While this is better than most descriptions of people with disabilities, there was also a subtle form of dehumanization in this description of people with Down syndrome—it was as if they were in fact a different species.

The biological origins of Down syndrome begin and end with the human reproductive process. Not the fun stuff but the invisible stuff. Down syndrome begins with cellular mitosis. To understand this, think of the cellular structure of the body as a Russian doll. You open up one doll and find another doll and so on. The human body consists of hundreds of thousands of cells; inside each cell, at its center, is a nucleus; within the nucleus are rod-shaped chromosomes that carry our genes; inside these chromosomes are our DNA and RNA. You get the picture. For the sake of understanding Down syndrome, we can stop at the chromosome. The typical human cell has twenty-three pairs of chromosomes, for a total of forty-six chromosomes.

Now comes the fun part. When two Russian dolls meet, fall in love (or drink too much vodka one night), and what happens happens, the resulting offspring has inherited half of his or her chromosomes from Mom and half from Dad. At this point, all is well with the so-called normal Russian doll, but with our brethren who have Down syndrome, this is where things get interesting. For reasons still largely unknown, the mom's or dad's cells, during a process called mitosis, acquire an extra chromosome. Each time a cell divides during the period of growth of that embryo, there are forty-seven, not forty-six, chromosomes, leading to the technical diagnosis of trisomy 21. There are actually two other forms of Down syndrome, resulting from a slightly different process, called translocation and mocisim. These are less common than nondisjunction trisomy 21, which accounts for 50 percent of Down syndrome in the world.

What effect does the additional chromosome have on the developing embryo and fetus? The irony is that while Down syndrome is a fairly significant genetic "aberration" its effects on the developing fetus are surprisingly subtle. There is very little known about why this extra genetic material causes the subtle changes that it causes, rather than the devastating changes most genetic errors cause on the biochemical system. But the bottom line is this: Down syndrome babies who die prematurely do not die due to Down syndrome. Most die of uncorrected heart defects. In 1968, the average life span for a child with Down syndrome was two years. By 1997, however, the average life span had shot up to fifty. This increase in life span is directly related to improvements in heart surgery.

All of this leads to two important points. First, the struggles of individuals with Down syndrome don't stem from their extra chromosome but mainly from how they are treated. Don't get me wrong, individuals with Down syndrome do face specific health challenges. Many face a greater likelihood of being diagnosed with leukemia or Alzheimer's later in life. But, from what I have learned, their greater struggle is against discrimination.

The second point is that Down syndrome is far from an aberrant human experience. In fact, it is connected to all of us. At the moment of procreation, every one of us is birthed as a result of a game of genetic roulette. Spin, spin, spin your chromosomes and see what comes up. The genetic process is dependent upon variance and diversity of genetic combinations. One writer has estimated that there are some 65 trillion different genetic combinations. While this variance is a great strength, genetic roulette does create chromosomal abnormalities. Down syndrome is one of the most common "errors" to both occur and survive to term.

The paradox is that we don't know what other genetic "errors" occurred in the history of human evolution that proved to be advantageous. Is my dyslexia an advantageous error? This all depends on your view of the world. Emerging systems theorists are looking at how even a supposed error in a complex process is intrinsic to the process. The bottom line is we don't know what role errors such as Down syndrome are playing in human development.

I'm not arguing that Down syndrome is one of those advantageous errors (though some research suggests it gives one a greater resistance to certain forms of cancer) but I do know this: Genetic variance is at the core of evolution.

The day Katie was diagnosed with Down syndrome, Candee said, "Tell me she's deaf, tell me she's blind, tell me she's crippled, just *don't* tell me she is retarded."

"I was devastated," Candee said to me as we walked out of the front door of her house. She paused after she said these words and her face completely changed. "Katie," she said, "revealed my dark side. She was a little crack of light that got in there and revealed my dark side." It is a dark side that most of us have.

Candee and I spent the next hour talking about her journey with Katie in a little cabin she called her "retreat." For the past year, Candee walked to this cabin almost every morning and her ritual had pressed a trail into the high grass that winded purposefully like a lifeline. The cabin where we spoke was important in her process of making meaning out of her experiences with Katie.

The cabin began life as a playhouse for the kids and was later turned into an outdoor kitchen in the late 1980s and then finally transformed into Candee's retreat when she began working on a master's degree in adult education. Not long before my visit, she decided to box up everything from Katie's life, all her reports, all her medical documents. She took the materials out to the cabin.

When we finally arrived at the cabin, I found a room, no more than two hundred square feet, cluttered with antique fabric and drafts of drawings. It was in this room that Candee had spread all of Katie's documents—the bureaucratic and medical ephemera of Katie's life— around her on the ground and tacked to the walls. "I tried to sense the experience," Candee said, referring to Katie's life.

The fabric that Candee had spread around the cabin was beautiful old material. Some of it seemed over a hundred years old. "This is all from good old Lillian," Candee said, pointing at the fabric. Candee had taken up quilting around the time Katie was born, and Lillian was an old quilting buddy of hers who had collected fabric throughout her long life. When she died in 1998 at the age of ninety-eight, her children asked Candee if she wanted any of this fabric as a way to remember her. As Candee and I stood in her cabin, Candee picked up a piece of paisley fabric and held it in her hand. "There are patterns to our lives, to our history," she said. "Perhaps these patterns can be found in these fabrics."

We spent the rest of the afternoon talking about Katie's early life. Katie was born on November 19, 1978. She was Candee's second child. The family's way of life at the time seemed a little off the grid, from what Candee said. They grew their own food. They made their own clothes and one year created all their own Christmas presents. This way of life wasn't all that radical in Seaman, Ohio, a place that is geographically and socially a part of Appalachia, where crafts and gardens are part of the local culture. Referring to her life at the time,

Candee said, "It was chosen for financial reasons and health reasons. We grew up believing you had to have a garden." Later she would say, "In Appalachian culture, you do it yourself or do without."

Katie was born in a local hospital. There were no problems with the pregnancy or with the delivery. Candee had a natural childbirth, as she had with her first child, without any of "whatever that stuff is that they stick into your back and paralyze you with." She took Katie home, wrapped her in a quilt that she had spent nine months making for her, and slipped into the role of a mother with a newborn once again. At this point, Candee noticed nothing unusual about Katie.

At two weeks old, however, it was state law in Ohio that all newborns return to the hospital for a phenylketonuria (PKU) test, used to determine an infant's risk of developing the PKU virus. After Katie had the test, a nurse pulled Candee aside and said, "That baby looks a little yella." The nurse believed that Katie might have jaundice. No one mentioned the possibility of Down syndrome.

Katie stayed in the hospital for a jaundice treatment. At the time doctors believed that babies would recuperate better off breast milk. "I didn't believe the no-breast-feeding bullshit," Candee said. After a week, Candee took Katie into Cincinnati to a pediatrician for a second opinion. The pediatrician examined Katie, called Candee into his office, and in a voice somewhere between a monotone and a whisper said, "Well, you don't have to worry about jaundice. We have another problem. This baby has Down syndrome."

After the diagnosis, Candee was numb and called everyone she knew looking for answers and guidance. She read every book she could find. "I read the wrong books," she said later. None of the books Candee read used the term *Mongoloid idiot*, as some still do to this day, but all painted a bleak picture. "These books said that Katie might have a vocabulary of ten words at best. That she might walk at ten, that her development would stop at seven." The pessimism that Candee encountered was not and is not unusual. Into the 1970s it was common for doctors and experts in the field to assert that children with Down syndrome had no capacity to bond with their parents, were incapable of learning, and would damage the family structure. The most common professional advice was for a family to institutionalize their child with Down syndrome.

To complicate matters, after a routine physical, Katie was diagnosed, at six months old, with a congenital heart defect; she had a hole in her heart. Candee and Gary took Katie to the children's hospital in Cincinnati to explore treatment options. Fortunately, the heart surgery Katie needed had a 90 percent success rate in children with Down syndrome, a success rate that is actually higher than that for kids without Down syndrome. At the children's hospital, however, a brash young cardiologist implied that Katie's life wasn't worth living. As the Basfords weighed the pros and cons of subjecting Katie to heart surgery, the surgeon offered an argument that, he believed, tipped the scales away from surgery. He told the family, "If you do not do the surgery, Katie won't be able to walk up a flight of stairs without being out of breath. And she may have a shortened life span. But then again, if you do the surgery, Katie will always have *Down syndrome.*"

Katie had open-heart surgery when she was two years old. At some point during the surgery, an attending nurse came into the family waiting room and escorted the entire family to the hospital chapel. Katie had been put on a heart-and-lung machine that breathed for her and pumped her body's blood supply. At the end of the procedure, Katie was taken off the machine, and her heart was supposed to beat on its own. But Katie's heart did not start up again. The surgeon did not expect Katie to live.

"I thought she was dying," Candee said. In the hospital's chapel, the family was encouraged to share memories about Katie. "I mean, we were talking about her in the past tense." They mourned for over thirty minutes, recalling Katie laughing in the morning when the cows got too close to her or her putting her arm at the side of her head when she slept. They realized that she had changed, already, every single person in the family. She had made an impact on the ways that all her family members saw their lives and life itself. She changed how they looked at and thought of others.

How do we value a life? Count all the fingers and toes. Look at the head and make sure it looks like every other kid's head. Think about the brain, make sure it will work like everyone else's. Is the value of a life just the sum of its parts? For Candee, after that moment when she was forced to confront the reality of her daughter's life, when she almost lost her daughter, many of her attitudes started to become less conventional. "We loved this kid so much," she told me. "We had learned so much."

The doctors gave Katie one more chance, putting her back on the machine, restarting her heart, and then taking her off again. The vast majority of the time, once a patient's heart has not started the first time, it does not start the second time. The patient dies. But Katie's heart began beating.

After Candee finished sharing these stories, in fits and starts, we walked back from the cabin through the open field toward the farmhouse. "I'm just a product of society," Candee said. "That [her response] was only brought on from society. It was brought on from the everyday images of what it means to be an American citizen."

After our walk back from the cabin, we had all decided that cards would be in our future later that night. The prospect of playing cards terrified me. I'm not a card player, and I hate to play anything that I can't win (a remnant from days of soccer). So I was very vocal that what we needed to do before we played was go shopping for the most important element of any card game: alcohol.

To the store we went, piling into Gary's old beat-up white truck and driving through the landscape that had been the backdrop of generations of Basford lives. As we drove, we passed old farms that Gary and Candee filled in with stories of the owners, their family, their crazy uncle Louis. But even in this small town Candee still had to fight for Katie's inclusion into the community. When Katie was old enough to go to school, it was recommended that Katie be sent to a segregated school named, without a hint of irony, Happy Hours. Candee refused to send her daughter to this school. Katie's entire education would be a fight for inclusion. It wasn't easy. "Want to know the truth?" she said to me as we drove. The school reacted with, "What's a retard girl doing in a place like this? The school thought I was in denial, an arrogant parent who thought that Katie didn't really have a difficulty." One middle school teacher actually said to Candee, "Do you realize I spent two weeks in the hospital because I knew I was going to have your daughter in my classroom?"

When we finally pulled up to the local store, everyone knew Candee and Gary and waved. Before we got out, Candee looked at me and said, "I think something invisible happens between people. We have only begun to tap into people's relationships. Someone's presence can shape all of us.

Candee said she believed that the dominant model of an American citizen is to consume, produce, and strive. In Candee's worldview, we have very little tolerance for individuals that don't fit this definition of a meaningful life. I wondered if the future existence of people with Down syndrome was threatened in this culture. "Is there a chance that we might not see people like Katie anymore?" I asked.

"Oh, yeah, that's a stated goal," Candee said without hesitation. She was referring to the fact that many genetic organizations and medical professionals have put Down syndrome on the top of their list of "curable" genetic diseases. In fact, many current genetic organizations were originally eugenic organizations that have changed their names, renounced the bad old days of state sterilization, and continued on the brave-new-world work of ridding the world of "diseases." The only "cure" for Down syndrome available now is abortion. Over 90 percent of pregnant women who are notified that their fetus has Down syndrome choose to have an abortion. Some time after our day together, the American College of Obstetricians and Gynecologists would recommend that all pregnant women regardless of age be screened for Down syndrome.

"What would the loss be if Down syndrome were wiped out?" I asked Candee and then immediately worried she might be offended. Candee answered me, not insulted but passionate. "It's like the rain forest," Candee said. "We don't know what the loss will be but if I believe my presence is tied to the presence of diverse individuals and these people are gone, I think we've become less human." After a pause, Candee paraphrased a quote from an author she admires. "When we are together," Candee said, "we become more of who we already are."

———

I spent the rest of the evening before dinner and Katie joined us after work, thinking about what Candee said and how it was relevant to my own life. I believed Candee's words deeply and had made the same arguments myself, for people with dyslexia and ADHD. I believed that these diverse experiences were a part of a complicated social and neurological fabric that we don't understand. But something about Candee's words cut me in half. I didn't know if my logic, my arguments, and my beliefs extended as far as Candee's. I believed that my dyslexia was worthwhile because it gave me gifts that helped me succeed. But what about someone like Katie—what if her role in the rain forest had little to do with success? Is someone valuable just because of their presence? I never believed that about myself. I believed I was of value for what I achieved.

Everyone could tell that I was in a foul mood during dinner. "Jon, you look sad," Katie said to me after we finished eating. (She was direct in a way most people are not.) I lied, "No. I'm just a little tired." "It's OK," she said. "It's OK to be sad." I excused myself and went upstairs and sat by myself for a while. I could hear them downstairs setting up for a game of cards. A card game was the last thing in the world that I wanted to play. I steadied myself, put on a brave face, and walked downstairs.

I was rewarded for my courage to participate with a game of hearts, which I had no idea how to play. "No thanks," I said. "I'll sit this one out." Hearts is complicated and I was surprised to see Katie dealt a hand. As I watched her, I noticed something that amazed me: It seemed Katie didn't know how to play hearts, or was simply terrible at it, and she didn't care.

She caught me watching her and smiled at me. "Why don't you play, Jon?" I smiled back, a little embarrassed. "I don't know how to play hearts, Katie," I said. "That's OK," she said, and then she leaned over and whispered in my ear, "I don't play all that well either."

She leaned back, looked at her hand, then at me, played a card, and laughed like we were insiders in on a cosmic joke. "Come on Jon, play." I shook my head again and stood up from the table. Katie put her cards down. "I don't like this game" she said. "Let's play crazy eights. OK?" Katie looked at me and seemed to wink. "Come sit back down next to me, Jon."

I gave in and was dealt a hand of crazy eights. I remember vividly looking over at the clock, and it was 10:30 p.m. as we began. Little did I know that this day would live on in infamy as the one having featured the world's longest hand of crazy eights. The game started slowly, and quite honestly mundanely, as any spectacularly competitive event does, I imagine. There is no strategy, there is no skill, and there is no *game* to crazy eights. It is really just an excuse to be with other human beings. This was Katie's game—and she was a master at it, though she never won a hand. At one point Katie put her cards down, adjusted her glasses, and said, "I love this. I love being here with you guys."

This was Katie—her presence like a conduit shifting energy, changing currents, plugging us in together. Buddhists believe the self is essentially whole only when intertwined with others. I don't know what time this hand of crazy eights ended. What I do know is because of Katie, no one was left out, no one won, no one lost, no one cared, and we were all more ourselves than we were before the game.

The next day, I realized something profound had happened during our game of crazy eights, something I didn't fully understand at the time, but which was subtly linked to Katie's presence. I stopped trying to win, something I had never done before. I wanted to understand what facilitated such a dramatic change. And there was only one place to go—to Katie.

Katie was up early and ready to go. She and I had made a date for a tour of the house, Katie-style. "Ready for a tour?" I asked. "Of course," Katie said enthusiastically. That was part of the essence of Katie—she was enthusiastic: about her farm and her family, about working at McDonald's, and about her life in general. She was excited about a simple walk around her house. Most people don't go through life like Katie. Many go through life bored, habituated to their surroundings, their successes, their good fortune. Not Katie. "Come on, Jonathan, hurry up. Don't you want to see my room!" she yelled.

Our first stop was in the middle of her room, and her tour style was like a spinning top. She pulled out pictures, books, CDs, and put them on her bed and back in rapid order. Things settled down, though, once we got to the first order of business and the most important element of any tour with Katie: the selection of touring music.

We stood in front of Katie's CD collection and ran our fingers down the plastic spines of the CDs, pulling them out one by one. She argued well for in *NSYNC. I made a case for Metallica. She countered brilliantly with Britney Spears. I winced. Then we settled, almost at the exact same time, on the perfect touring music: Justin Timberlake's "Rock Your Body." Officially, JT was *all* Katie's idea and I merely acquiesced for her sake. Unofficially, I wrenched JT's CD from Katie's hands and rushed it over to the stereo with bated breath. I'm a big closeted JT fan.

Music was a huge part of Katie's life, but it wasn't something she used to be a part of a group or as a way to claim a particular identity. It was just something she loved. In fact, after our day together Katie would declare that she was going to create her own band. Did she play any instruments? Sure, but not well. This was irrelevant. As the tour of Katie's room commenced, I followed her around. She danced, her feet moving in little tight circles, like an old woman doing the polka, or foxtrot. That was what she looked like to me: not a child but an old woman who had lived life and didn't give a shit about what other people thought. With JT playing, I couldn't help myself. I rocked my body and all of sudden Katie and I were dancing around her room. I was not an out and proud JT fan. I was certainly not a public dancer. But with Katie I was all these things, because I knew Katie would never laugh at anyone.

After a while of dancing and pulling out books and music randomly, I spotted something in her bookshelf. The book was titled *Katie's Book of Life*. "What's this?" I asked her. "I'm writing this and my boyfriend's, too," Katie said. The book was huge, crudely bound, and stamped in red ink "Draft." The pages were overflowing—I could see the edges of photos, clippings, and the marks of Katie's handwriting. "Can we look at that?" I asked. "Of course," Katie replied.

We spent the next half hour looking through Katie's book of life. She pointed to one picture and said, "This is one of my favorite teachers . . . my science teacher . . . she had helped me." Katie then sat in the chair and read from another passage, "Me I use the Abslide . . . the Abslide, for me, because I'm on a diet. . . . I'll probably use like a ab-swing to flatten my abs."

I looked at her puzzled. "Why are you on a diet?" I asked. Without hesitation Katie replied, "Yes, because somebody told me I couldn't eat bacon." I was fascinated by this self-consciousness. Was Katie just like the rest of us, worried always about being fat and ugly? "Are you unhappy with the way you look?" I asked. Katie responded like many young women in their twenties would, somewhere between a yes and no. "I get bloated," she said.

Katie's book of life was filled with all of the human flaws, insecurities, and petty desires that any honest book would be filled with. In the world of Down syndrome that is a radical statement for Katie to make. Often people like Katie aren't seen as real people; they are seen as little angels, perpetually happy, and not like us. But in Katie's book she worries about how she looks, she listens to boy bands, she gets bloated.

"What is this?" I asked, pointing to picture of her and another group of young people in what appeared to be a New England backdrop. "This is a college trip," Katie said. I laughed, "This is where you got loaded, right?" "Jonathan!" Katie yelled. "Where did you hear that?" "Your mom," I replied. Katie had in fact gone to New England with a group of students from her local college. It was an amazing trip for her and much of it was documented in her book of life. Her mom wasn't there; she traveled just like every one else and did just what everyone else did at night. She got drunk off of an unspecified brand of beer, though she was very clear it was not Bud Light. "Yes," she said sheepishly, then added out of the corner of her mouth, "I don't like Bud Light!"

The rest of Katie's book of life doesn't cohere into a narrative or a story—at least in the traditional sense. Katie's book of life is much more a collection of friends, family, and work. There are pictures of a friend's baby shower, her brother's wedding, ex-boyfriends, and descriptions of her perfect man. The book was a document of a woman striving to live a typical or ordinary life.

There was one hitch, though. In Katie's book and all around her room was a testament to the power of popular culture. Recently, Katie had begun drawing portraits of celebrities. I wondered if Katie was caught up in this desire and myth for the exceptional life like many of us. We flipped through her portraits and stopped on one that's labeled Joey Fatone (of *NSYNC). "That looks like you," she said. In fact, as we flipped through the rest of the photos, most of the "famous" people looked alike.

It quickly became apparent that Katie had an elastic definition of "celebrity." She had done a drawing of her father. "Is he famous?" I asked. "Jonathan!" she yelled and then smiled and said, "To me he is." To Katie, one of her teachers was famous; her brother was famous; Christopher was famous. Looking at these pictures I realized something that I had felt the night before but hadn't put into words. In Katie's world, there is no hierarchy of human worth.

Katie's story and her book of life had come down to a question we all ask ourselves at some point: What is a meaningful life? That was Katie's challenge to me because to me a meaningful life was the exceptional life. But it wasn't to Katie. "What is a meaningful life to you?" I asked her. She didn't respond in words. She pointed to the book, flipped through the pictures of her friends, her work, her school, her family. "The book of life is just huge, isn't it?" I said to her after she had flipped through most of the pages. She smiled broadly and said, "Yes, it is."

Before our day ended I sat with Candee, drinking coffee and talking about Katie. I was moved by her desire to live an ordinary life, but I was worried this wasn't possible in America. Candee had the same concerns. I would learn later that Katie was let go from McDonald's, not officially fired just never scheduled again, after six years of work with near perfect performance and attendance.

Candee was terrified that Katie would always be poor, as her daughter does not accept SSI or any other aid from the federal government. According to Candee, if Katie accepted SSI, she could earn no more than seventy dollars a month from a job; if she made more than that amount, she would lose SSI money. To remain eligible for state

Medicare in Ohio, Katie could accumulate no more than a thousand dollars' worth of assets. So Katie can't even own a cheap, used car. The Basfords had been told not to include Katie in their will, because this "wealth" would threaten her future ability to get SSI and Medicaid.

Government work programs are equally problematic. According to Candee, Katie's home county—Franklin County in Ohio—spent eight thousand dollars per person to fund a sheltered workshop that paid workers with disabilities under the minimum wage. Summing it all up, Candee said, "We have a system set up to employ a whole bunch of people, and then we will give people with disabilities just enough money to make them poor."

Katie's space in the community college, one of her best outlets for socialization, was also evaporating. Because of a complicated legal loophole, she is not eligible to receive special accommodations in her classes without identifying herself as a student with a disability. But if she self-identifies as a student with Down syndrome, she will be considered ineligible for financial aid and accommodations because, based on an assumption of her "low IQ," she would be considered to have no "ability to benefit" from higher education.

Over coffee, I asked Candee, "How do we help Katie?" Candee laughed in a way that made me feel like I had said something wrong. "Did I say something that offended you?" I asked. "No," she said with resignation. "I understand where that question comes from—I used to ask myself the same question. How can I help or fix Katie? But Katie isn't the one who needs to be fixed."

Candee wasn't being flippant or critical of me but of the cultural consciousness that looks at Katie's life through the lens of what's wrong with Katie. In some ways, this was the real battle that Candee waged after Katie's heart started again. The first year of Katie's life, Candee tried her best to fix her daughter. She counted Katie's steps. She compared Katie's development to "normal" kids. She bought training devices shaped like toys. She was instructed to buy a book called *How to Train Your Down Syndrome Child.*

Every interaction was instructional. Every moment, an opportunity for teaching. And, in Candee's mind, "it accomplished not a goddamn thing. It is the myth that drives the pyramid scheme of the service industry. I realized," Candee said, "that I had not been Katie's mother. I had been her trainer, and I had been sucked in."

How did she get out? I needed to know. But, like most answers to hard questions, Candee's answer wasn't simple. "Let me show you something," she said to me as she left the room. She came back with a series of paintings she had made about her experiences with Katie that would later be turned into a book called *We Dance Together.* "This is the best answer I have for you," she said, pointing to a painting in progress called *A Conversation with Katie.*

This visual essay recounted a time when Candee had interviewed Katie for a publication on disabilities. Candee asked Katie what she could do to help her, to support her dreams. Katie responded, "You can teach me to dance." Candee was at a loss at first. She didn't get it. "Teach you to dance? What good does that do?" Katie smiled and said, "If you teach me to dance, then we can dance together."

It wasn't about helping Katie—it was about Katie helping us be connected. "I just think it's a shame that we believe that we are individuals in the world. Someone's presence can shape all of us," Candee said.

After breakfast, there was not much more to do except say our good-byes, but no one really wanted to say those. We took our time cleaning the kitchen and tried to cling to the few minutes we had left together.

"Dude, let's hit that trampoline," Kelly said after the dishes were washed and put away. Katie and I followed her outside. Kelly got on the trampoline first, but unfortunately her jump was truly pathetic. "Do a flip," I yelled, in the tone of voice a brother uses when he is encouraging his sister to possibly break her neck. "No fucking way!" Kelly yelled as she crumbled into an ungraceful pile.

"It is better if you jump together," Katie said. So Kelly and I jumped together, our bodies slowly adjusting to each other's weight. Then Katie joined us. We had only a few more minutes left, so Kelly, Katie, and I threw our bodies in the air and we fell into an unspoken rhythm, each of us using our weight to throw the other one up a little higher than we could ever go simply on our own.

13

Black Rock City's Bell Tree

SEAMAN, OH—SEATTLE, WA

The drive out of Ohio and into Michigan was on a two-lane highway that took us from the Appalachian South to the heart of the industrial Midwest in just a few hours. The road was lined with attractive but emptied-out towns, decimated by Ohio's decadelong recession. The towns had antiquated names such as Yellow Springs that spoke of other eras. I promised myself I wouldn't forget these places as so much of the rest of the country has. These are towns that have been left behind as the world moved on.

It was August 16 when we left the Basfords and we had no place to be until the twenty-fourth, when we planned to park the bus for seven days in the middle of the Nevada desert to experience an event called Burning Man. The question of what Burning Man actually *is* is the subject of much debate. First the official Web site–sanctioned definition: Burning Man is "an annual arts festival and temporary community based on radical self-expression and self-reliance in the Black Rock Desert of Nevada." Thirty thousand–plus people from around the world build a city from the ground up over the course of a week. At the center of the city is a six-story wooden figure that is burned to the ground at the conclusion of the week. The burning of this man is the only organizing principle of the experience. There are no planned events, no planned entertainment, no commerce, and—with the exception of guidelines to prevent environmental degradation and gratuitous violence—there are no rules.

Burning Man had become my obsession. It had grown so large in my mind that I firmly believed that if I did not make it there, my entire trip would be a failure. My obsession with Burning Man, however, had little to do with the official Web-sanctioned description. Burning Man became my holy grail after a conversation with a dyslexic New York photographer named Peter, who had had a terrible time in school. Peter had attended Burning Man and regaled me with tales of mass nudity, orgies; it seemed a kind of throwback to seventies-type bacchanalia. But this hedonism really didn't interest me all that much. (OK, this interested me just a little bit.) What grabbed me were Peter's stories of art and transformation. Burning Man was essentially a huge public and performance art experience. Cars were transformed into mobile art experiences. Worlds were created. The year Peter attended, a man from Maine had towed a huge, fifteen-foot-tall boulder thousands of miles and then balanced it on a thin pedestal in the middle of the desert.

Burning Man changed Peter. He told me he went through his life, as a result of his school experience, with suffocating anxiety and social phobia. He thought he was stupid. This all changed, he said, at Burning Man. When I asked him how, he couldn't really answer. All he said was, "You'll see."

A place that would change me—that's what I wanted. That was worth seeking. I had been hoping to be transformed by riding this bus; I wanted to shed my old self and come out on the other end new. What better place than Burning Man to burn away the past and build a future? We all have those places that we think will make us better, places we believe will change us. Burning Man was that place for me. Or so I believed.

The obvious question, however, is if the Nevada desert, due west from Seaman, Ohio, was our next stop, why the hell did we head due north toward the Upper Peninsula of Michigan? This route, quite frankly, took us thousands of miles out of our way. I had all sorts of answers to this question: *I wanted to see the Upper Peninsula, I wanted to see an outsider sculpture garden made of concrete in rural Wisconsin, blah blah blah.* All of that was bullshit. The reason for this diversion was quite simple: I was desperate to keep this trip going for as long as humanly possible. I didn't know who I was if I wasn't chasing the horizon, if I wasn't the hero who overcame.

As I drove through Michigan, thinking about Burning Man, I listened to Kelly and Christopher talk about Kelly's early life—her depression, growing up in a housing project, all the chaos and pain.

Kelly's response to our lives could not have been any more different than mine. Mine was to strive, to fit into all the so-called perfect conventional patterns. To reinvent myself, to change, to try to be the hero. Kelly's was to resist, challenge.

"What would happen if you had accepted the status quo, normalcy as an idea?" Christopher asked her. "I'd be hosed!" Kelly yelled out. "That's how I ended up fourteen, depressed, wanting to be dead. I was evaluating myself by their measure. Now I refuse to let that define my life. At some point we all *chose* to believe that we were not abnormal but exceptional. We chose to believe that we weren't poor white trash, but really the Kennedys of our kind, you know."

Kelly's last line got me. "Isn't that its own kind of trap?" I asked her. "If anything, I grew up feeling that to be loved in our family I had to be doing something exceptional." Kelly didn't answer that question right away. On the trip so far, it seemed that she was struggling with just this family trap: that she should be doing *something important* with her life. I felt conflicted—maybe Kelly should do something exceptional with her life, like follow through on her plan to go into the Peace Corps. But, then again, another part of me felt that Kelly had already led a meaningful life on her own terms. Maybe achievement didn't matter as much as I had believed.

"Everyone's trapped," Kelly finally said in response to my query. CPK put down the camera and laughed. "What makes you so high and mighty, lady?" I watched CPK gesticulate wildly. He had already changed so much on the bus. He had grown his own style of goatee, which was in the spotty, heroin-chic genre of facial hair. CPK had started out on this bus with a detached documentary filmmaker air. But two weeks later he was arguing passionately with Kelly about the meaning of life. Not only was he arguing passionately, he was also flirting with Kelly. On the short bus, objectivity doesn't exist.

"Jonny's in the box," Kelly said pointing to me. "Jonny's got the success monkey on him." She had never said that directly to me but she was right. I laughed uncomfortably. "No way," I joked. "I'm dropping out of society." I had always had that dream. That at some point I would disappear. "Don't worry, Jonny," Kelly said. "You'll get out of your box, dude!" I immediately saw where she was going. "Yeah," I said, "out of my box, and—" Kelly finished my sentence, "and into another one."

Everyone laughed. But I wondered: Was Kelly right? Even if you run from normalcy, can it still influence you, are you still trapped? And, if so, how do you escape? I think we all hoped Burning Man would have the answers.

The next morning, Kelly's eyes were red from the steam of her coffee and from crying the night before. "Love affair," Kelly said, confirming what I had suspected for some time now. She was in love with Christopher and had said as much to him the night before. But it was unclear if Chris was like-minded about the love thing.

"Insane conversations," Kelly said, referring to the talk of the night before. There was nothing more to say. I felt terrible for Kelly but, at the same time, at least she was out there, at least she had the courage to tell Christopher how she felt. After years of family and personal crisis, Kelly and I had developed a kind of shorthand, like the secret language of twins. "But what are we going to do? All we can do is drive to the Upper Peninsula and see what happens. Nothing we can do." Kelly, like everyone who rides the bus long enough, had given in to the inevitable tedium and high and lows of this journey. "I'm with you, dude," she said as she took a huge sip of coffee and rubbed her dry eyes.

Our drive that day took us over the Mackinaw Bridge into the Upper Peninsula, where we headed due west, toward St. Paul, Minnesota. The UP is a desolate, cold, and windy landscape of low trees expanding in every direction. The sky was glassy and low and claustrophobic; looking at it was like viewing the world with a clear plastic bag pulled over your head. The driving was tough. It took us over ten hours to get to St. Paul. Our moods, Kelly's rejection, the miles, tightened like cramped muscles. It felt very familiar, this sense of pending doom. I grew up with this feeling. Before we turned west, I said out loud, to no one in particular, "Back to the driving, where my life makes sense."

Our host in St. Paul was Dan, a friend of mine whom I lovingly referred to as Gay Dan. Dan's childhood home was, let's just say, a tad off the Minnesota Nice mainstream. Dan had a sizable collection of Roman-inspired gay porn (think gladiators) hidden under his bed, but clearly visible from the futon where I was to sleep. Dan's parents, Ruth and Karl, were both professors at Carleton College and were card-carrying academic eccentrics. At the time of our visit, their bathroom was covered with stacks of the *New Yorker,* the *Economist,* and the *Times Literary Supplement.* Ruth and Karl peppered conversations with long bouts of French. But they weren't pretentious. They were my kind of freaks.

The morning after we arrived, we had breakfast with Dan, Ruth, and Karl, an experience in itself. The meal consisted of eggs, sausages, and bagels and a two-hour seminar in French history, torts, and Brechtian liminalism. I kept thinking I had lost my syllabus. Karl passionately held forth on his area of expertise, an obscure French duchess whom he had been studying for the past few decades. Much to my surprise, however, the conversation abruptly turned to, of all things, Burning Man. It seemed that many a Carleton student made the annual pilgrimage to Burning Man, and Karl and Ruth were fascinated with their accounts of the mayhem. Karl believed that Burning Man had deep historical roots and was a truly significant gathering.

"It is a timeless ritual, really," he said between bites of a bagel. "Just one more modern manifestation of a very old urge."

"What is this urge?" I asked him, curious because of my own attraction to the idea of Burning Man. "The urge for self-destruction and self-creation, of course," Karl responded. He believed that Burning Man was a modern manifestation of a medieval peasant festival in which the king was burned in effigy. He smiled, his cup of coffee close to his mouth. "I wonder," he said, "why are *you* going?"

It was a good question. What did I want to burn? I had actually brought with me, though I didn't tell anyone, a bunch of old pictures from my childhood from the time where school was going bad. I wanted to burn these old selves, set them on fire, be done with them, and be someone new at the other end. But I didn't tell Karl that. "For all those deep historical reasons," I said. He laughed. "Of course," he said and then added, "and to get laid."

We lost the traffic about an hour after we left our friends. The Twin City sprawl gave way to farmland spread out before us like a naked spine in the sun. The sky was filled with light, a big western sky, seaming the two halves of the country together. We were finally back on a more sensible route toward Burning Man, and our goal that day was to spend the night in Nebraska, then head on to Denver, over the Rocky Mountains, then north into the Nevada desert.

We spent that night in Hardington, Nebraska, a farming town of no more than eight hundred people. Christopher's father was born and raised in Hardington. His dad had moved long ago, but he still had family there. It was almost midnight when we passed through the sliver of South Dakota that dropped us into the Nebraska Corn Belt. Exhausted, I could hardly see. I was sweating profusely and had a shooting pain in the back of my neck. "Dude, you don't look so good," Kelly said to me when we finally pulled up to our motel. "I just need a shower," I told her, but I wasn't so sure.

That was the last thing I remember.

I would learn later that I had a fever of 104 degrees for the first two days we stayed in Hardington. My memory comes back toward the end of our second day, when Kelly and Chris decided that I needed to go to the local hospital. I was adamantly opposed to this, but supposedly the chatting classes of Hardington, a group of old ladies who knew Chris's father, had decided that I had West Nile virus and was a public health risk. It was imperative that I see a man known in town only as Dr. Mark.

Dr. Mark was a good-looking man in his late thirties, decked out in country doctor chic: khakis, athletic shoes, and a terrible tie. He was the kind of man who liked nothing more than a good firm handshake. "What was that?" he asked after I had shook his hand in my usual manner. "That's not a shake," he said. I nodded sickly and tried again. "That was more like it," he said. After that rite of passage, Dr. Mark got down to the business of the patronizing doctor exam. Then Dr. Mark came to a diagnosis. "You very well could have West Nile virus," he concluded. "But," he said, "it doesn't matter because by the time you have the test results back, you'll have left town and either you'll be better or you'll be dead."

Dr. Mark found the last part of his diagnosis extremely humorous. "Nothing like a good chuckle," he said. "I'm just kidding. You won't die," he said. "In all seriousness, find a place to rest for ten days or two weeks, and you'll be better." I felt Burning Man slipping away, and I was filled with a sense of failure. "Wait," I said, "what else can I do?"

"My recommendation is that you stop traveling for two weeks or so, and that you don't go off into the desert." The humor was over. "You could get very sick."

"I hear you, Dr. Mark." I began. "Just tell me what else I could do if I really needed to go to Burning Man." Dr. Mark looked at me with a deadpan face. "OK," he said. "You take as much vitamin C as you possibly can handle." "How much C should I take?" I asked dismissively. Dr. Mark was not joking. This was serious medical advice. "You should take vitamin C until you have to shit."

Dr. Mark's regimen was certainly not sealed with the FDA stamp of approval. But we left Hardington the next morning at 6:00 a.m. with a lifetime's worth of vitamin C. Black Rock City was our next stop.

We made it to Burning Man after a tedious three-day drive over the Rocky Mountains, during which I slowly recovered from my illness. It was pitch black when we found the small one-lane state highway that peeled away from Reno, Nevada, and into the Black Rock Desert. At the end of this road was Burning Man.

The traffic was terrible as we got closer to the city. All we could see was the glow of electric lights mixing with the dust and dry desert air. We could hear a faint sound of music, but only the bass. At end of the road might just as well have been a tribal ceremony in Africa. The license plates were from all over the country: Michigan and Minnesota and Kansas and California—all of the places I had traveled so far, as if somehow all that I had collected on this journey was spilling out here in the desert. They had all come to escape normalcy. I was not as alone in this search as I had thought.

After an hour of waiting in line we pulled up to the entrance and I handed a man three tickets. The man had on a furry jumper that made him look a little like a *Star Wars* character. I couldn't tell his age, where he was from, or decipher his accent. For all I knew, he was born and raised at Burning Man. He tore our tickets, looked at me, and then at Bob Henry. "A short bus, huh?" he asked. I nodded. "You know it?" I asked. "Know it?" he said over the roar of the city. "I rode it!" He laughed and then said, "Welcome home."

If Burning Man was home, then I have never been home in my entire life. It took me and my crew one full day to begin to make sense of the visual and physical environment we had found ourselves in. Our first night, we couldn't make sense out of the city. It was fragmented and unruly like a stream of consciousness narrative. We had pulled into our camp in the middle of a sangria party. By camp, I mean an area that had a full kitchen, a self-suspended canopy for a roof, and a thirty-foot bar. Most camps had a theme (my personal favorite was "nap time"). Ours was called the lamp lighters, and it was our responsibility each night to place gas lanterns throughout the "streets" of Black Rock City to illuminate the way. And, by "sangria" I mean wine, limes, oranges, and some unidentified form of hallucinogen. The rest of that first night was a blur. I slept on the desert floor, Kelly on top of Bob Henry, and we still don't know where CPK ended up. A true Burning Man homecoming.

The next morning we slept in, and things looked different in the daylight. The city was in constant flux, like a human body regenerating itself and decaying at the same time. We got dressed and then set up our tent. A woman in her forties named Sue helped us. She was there with her daughter. "I wanted to experience this with her," she said to me as we pounded in the stakes for our tent. "She loves it here," Sue said. Her daughter said she was more herself at Burning Man than anywhere else.

We got a better sense of the city at dusk when the heat broke and people emerged from their hangovers. This was a nocturnal place, and as the sun set the desert filled with a hum of humans moving together and looking for the space between each other but never that far from anyone. Kelly, CPK, and I walked that night all around the camp, just trying to get our minds around what was happening. It was almost impossible to get our bearings. All we could see was that the city was laid out in concentric circles, with the man in the exact center.

We wandered around, giddy like children on a sugar high, over-whelmed by the sensory experience. Burning Man was the imagination and collective unconscious embodied, hooked up to a generator, and set to roam an ancient lakebed for six days. Cars were on fire. A life-size replica of Mad Max's Thunderdome held "jousting" matches as people hung from the area. A Buddhist monk wandered from camp to camp meditating. That night affirmed to me why we had traveled so far to get here. This place blew open normal, but I didn't yet know how I could tap into this destructive and creative energy. After an hour of wandering, we finally reached the man, stood at his feet, and looked up. He was wired in fluorescent blue lights, his arms outstretched. I thought of the pictures I had brought. Here, I thought, I would let go of these old selves. But first, I had to experience being someone new, living without regard to the norms, for the next five days.

The next morning, the sun was beating down on our camp and the temperature must have been at least one hundred degrees. What to do, I thought. How does one go about living a life without norms? That was the challenge of this place. If there are no prohibitions, no man-dates, no imperatives, what do you do? Who are you? Maybe not knowing was the point. After the heat broke that afternoon I wan-dered around in a haze, lost in the city.

My first act of defiance was a haircut. I decided that I needed a mohawk and that CPK was the man to give it to me. "Yeah!" he said, "awesome!" Christopher didn't seem to have this desperate need to reinvent himself. He was in the middle of the desert, surrounded by naked people, and he seemed like the same old guy. He enthusiasti-cally set up a mock barber stool in the back of the bus and pulled out his electric razor (I was half expecting him to pull out steaming hot towels as well). I was actually terrified to have my head shaved. I'd had short hair before, but if CPK gave me a mohawk I would still have it the next time I gave a professional presentation. I watched clumps of hair fall to the ground. "That is a fucking hawk!" CPK said when he finished. "You are ready for burning!"

The trouble was that after the mohawk I felt like myself again, the same old me with a terrible haircut. I felt anxiety come up in my chest. Would I fail at this—would I fail at escaping normal where there was no normal? That would have been pathetic. I felt increasingly desperate to fit in at Burning Man and it showed. One night my crew and I cooked an elaborate dinner of Machsoo, a dish that Christopher had researched on the Internet. The dish required extraordinary measures to prepare. We had to haul hundreds of ears of corn from Denver and shuck them ourselves to make the meal properly. I figured maybe I needed the right outfit to go with my hair. I donned a sarong.

The night before Becky arrived I felt lost. I had screwed this up. I had traveled all this way, only to find myself at the end of the tunnel, no different. That night I got drunk and stole someone's bike. I had forgotten my sandals, so the metal pedals cut into the soles of my feet. I rode the bike as far as I could to keep moving. I crashed somewhere outside the heart of the city. The soles of my feet were bleeding, and I lay on the desert floor and cried.

The next night Becky arrived. I was nervous and walked out to the front gate early to meet her. I greeted her with my newly shorn mohawk and bright green sarong. She looked a little taken aback at first and then quickly said, "So where do we camp?" This was not the woman who I thought was going to break up with me back at *The Lightning Field* because we had no en suite bathroom. Outhouse (and now nasty Porta-Potties) be damned, Becky was ready for the burn. Unlike me, Becky hadn't come here to be changed. She had come to be with me as I was. She wasn't looking for me to change.

I felt better the next day, as I always did with Becky. But I still felt like I had failed at Burning Man. There were just a couple of days before the burn and I still had not come to terms with this experience. I walked to the center of the city where they sold ice and coffee, the only two products officially sanctioned for commerce. When I got to the front of the line, I saw a sticker on the cash register that said "resist normalcy."

The sticker seemed trite. I watched all these people who had in some way come to free themselves from normalcy like I had. The irony was, as everyone palpably resisted normalcy, I could feel normalcy coming back to life. I wasn't shocked by the public sex; I wasn't amazed by the art cars. Burning Man had its own hierarchies and cliques of cool. There were "in" groups and "out" groups. The most radical thing one could do at Burning Man would have been to wear a business suit, stay sober, and trade stocks.

Burning Man had become, of all things, normal.

I went back to the camp and watched the day change. I spotted Gary, a man I had met the day before, waving to me. He was in a themed camp where families with children stayed. The first time I met Gary I figured only a degenerate would bring his child to a place like this. I waved back to Gary and watched him play with his daughter. He had on hot pink furry leg warmers and held his daughter's hands, and they stretched out away from each other. The dust blew in and they came in and out of focus, appearing and disappearing in the storm. The sun lit up the air like gas on fire. Gary and his daughter weren't fighting anything. They seemed to have found what I was looking for.

By the end of the week everyone was tired. So was Burning Man. We had experienced in six days the life cycle of a city. We saw it born from the desert of a lake bed, grow, mature, age, and then decay. On day six, the toilets were overflowing, people lined up at the medical tent, and a new crowd of day-tripping Los Angelenos had arrived to stare at naked people and get high. But I still held out hope that the burn would change me. If I could just burn these old parts of myself, it would be OK, I would be different than what I was.

On the day of the burn we walked back to the man to say good-bye and to visit what was known as the mourning temple. This temple was directly behind the man and made entirely of wood. It would be burned the night after the man. It was tradition for people to write things on the walls of the temple.

There was a wedding ceremony going on, and the air was filled with music and dust and the smell of sweat. I read a few things written on the side of the temple and stopped on a printed note and read it twice. There was a picture on the note of a middle-aged black man with his arms around a woman. The man was a janitor at a high school. He had died, and the kids who knew him at school wanted to say good-bye. "Thank you for keeping our school clean," one student wrote. "Thank you for not being mean to me," wrote another. And then, "You were the only person who said hello to me."

By the time I finished the note, tears were streaming down my face. The tears were mixed with dust and sweat and all the toxins I had gathered in my skin over the past two months.

The burn was changing in my mind. It was becoming more complicated. Was it the place to burn bad memories and stories? Or was it a place to make an offering of love and gratitude? Maybe it was both. Maybe it didn't have to be a funeral pyre for my imperfect self. The bottom line is the burn would be what I made it. I sat down outside the temple and wrote on a piece of paper, "Control yourself." "What's your problem?" "What's wrong with you?" "Dumb jock." These were all the things I had been told about myself for so long. I folded up this piece of paper and put it in my pocket with my old pictures, representations of parts of my life that I thought I had to forget and let go of to become someone new. One of these, both of these, might go into the fire. Either way, I was ready for the burn.

The night of the burn, we boarded a not-so-safe-looking truck that had a raised platform that put us at eye level with the man's wooden and hollow center. After we got to the center of the city, I turned and looked out behind us, where thirty thousand people had been living. The desert was dark and empty, pulsating with entropy. The truck was filled with limbs and people talking too fast or being too quiet. We didn't know any of the other bodies pressed against us, but we passed around a bottle of wine and a bag of kettle chips. The air was crisp, cold, and heavy with the smell of wood and smoke. We had all come here to see whatever it was that loomed over our lives burn to the ground.

And then it started. A ritualistic line of fire dancers circled the man, rhythmically moving their bodies. The crowd surged forward and back like a collective deep breath. Another line of fire dancers came out, circling the man from behind, surrounding him like fireflies. Then the dancers pulled back and the air became quiet. I could hear the sounds of my feet shifting on the planks.

The man raised his hands; the first fire started. Then the second. The crowd pulled back like water receding before a tsunami. The man exploded and the crowd rushed forward toward the flames. I saw a man I knew in the crowd named John. He had come from San Diego with a lock of his partner's hair. His partner had died of AIDS. John ran toward the flames and threw his scars, his love, the dead part of himself into the fire to burn.

I pulled out my photos and my note. I looked at the kid who felt so anxious in elementary school. I looked at the kid in high school. I wanted to burn the anxiety, the doubt, the violence, all the things I thought were myself. I prepared to throw the pictures toward the fire but then I saw another picture in the pile that I hadn't intended to bring. It was of me and my dad, at Disneyland, before I had started school. I'm wearing a Mickey Mouse hat and I'm sitting in my dad's lap. I looked at this kid in the picture—he was happy. He was OK; he wasn't gone. I looked at the other pictures that I had wanted to burn and changed my mind.

I put the pictures back in my pocket. I didn't want to throw myself away anymore. I pulled out the note I had written at the temple and read it again: "Control yourself," "What's wrong with you?" These were all the things that kept me striving for someone else's idea of a good life. I crumbled up the piece of paper, threw it into the fire, and watched it burn.

That night would be the last night that Kelly, Becky, and Christopher would all ride the short bus with me, and I wanted it to last. After the burn we sat in the bus and passed around a bag of sea-salt-and-vinegar chips. I had given Kelly a new nickname that she hated: Confucius. "Confucius," I said, "what's your wisdom?" "Fuck you," she said. Kelly filled the bus with laughter just like my mom's. She tilted her head back and closed her eyes. As I listened to Kelly laugh, I thought about the end of this trip and about going home, not to L.A. but to New York, where I would make my life. It was terrifying for me to think about the end of this journey. I couldn't stand sitting around in the bus anymore. I had to go, to do something. "Let's go find the Bell Tree," I said to the group. Everyone nodded, though I'm sure they would have been happy to just pass the night talking.

It was unclear whether or not the Bell Tree actually existed. People had talked about it all week, but we had never met anyone who had actually seen the thing. It was described as simply a plaster tree with bells on its limbs, which hardly sounds like it warranted a pilgrimage, but it was out there to be seen so I wanted to see it. I had a general idea that the Bell Tree was at the very edge of Burning Man near the perimeter fence a quarter of a mile away from the center of the city. We had one fact to guide us: a blue light supposedly surrounded the Bell Tree.

We set out on foot for the Bell Tree, back through the center of the city, with a bottle of wine, covered in dirt, sweat, and ash. The man was gone now, the fire from the burn replaced with smoldering embers where people congregated and stood holding hands and singing songs with no lyrics. The embers smoldered like the last hot breath of something dying. The man's absence changed things. The sky was gray. The city had lost its center. There was nothing more to look up at, only bodies to look around.

We meandered for half an hour, out into the desert, until we found ourselves at the perimeter fence. It was dark, and cold, and the sky was lit like a halogen lamp with stars. All that was left of the city was a faint vibration of techno music, losing its sonic hold out there in the desert night. It was beautiful away from the city, but the Bell Tree was nowhere to be found. No one really seemed to care, but I wanted to keep going. Nothing had changed. After all the miles, I still needed to keep moving, keep striving toward something. "Trust me," I said, "when we get there the Bell Tree is gonna blow your mind."

After another fifteen minutes of walking, Becky turned to me and said, "The light went out. There is no way we're going to find this thing." She was more than a little annoyed, and it had nothing to do with the Bell Tree. The next day Becky would leave, return to New York and journalism school. I had a choice in front of me. I could head to Seattle, as planned, where I would finally turn the bus south and head home. Or I could lengthen my trip; there were more stories that I wanted to hear, one back in Denver and another in Montana. I could go back, adding thousands of miles and at the very least six more weeks to my trip. I didn't know what I would do.

"Confucius," I said to Kelly. "What is your wisdom?" "I think the light went out, but we can keep looking if you want." Everyone else was just happy to be together. But not me. "Y'all ever heard the one about the Chinese monk who rode around the country on the mule?" I asked the group as we walked around the desert searching for this bullshit tree. No one had heard of the monk, so I told them the story. Thousands of years ago, a monk was told by a Chinese emperor to search the country and bring him a mule. The monk set out on his quest and traveled the circumference of the known world. Remarkably, the monk could not find a mule to bring the emperor. Years later, he returned to and bowed before the emperor to confess his failure. The emperor laughed and said to the monk, "You haven't failed," pointing to the mule that the monk had been riding on for the past two years.

I looked around at my little band of freaks and suddenly I felt OK. All the anxiety that I had as a kid, and which I carried in my synapses and brain tissue, was leaving my body. I wasn't a freak here, with these people I loved. I still didn't know what I was, but I wasn't a striver anymore. Whatever I was, or would be, wasn't out there anymore.

I stopped walking and I looked at the sky. Mars was the closest it had been in a thousand years that night. Becky laughed and looked beautiful. This moment would never happen again. "I'm cool," I said to everyone. "We can go back. Bye-bye, Bell Tree." We took two steps back toward the camp and ran into the Bell Tree. We were right in front of it. "Confucius," I said to Kelly, "what's your wisdom?"

"Fuckin' A bubba," Kelly said.

"You're a wise woman," I said.

When I woke, the smoke from the burn was still heavy in the air and clung to my skin, mixing with the sweat left over from the day before. My hair was white with ash and dust from the desert. I could have been a ghost. We got up early, at 5:30 a.m., and the sky was light on the edges but still dark in the center. Mars was bright in the distance but had begun its slow orbit away from us. I was tired and a little hungover, but the cold woke me up and, in less than ten minutes, our camp was gone and the sky had changed again. The dark center turned shades of white and blue as the sun rose over the mountains to the east. I knew I wouldn't be back to Burning Man again, though we all said we would.

We drove to Reno that morning and found a hotel for brunch before Becky drove her rental car to the airport. Reno is basically in a coma; it's like a body hooked up to a life support that is barely bleeping. The life remaining is artificial. When we sat down to brunch, I felt something I hadn't felt in the six days at Burning Man. Every last person was staring. Of course, I hadn't shaved in two months; nor had we showered in nearly a week. We were covered in dust. We were freaks again.

I walked Becky out to her rental car after brunch. I started to explain to her that I had decided *not* to keep this trip going any longer than I had to. I was going to Seattle with Kelly and then home. But she didn't give me a moment to speak. "You come home when you're done, OK? I love you, you short-bus riding fool."

That night, I slept the longest continuous number of hours that I've ever slept in my life—almost twenty. The next day it was time to say good-bye to Christopher. We had planned an elaborate night of drinking. We had dinner, and our departing friend ordered an ill-advised piece of cake for dessert. It didn't go down well. Later he lay on the bed promising to rally. Then he got out of bed, in his boxers, assumed a gym teacher–worthy jumping-jack stance with impeccable right-angle form. "I'm just going to jack it out, man," he said. "That's all I need, a few perfect jacks, move this cake right through me." And that is what CPK proceeded to do. He stood up and executed one perfect jumping jack after the other, in the middle of a hotel room in Reno, Nevada. I'd miss him.

Kelly and I left the next day for Seattle, where she would fly home to L.A. Our first night out of Reno, in Bend, Oregon, Kelly called my mom and learned of her Peace Corps assignment. We were sitting in a less-than-luxurious Hampton Inn, and Kelly's face crumpled in the yellow light from the desk lamp. "It's not good," she said. Kelly had been assigned to a series of atolls in the Pacific. It would be difficult, nearly impossible, for her to travel home from this place. I wouldn't see her for two years.

Kelly and I said good-bye in the Seattle airport. I had been wrong about Kelly. She didn't have to do anything "important" with her life— she didn't have to go into the Peace Corps, she didn't have to change. After all that I had experienced on the bus, I wanted to tell Kelly that a life grounded in relationships was a good life . . . was the best life.

"Confucius," I said one last time as we stood in the Seattle airport. "What's your wisdom?" She laughed and then smiled. "Normal people suck," she said. "Don't you ever forget that *you* taught me that." I gave her a hug, and then we said good-bye the way we always do. "Later, dude," I said. "Later, dude."

PART THREE

The Eccentrics

Seattle, WA—Los Angeles, CA

14

Driftwood Beach

SEATTLE, WA–DAVIS, CA

Like that, my trip was almost over. I had left the bus in Seattle for a week to go back to New York and returned on September 20. On my way back, I stopped in San Francisco to pick up my last passenger. His given name, believe it or not, was Miles Davis. Miles was fifteen years old, half black, half Jewish, and all LD/ADHD. Not long before we traveled together, he had changed his name to Alec. I still don't know why, but I have to admit it was a bit of a cruel joke on his parents' part to name him after the great jazz musician. Alec, though, will always be Miles to me.

I knew Miles through his mom, Leah, a bona fide freak who was one of the first people to support my career as a public speaker. She had grown up around her folks' thrift store on Pico Boulevard in L.A. Her father was an aspiring artist and her mother had bipolar disorder. Leah, maybe five feet tall on a good day, was like an East Coast yenta with a surfer's accent. She hated school and rebelled fiercely against all forms of authority. In 2001, she organized a week of speeches in San Diego for me. I stayed at their house and got to know Miles, who was being destroyed by school. It showed in so many familiar ways. He stayed home most days during my visit, and we hung out. He was a brilliant and hurting little kid.

That week I got a sense of Miles's natural wit and sarcasm. Leah told me a story about when Miles was ten years old. She had left him alone in the house to run an errand. She returned to find Miles lying on the floor in what appeared to be a huge bloodstain next to a bloodied butcher's knife. Leah began crying hysterically and called the cops. The bloody pool turned out to be ketchup. When I met him, Miles hadn't yet lost all of himself to this struggle.

When I got off my plane in San Francisco, though, that day in September, I didn't see the Miles I knew. Standing next to Leah was the faint outline of a kid who seemed vaguely familiar, a little boy with a body swimming in a stew of adolescence and black clothing. Miles had on black plastic raver pants spilling over his shoes, a black shirt held together at the shoulder seams with oversized safety pins, and, to top it all off, a black Parisian existentialist-style beret gingerly placed on the top of his blond-tipped black Afro. On the back of Miles's black backpack was an upside-down American flag, the military sign for distress.

"You don't answer your fucking phone, do you?" Miles said to me when I got off the plane. I gave him a hug. I had extended Miles a half-hearted invitation to join me on this trip at the beginning of the summer, but I never thought he would actually get his ass on the bus. Yet Miles was motivated, and he called me at least once a week throughout the entire summer. I, as usual, didn't answer the phone.

"Good to see you too, man," I said, as Leah greeted me the way she always did, with a huge "DUUUUUUUDE." She sounded like a seasoned surfer. I couldn't chat long, though; we were in a hurry to catch our flight to Seattle.

"OK, honey," Leah said to Miles. "Here is all the money you have. Don't get arrested. Don't drink too much. And don't piss Jon off." She took him in her arms.

"I don't know when we'll be back," I said to Leah. "It's cool," she said. "His school starts in ten days, and he has to decide by then whether he wants to go back or not. It's up to him." And with that, Leah hugged me and sent us on our way the only way she knew how: "DUUUUUUUUUDES, have a great trip," she yelled.

The flight to Seattle, to pick up the bus, was quick, easy, and quiet. Miles sat next to me and put his headphones on and didn't say a word. Miles's journey is marked with the familiar plot points of any LD story: the painful reading out loud, the futile attempts at spelling. But for Miles, I think there were a few moments that truly defined his experience—events that he was still struggling to make sense of and process.

Miles dreamt of being a fighter pilot; maybe he got this idea from the planes he could hear flying at night from the air force base near his childhood home in San Diego. Miles told his fifth-grade teacher about his dream and that he wanted to go to Annapolis for college. The teacher laughed at him and then pulled out one of his assignments and held it in front of the class. "Your mom does your homework," she told the class. That year Miles failed math. When given an IQ test, he was in the ninety-ninth percentile for mathematical reasoning. He failed because his mom had to write out the answers on his homework, and that was unacceptable to his teacher.

In elementary school, Miles wrote a note to a kid sitting next to him, asking his name. But Miles misspelled "what," "your," and "name." The kid turned back to Miles and said, "Why should I tell you my name? You can't spell. You're stupid."

These degrading moments and years of humiliation had changed him. He didn't talk as much as he used to, and he seemed deeply depressed. Later Miles told me he had, not long before, moved into the basement of his family's house and painted it black. He wasn't sleeping at night, and he couldn't get out of bed during the day. Miles was in transition, and who he would be was sort of up for grabs. He might not make it. I can't claim to know all that this kid was struggling with, but I do know that he was torn up by being accused, through his whole life, of not being who he really was.

Miles is gifted, extremely so, with an IQ of well over the superior range. Yet, at the age of fifteen, his phonetic awareness was at an elementary school level. Many people, including many educators, cannot get their minds around the paradox of a brilliant kid who can't do certain seemingly simple tasks. So where was he told that he was gifted and with a high IQ? Miles was told that he wasn't, in fact, gifted and that he wasn't actually all that smart. Miles was led to believe that he was a fraud. Leah, of course, gave the school hell for this when it became clear that people were telling her smart boy that he was, unfortunately, just lazy.

Our culture often conflates giftedness with academic achievement. But nothing could be farther from the truth. Truly gifted individuals often don't do well in school at all. I was told the same thing as Miles, and I struggled with the question giving him so much grief: Were they right? All of these things—Miles, the question, the doubts, the struggle—would be my traveling companions for the next two weeks.

Our first night together, Miles and I stayed at the W Hotel in downtown Seattle. I craved one last night of comfort before we headed down 101, where we'd be camping, without a hint of luxury, most nights. That night in the fancy hotel, I woke up at 3:30 a.m. to find Miles, wide awake, wearing the same clothes he had on that day, watching porno on TV. "What the fuck are you doing?" I yelled across our hip bedspread. "Watching porno," Miles replied.

"No shit," I said. "You trying to be a pain in the ass, man?" "No," he responded, "but you know, as they say, ask a stupid question, you get a stupid answer." The next morning when we checked out of the hotel, I found out that Miles had actually rented *eleven* pornos, at fourteen dollars a pop. In one night, he had spent half of his money for the entire trip.

That afternoon, we got back on the road. Our plan was to spend the night in Port Angeles, Washington. Miles had a family friend in Port Angeles whom he called Uncle Anton. We took a ferry across Puget Sound, which was rough and white. The sky shook with gray storm clouds speeding south down the coast to a storm that wasn't real yet but would soon be. For most of the ride, Miles sat alone with his headphones on, but halfway across the sound he took them off and came and sat next to me.

"I heard shit's not going too well for you, man," I said to him over the sounds of the approaching storm. "Fucking cow town that I live in," Miles said. "They beat me up because of the flag," Miles added. He was referring to the upside-down American flag that he wore on his backpack. Before we left, Leah told me that Miles had recently been assaulted by a group of local kids. I think there was more to it than the flags. The kids who beat him up used racial slurs. Miles was also failing classes. "Why don't you just split, man, you know, enroll in a community college?" I asked him. "Get the fuck out of that conformity factory."

"I don't know," Miles said as he took off and put on his black beret. He was quiet for a while, his eyes watching the shallow horizon of storm clouds and fall air. "You know, my friends and stuff. But I don't want to just be the freak kid in college, you know."

Miles and I didn't talk for the rest of the ferry ride. We just sat there, watching the rise and fall of the horizon covered in mist. I thought about Miles's dilemma. Did Miles really need to change something essential about himself? Watching my friend in his uniform of noncompliance, I thought he just needed to get that kid back who was being churned up and turned into something he was not.

Before we got to the other side of the sound, I turned to Miles and said, "You ever heard of Goethe?"

"Who?" Miles yelled over the sound of the waves and wind.

"Fucking Goethe, man, don't you know shit?" I teased. "I'm just fucking with you, man. I had no idea who Goethe was until I asked my shrink one day what holds someone's self together."

Miles looked at me intensely. "What did the shrink say?"

"He said Goethe believed that there was something at the center of ourselves that he called the knot that binds."

"OK, what is this knot?"

This was a good question. "That is exactly what I asked the shrink," I told Miles.

"And what did he say?"

"The shrink said, and I quote, 'I have no fucking idea.'"

Miles burst out laughing, "Oh, that's fucking helpful, dude. I bet he charged you a hundred dollars for that advice."

The world had changed when we got to the other side of the sound. It was no longer summer, and the day was filled in like a child's drawing with cold clear afternoon light tinged with the blue gray of fall. The highest peaks were already covered with snow, as they would be for the rest of the year. For the first time, the trip felt old.

We stayed that night in Port Angeles with Uncle Anton and his family. "They don't approve of what I'm doing," Miles said cryptically as we pulled up to Anton's house. "School, the trip, what?" I asked.

"Sure," Miles said, waving his hand to include all of it. "They think I should be back in school."

Yet for all their alleged cognitive dissonance about Miles's education and choices, Anton and his wife were gracious hosts and seemed very supportive. They fed us, housed us, and perhaps most importantly gave us access to cleaning supplies to rescue Bob Henry from the debauchery of the Black Rock Desert.

Miles and I spent most of that night cleaning out the bus. It was late and cold that far north, and the fog covered the tops of the mountains. The bus was parked under a streetlight that illuminated it like a beam of light from a spaceship capturing humans for extraterrestrial experiments. Bob Henry was utterly filthy, covered in white dust from the desert that was impossible to sweep away. The harder Miles swept, the more the dust scattered through the air, floating around our bodies only to settle in the same place again. "Forget the dust, dude," I said. "Let it be."

Miles put his broom down and tried, unsuccessfully, to shake the dust out of his hair. "What are you going to do with this thing when you're done, Jon?" he asked, shaking himself out like a rug. "You mean Bob Henry!" I snapped, surprising myself. "Wow, dude, too much driving," Miles said. I laughed at myself. How was Miles to know that the bus wasn't a thing, that this wasn't even a bus anymore, that this vehicle now felt like a part of who I was? "So what are you going to do with *Bob Henry* when you're done?" Miles asked again, with a sarcastic sneer.

This was a good question—one that I had put out of my mind. I had started this trip knowing exactly how it would end. I would leave BH in front of my old elementary school as a sort of statement. But I wasn't so sure about that ending anymore. I shook my head. "I don't know," I said to Miles. "I might just leave it somewhere." Miles didn't equivocate. "I'd burn the fucker!" he said.

I understood Miles's anger, his rage at all this bus represented. But

I didn't feel that anger anymore. Anger had for a long time been rocket fuel for me, but I had left that rage in the desert. I really wanted to move beyond those old resentments.

I couldn't burn Bob Henry. I looked around the bus at all that I had collected over the past three months. Above the driver's seat was a picture of Ashley sitting on the beach. Next to this picture was the picture of me and my dad at Disneyland. On the floor was a copy of *the Kent*. Burning Man was everywhere. And Cookie's mural reflected in the rearview mirror. All these people, all of their values and beliefs and worlds of resistance, had been brought into my life *because* of this bus.

The next morning, our plan was to drive directly down the Washington and Oregon coast and then head inland for my next stop in Davis, California, where I would spend a day with a man named Jeff Woodhead. He was a poet, specializing in short-form haiku and the distinguished literary form of the list. I had learned about Jeff through a local reporter in Davis. She had written an article in which she described him in almost spiritual terms. It was unclear if Jeff was mentally ill or autistic. She rendered no judgment, just described him as strange and eccentric. Jeff was our next official stop.

The morning after we arrived in Port Angeles, however, I got an e-mail from an artist named Sarah, who lived in Olympia, Washington. I had met Sarah over the Internet and I admired her work and wanted to meet her in person. The e-mail I received that morning was the first that I had gotten from her in months. She wrote, "Sorry to be out of touch for so long. I don't do e-mail much. I think yard sales are a better way to communicate. If you are still in the Northwest, maybe we could have coffee."

I would drive weeks in any direction to see someone who believed in the power of yard sales as a form of mass communication. I called Sarah and arranged to meet her for coffee in downtown Olympia.

It was a beautiful drive to Olympia on a road that curved and twisted like a child's drawing on hot summer asphalt. Miles and I didn't talk much on the way. He was bored, I assumed, and he was up every few minutes shifting positions, waiting for something to happen. His was a familiar restlessness; I had experienced something similar all my life. I had it when I first got on the bus, scanning the horizon for something I couldn't quite name. I wanted to tell him that the driving, the little towns, the stops for gas were all there was, that nothing happened on a journey except the traveling itself. I didn't have the heart, though. He would have to learn that himself.

"OK, dude, this is where we part ways," I said to Miles after we parked in downtown Olympia. I had explained to him earlier that I wanted to see Sarah on my own. Miles nodded and counted the money in his wallet. "And no," I said, "I have no money for you."

Before we parted ways, though, a young man ran up to the back of the bus. "What are *you* doing here?" he yelled as he pointed at our vehicle. I couldn't tell how old he was, but he had on thick glasses, the kind that Katie wore. This kid was clearly one of her Down syndrome brethren. When Miles and I didn't respond right away, he repeated his query. "I said what are you doing here!" he yelled at Miles, his voice shaking somewhere between anger and fear.

"Nothing, man, don't worry," I said.

"Are you here to take me away?" he responded.

"What?" I said. He was pointing at the bus. "Oh, no, no, this isn't really a school bus; it is an RV now. Check it out," I said as I opened the back of the vehicle. The young man tiptoed up the stairs and turned his head around the bend without bringing his entire body into the bus.

He looked back at me and said, "You're not here to pick me up again, are you? I don't want to go."

"No," I said.

He relaxed his face and blew out like he had been holding his breath. "It's messy," he said, and then he left.

"Shit, that kid was terrified," Miles said to me.

I nodded my head.

I put my hand on Miles's shoulder. "You know, sometimes I think they are still coming for me."

Miles nodded. "But they aren't anymore, right?"

"No, they fucking aren't."

"Maybe we're coming for them," Miles said.

The coffee shop where I met Sarah felt like a hippie commune.

Folks looked more like people from Berkeley than people from Berkeley. Sarah was late, so I ordered an organic Chai latte and found a seat. Not only is Olympia the capital of Washington State, but it is a small mecca for hippies, radicals, and generally folks of an alternative persuasion. It was the kind of town where it was hard to be a freak.

It was well past five by the time Sarah and I were done talking. Miles had called me many, many times, leaving progressively more disgruntled messages. As it was too late for Miles and me to continue on down the Oregon coast, Sarah invited us to stay the night in her house just outside of downtown.

"Where you been?" Miles said when he got into the bus. "I've been calling."

He quickly got over it when I pointed to the back of the bus and said, "Miles, this is Sarah."

"Hi, Miles," she said.

He was clearly stunned, fumbling over a few words before sitting down.

"Miles, say hi to Sarah," I invited him.

"Hi" was all Miles could mumble as he stared at Sarah. I think that, in that moment, Miles might have fallen in love. He certainly calmed down considerably.

The rest of the night passed like a scene from *Slackers*. Sarah's house was not fancy but had a certain charm. Sarah lived with her sister, her genetic opposite, who was built like a pipe fitter, had huge curly hair, and thick-rimmed glasses. Sarah's sister had lived quite a life. For the past ten years she had spent her summers doing migrant farm work, and she had traveled the country by train, as a hobo. When she was in third grade, nine years old, she walked out of class, walked downtown, and boarded a bus from Portland, Oregon, to San Francisco. Just for fun. She was gone for three days.

"Gone for three days?" Miles said with a stunned look on his face. "I mean you just up and split?" Sarah's sister nodded her head. "You could do that," I said to Miles. "Just get up and split." He laughed. "I just might—and come live with you in New York."

Sarah and her sister owned no furniture, so that night I brought out our dusty lawn chairs and opened the last bottles of wine from the coolers that survived the desert. We all drank wine and listened to old folk music on a shitty stereo in an empty room warmed by our stories. The sun was almost up when Miles and I went to bed. If you can call it that. We laid out my sleeping bags from Burning Man, still covered in dust, in the middle of the living room. As I got ready to go to sleep I thought I heard him crying. "You all right?" I asked. He didn't say anything. He rolled over on his side, away from me. "I'm fine, you know, OK." I didn't believe him. I put my hand out over the brown shag carpet and rested it on his shoulder. "Shit will get better, Miles. It will," I said. "You think so?" he asked. "You know I couldn't get out of bed this summer. I couldn't move. I was just so sad." There was nothing to say to that. We both went to sleep, my hand still on his shoulder.

The next day was the first really cold morning of the trip. The air was filled with the kind of cold that comes in between the seasons to push summer farther from fall.

For the next three days it was just Miles and me. No stops, no plans, just 101 and the coast of Oregon and then California. The drive that first afternoon was easy and seductive, filled with the landscape colors and smells of clashing ecologies. We began in Portland, where the air was still a relic of a fading season, the last of the summer's heat and humidity trapped in creases between the river and the city's concrete. Then we entered the heart of the Willamette River valley, a place that was in between summer and fall. On the other side was the Pacific Ocean, where my trip had begun months earlier and where it would end in five days. It had come down to the digits on one hand.

When we found 101, Miles had crept up behind the driver's seat. "No hotels or motels for the rest of the trip, OK, dude?" Miles said to me. "I have a motel phobia," he added.

"You have a what?" I yelled over the bus engine.

Miles was in a better mood, acting like a smart-ass kid, which was not a bad sign. "A phobia," Miles said. "Should I spell it for you? Oh, wait. I can't spell *phobia*. Should I sound it out? Oh, shit, I can't sound it out—PHOBIA, OK, Jon?"

Miles, it seemed, had found something in Olympia that made his life hurt a little less. Or at the very least, Miles found a raw outline of a future that didn't completely suck, where he wouldn't be a freak and wouldn't be like everyone else. Sometimes that is all that matters.

"Miles," I said before he sat back down. "I want you to know something. There isn't anything wrong with you, man. You need to know that. You don't need to change shit about yourself." Miles didn't say anything, and so I added, "And you realize that the W is considered a *hotel*."

"Oh," Miles responded. "OK, no hotels or motels except the W." He laughed, and then he looked at me and said, "Do you think I could visit Sarah again?"

"I think she'd love that, man."

Miles and I ended our drive down the Oregon coast by spending the night not in a motel, hotel, or W but on, of all places, Driftwood Beach. Before we set up camp, Miles and I walked on the beach together and got lost in the fog that had settled over the sand and the dunes and the shifting line between the ocean and the land. The beach was long and cold, and the sand was hard like a field after an ice storm. The sound of the ocean was muffled; I could hear it rumbling like a stomach growling in the distance.

The thing about fog, though, is that when it breaks it's like a portal has opened up in the world. The fog on Driftwood Beach opened for a moment, and I saw stretching out in front of me hundreds of pieces of driftwood that the ocean had deposited in its wake. I picked up a piece. It was still cold from the ocean and worn down. The ocean had worked its way through and around this solid fragment of wood; what had half destroyed this wood had also made it beautiful. All the driftwood on the beach was dented, broken, twisted into exquisite shapes balancing on their sides in the fog until they were washed away. The tide was coming in, and I gathered as many pieces as I could carry home.

Miles had found something as well, in the fog on Driftwood Beach. He ran up to me and he had in his hand a piece of seaweed that looked like a whip. "Check this shit out," he said as he snapped the moist air. "You try."

I picked up the whip, and I gave it a half-ass swing and lashed myself on the back. I ran around in circles yelling as Miles laughed. He was alive now, filled with anger and rage, the kind that can, if used right, heal and transform a hurting kid. I knew this anger well. But it wasn't in me anymore. I needed something else. I needed beautiful pieces of driftwood. "Dude, I am done with this shit," I said, as I handed the whip back to Miles.

Miles smacked the side of the short bus with the whip, cutting through the thick fog like a flashlight. He swung it around and yelled out into the deadening air.

If he could only hold on to this, I thought, he would be OK. I put my driftwood in the back of the bus and Miles took the piece of seaweed with him. It's funny what you find in the fog.

15

Things Not to Share—at First

Jeff Woodhead

DAVIS, CA

I was told by the local reporter in Davis, California, who had turned
me on to Jeff Woodhead's story that he was a rather "difficult" sort of
personality to understand. Even duly warned, I did not realize what
she meant until *halfway* through my day with him, in the most literal
sense. Jeff had timed our day together down to the second and
informed me, as we ate lunch at Togo's (a California sandwich chain),
that "our day is halfway over." "Difficult" to understand didn't quite
seem to cover it.

At that moment, Jeff was sitting across from me eyeing a turkey
sandwich of the exact same sort, he informed me, that he ordered
every day. While at Togo's, in no particular order, Jeff spoke at length
about his friends, his math, his poetry, his need to take a shower, his
belief that one should never wash clean clothes, only dirty, and his
notion that extra dietary salt was not detrimental to one's health. It
was somewhere between Jeff's laundry and his non sequitur on salt
that I realized the scope of my problem:

I had no way to make sense of Jeff.

I took a bite of my turkey sandwich and thought about what to do.
I could leave, but I didn't want to. I could press Jeff about his past and
his clinical diagnosis. Suddenly his voice broke into my thoughts: "His

name is Jeff and my name is Jeff, and they like me at Togo's," Jeff said. "What?" I asked, lost in my deliberation. "Togo's, they like me here. Do you want to see the rest of Davis?"

I looked at Jeff and took stock of what I knew about him thus far: He was forty-six and had not held a job since the 1980s. He was known all around the city of Davis, a typical California college community, for his deep love of math. He believed if you really wanted to learn something you should read children's books. He believed that an ethical life meant not being cruel. He collected friends' autographs in an autograph book. He corresponded with famous mathematicians. He loved his Hewlett Packard graphing calculator like one might love a pet. While none of these facts really coalesced into a narrative, somewhere in them was the experience and mind, if not the *story*, of one of the most singular people I had ever met. I nodded *yes* to Jeff's offer of a tour of Davis.

My experience with Jeff had not actually begun at Togo's. Nor did my day start on such unsound narrative footing. In all honesty, from the moment that I spoke with Jeff on the phone, I thought I knew without a doubt what his story was all about. It was the morning of September 27 when I phoned to get directions to his apartment in Davis. The sound of Jeff's voice was the first hint that he was a little off the mainstream; it was so strange and distracting that I had to ask him to repeat his directions three times. His speech was so mechanical and stilted that I was reminded of my dad's flat intonation on my family's early answering machines in the 1980s. Jeff's voice, at certain moments, rose to very high tones like a computer on helium. Then it fell. Its rhythm was also erratic. He would slow down, awkwardly at times, and then would speed up like an out-of-control train gathering steam. Surprisingly, Jeff's pitch was soft, so much so that I worried his voice would crack if he stumbled on a heavy consonant. Once I eventually adjusted my expectations of what a voice should sound like, I found Jeff's voice to be as beautifully strange as a Glenn Gould performance.

I listened carefully as Jeff proceeded to give me incredibly specific—one might say ritualistic—directions to his apartment. These were broken down not just by streets and highways and local land-marks, in other words, the usual sorts of thing. No. Jeff had done all of this and more. He had broken his directions down to mile markers (their locations rendered in exquisite detail) and estimated the time it would take me to move through each section of the directions. Down to the second. When I pulled into his parking lot, my cell phone rang. "You should have been here a minute ago," Jeff said. I assured him that his directions were fine, that I had just driven a little slowly.

Jeff lived in a gray, concrete bilevel complex that boasted all the architectural distinction of most standardized subsidized housing. He lived on disability, and his apartment was financed, in part, by the state. I walked up the two flights of stairs and found my host standing at the top, holding his watch. "Hi, I'm Jeff," he said. He looked a little like an old Irish priest with his reddish brown hair, which was graying on the sides. He was about five-foot-ten, and gravity was doing its work on his face and the middle of his body. I put out my hand, but he had already turned away and was headed toward his apartment. Shuffling awkwardly to the side, he held the door open for me.

"This is my girlfriend, Andréa. She wanted to meet you." Sitting on the couch was a woman with coal black hair whom I estimated to be in her mid- to late forties. Shaking her hand, I sat down next to Jeff. There was very little small talk. None in fact.

Jeff started the conversation with the not-quite-standard meet-and-greet topic of infidelity. "We've been together for a while. I love Andréa. She makes me feel good," he said, with no warm-up or transition. Then he gulped like a goldfish and blew out, "Though I've cheated." I blanched as Andréa nodded her head. "But," he continued, "she has cheated too. That is OK, though, because I know how to forgive. I expect my friends to be who they are, not who I expect them to be."

Over the next ten minutes, I was given a very personal overview of Jeff and Andréa's relationship. They had met over twenty-two years ago at a halfway house for people with mental illness and disabilities. (Andréa told me that she had experienced a breakdown.) From the beginning, Jeff was the pursuer, although Andréa resisted at first.

"He grated on me at the start," she said. But Jeff had no doubts: "I liked her the first time I met her, and I asked her to date me, and she

had decided she had to make a list of characteristics of someone she
was looking to date. But she did decide to date me." I would learn later
that Jeff is an epic list maker. But he did not need to make a list about
Andréa. "I decided that I did not have to rationally think. My impres-
sion, it turns out, is that love can be at first sight." An odd, wholly Jeff
way to express a very old idea.

Despite the unconventionality of their relationship, I was quite
moved by the way Jeff talked about it. Clearly, his feelings for Andréa
were real. To be honest, I was surprised and happy that Jeff had anyone in his life, much less someone like Andréa, who, despite her history
of mental illness, would be considered cognitively normal. She had
issues, perhaps chemical, but she was quite different from Jeff, who
was, both cognitively and personally, one of the most unique men I had
ever spent time with.

As Jeff and Andréa talked about their relationship, I scanned Jeff's
apartment. It was covered with stacks of books ranging in subject from
advanced math to self-help such as *Soaring with Your Strengths*. Next
to some of these books appeared to be one of Jeff's old business cards.
It read:

MR. JEFF WOODHEAD
AMATEUR COMPUTER PROGRAMMER
1-503-777-8423

Basic, Rpl, Rpn for Hp-42's & HP48GX Computers
Computing since 1980

While I was impressed with the fact that Jeff had been computing
since 1980, no one in his or her right mind would consider him a computer programmer, not in any situation I could imagine, beyond my
ninth-grade algebra class. He referred to these graphing calculations
throughout our day together as simply "computers," revealing that he
was, perhaps, just a little behind the technological bell curve.

"So Andréa has only three minutes left to spend with us," he said
out of the blue. He knew exactly how much time had passed. He had

been timing everything thus far. After his prompt, Andréa prepared to leave. I said good-bye, and we shook hands, and she quietly disappeared.

Jeff sat back down on the couch. "So," I asked him, "what should we do?" "I want to show you some places that I hang out in Davis," he replied.

"Sounds good," I said, and before I could finish my sentence Jeff was up, packing his backpack. He filled it with maybe five or six books and then said, "I'm ready." This is the point where he informed me, very loudly, that he was "totally against washing clean clothes. I think it's good to wash dirty clothes," he remarked. What *kind* of human was in front of me? I thought.

As Jeff and I stood out in front of his apartment, we talked about the first stop on our tour of Davis. This conversation, however, did not unfold like any traditional exchange. A talk with Jeff doesn't proceed in a straight line, but darts and weaves like the brushstrokes of an abstract painting. Jeff informed me that his "is different from hers." What *his* referred to was left unspecified. I suspected that he was speaking about his diagnosis, but he didn't elaborate.

I didn't have time to push the issue because this statement was quickly followed by a long deliberation on which route we should take to get to Togo's. I was under the assumption that this would be a fairly brief conversation. Davis is a small town. Togo's is located maybe five minutes away. Wrong. Jeff had many different routes to choose from. He and I spent maybe ten minutes deliberating, listing their pros and cons (I played along, faking a familiarity with the geography). Finally, we settled on how to proceed. I don't remember which way we chose because none of these routes was very different. Before I took my first step, Jeff started the stopwatch function on his black Casio watch. He was timing our walk.

Later I would ask him about his need to time everything, to hold on to every minute. He didn't seem offended, but he did act like I was exaggerating, like his whole timing of my trip didn't happen. "I did that with you?" he asked. He did, I explained, then asked why he did this. "It is sort of a comforting habit," he said. "It doesn't mean something. If you can get information, then why not, I figure. If I time it and I don't need to know, then I can erase it. It is a habit that is comforting to let me know how fast I do it. I don't do it all the time. To what extent is it like anything you can make a pro/con list about?"

By the time Jeff and I actually arrived at Togo's, I had reached the conclusion that Jeff's habit went beyond what he could explain. I later learned that he had timed many walks he had taken in an effort to improve and maximize his efficiency.

While Jeff and I were eating lunch, I got a glimpse of a chart that he had written in his notebook. Reproduced here, it itemized how he had used every hour in a given week.

3:40 P.M.

-

-

-1-14-2003 DREA'S TUE

WEEK-7 DAYS	USE	BALANCE
WEEK-7 DAYS		168
SLEEP 8 HRS/DAY	56	112
EAT	7	105
COMPUTE	15	90
NAP	21	69
JOURNAL	21	48
READ	14	34
FOOD SHOP	1	33
VISIT DOWNTOWN	3	30
CALL FRIENDS	6	24
THERAPY	1	23
GET POSTAGE	.30	22.70
GET BISTRO SODAS	2	20.70
SEE TYKLE	2.70	18.00
WRITE LETTERS	3	15
PRAISE PEOPLE	4	11
SEX	2	9
BOOKLET WRITING	2	7

WALKING	1	6
BICYCLING	1	5
GET MAIL	.30	4.70
PREPARE AND TAKE MEDS	.70	4
SEE BRUCE D	3	1
TAKE SHOWERS	1	0

As Jeff and I ate our sandwiches, I pondered his quirks, his voice, and his social awkwardness. Jeff reminded me of a Cambridge University mathematician I had read about, a man who loved efficiency so much that he sprinted everywhere he went, regardless of whether he was in a hurry. He sprinted to the bathroom. He sprinted to his colleague's office down the hall. Wherever he went, he sprinted. This man is believed to have a form of high-functioning autism known as Asperger syndrome.

The trouble, however, with classifying Jeff's behavior within the categories of autism or what is known as Asperger syndrome (a distinction I'll get to in a moment), is that these categories are murky at best. They are not conceptualized as experiences or isolated neurological "disorders"; they refer to *types* of humans. It is common in the field of autism to invert the traditional politically correct sorts of phrasing and claim that an individual does not *have* autism but *is* autistic—like a cognitive nationality. Likewise, the rest of us are considered by autism advocates (boldly and heroically in my mind) as neuro-*typical*. For this reason, discourse on autism and Asperger syndrome brings us to an edge and tipping point. Depending on your perspective, autism is a human experience that is either an actual cognitive impairment or a relativist cognitive difference, pathologized by us neuro-typicals.

Let me acknowledge up front that there is much confusion about what autism and Asperger syndrome are and what range of humans fit these labels. About the only thing that is clear and undisputed is the discursive history of autism. The types of people we now call autistic have been around since the beginning of time. Autism as a designated condition, however, was not "discovered" until the 1940s when Drs.

Leo Kanner and Hans Asperger, who were working on two different continents, unknown to each other, published the first scientific reports on autism and what came to be known as Asperger syndrome.

Dr. Kanner, a child psychiatrist, was a Viennese immigrant working at Johns Hopkins University. In the course of his work, in the 1940s, he came upon a group of eleven boys who were described by professionals and parents as in their "own world." Through observations, Dr. Kanner noted that these boys were radically disconnected from typical or normal human language and emotional experience. To him, these young men were tragically and pathologically lost in the self. He called this experience of self-immersion autism, after the Greek word for self, *autos*. In 1943 he published "Autistic Disturbances of Affective Contact," the founding text of what is now known as "classical infantile autism." The child described in this paper is perhaps what most of the public imagines when they hear the word *autism:* a nonverbal child suffering from involuntary verbal and physical tics painfully disconnected from the human experience.

At almost the same time, Dr. Asperger was working with a similar but slightly different group of young boys. He ran a clinic at the University of Vienna that specialized in difficult boys. One group of boys, like Kanner's, suffered significant language delays and abnormalities and also exhibited similar physical tics. Asperger's boys, however, presented a paradox. Many of these boys could not feed themselves but could do calculus. Some could not answer simple questions yet were endowed with musical gifts. Asperger concluded, unlike Kanner, that this human experience may constitute an "originality of thought and experience, which may well lead to exceptional achievements in later life." Asperger's work, however, was lost in the 1944 bombing of Vienna and was not formally published in English until the 1980s. At the time of publication, a new diagnosis was born: Asperger syndrome.

Are autism and Asperger syndrome the same thing? The answer is yes, no, and we don't know. According to the writer and neurologist Oliver Sacks in his book *An Anthropologist on Mars*, work throughout the 1970s in the emerging discipline of cognitive physiology identified a triad of impairments that constitutes all cases of autism, including Asperger syndrome. The following had to be present for a diagnosis:

impairment of social interaction with others; impairment of verbal and nonverbal communication; and impairment of play and imaginative activities. This triad is fairly well accepted in current academic research as well as in the *Diagnostic Statistical Manual (DSM)* and allows that autism can come in mild to severe forms. Seen through this lens, autism is the root biological experience, and Asperger syndrome is just a milder form of it.

On the other hand, there is an emerging academic opinion, led in part by Uta Firth, a professor in cognitive development at the University of London, that Asperger syndrome is an autonomous biological experience. Even though some researchers agree, they still use the language of high-functioning autism to describe Asperger syndrome. There are many good studies *suggesting* the biological roots of autism and Asperger syndrome, but none of this research is definitive. We don't know for certain what causes classical infantile autism, much less high-functioning autism. Without this clarity it is difficult, if not impossible, to know where to draw the line between autism, Asperger syndrome, and just plain old strange human behavior.

The danger, however, is that we, as a culture, never draw the line. The conceptual confusion over autism, Asperger syndrome, and human eccentricity has been resolved by what, in my opinion, is one of the most dangerous of psychiatric concepts and intellectual crutches: the continuum. It is commonly asserted by academic, professional, and parent groups alike that autism is a "spectrum." Survey any local bookstore and you will see many books referring to the Autism Spectrum Disorders. The *DSM* itself resolves this confusion by grouping the two terms under the diagnostic category Pervasive Developmental Disorders (PDD). Where did autism go? Are you confused yet?

According to the *DSM*, the PDD spectrum contains all deficits and developmental delays in communication (both verbal and nonverbal) skills, social skills, and cognitive skills. On this continuum are classical infantile autism, mild-functioning autism, high-functioning autism, Asperger syndrome, and my own favorite PDD—Not Otherwise Specified (PDD-NOS). What is PDD-NOS? Only a fine-tuned clinical eye can spot that one. According to one book for parents, *A Parent's Guide to Asperger Syndrome and High-Functioning Autism*, PDD-NOS is when a child "has some autistic like behavior but does not meet the definition of either high-functioning autism or Asperger syndrome."

It is important to note that NOS is not limited to PDD, but also applied to mood disorders and every other diagnostic category. In other words, you can have a disorder not otherwise specified in all areas of the *DSM*. Now we come to the real cultural dilemma at the heart of the autism discourse. With Not Otherwise Specified as a diagnostic category, our culture has a sickness for every scientist, mathematics lover, dork, geek, artist, introvert, and extrovert. In short, we have a category for every shade of human experience out there. I have no idea who you are; I don't know your life, but I'll bet real money that if you spent enough time with a shrink there would be a spot for you on this Not Otherwise Specified spectrum.

So here is where our journey through the discourse of autism ends. We started with a population of kids who, according to the original researchers, required few diagnostic tools to see that they were "different." These children were impaired and in need of care. We conclude, however, with a continuum that takes these children as its starting point but ends wide-open. Here is a definition of *autism* from the same book that gave us a definition of PDD-NOS: "Autism is the most common and typical of PDD's, ranging in severity from those who are very handicapped (nonverbal and totally aloof) to those who are only mildly socially awkward, are slightly unusual in their conversation style and have special interests."

The autism spectrum gives us a way to name one of the things we humans hate the most: the unknowable. The spectrum idea explains why some people are rude; why some kids talk to themselves; why some people don't make eye contact. And it is one of those categories that helps me understand why a man would time our walks together. I had deep philosophical concerns about an amorphous category like Asperger syndrome, but it fit Jeff.

I did not have the courage to ask Jeff directly about autism or Asperger syndrome until well into the middle of our day together, after lunch. At that point I had fragments of Jeff's personal history swimming in my brain. I ran them through my mind, trying to put them into some coherent order. I failed. Without the confirmation and frame of the autism label, Jeff made no sense to me.

Here is what I pieced together, after the fact, from the fragments of narrative. These pieces have been put in some semblance of a story only after follow-up interviews with Jeff and with his younger brother, Allan. Every single person that I interviewed expressed confusion about Jeff's cognitive profile and diagnosis. Some used words like *autism*. Others used the language of mental illness, which in Jeff's generation was a common misinterpretation of the autism spectrum. Everyone I spoke with, however, said that Jeff was odd, strange, and "really smart but not in many things."

If I, or anyone else, was going to understand Jeff, I had to understand the man in his own words. At one point in our day together, Jeff told me that his childhood was a "living hell. It taught me not to look back." Indeed, Jeff told me very little about his past. The following personal history, while reported in the third person, is in Jeff's own language, cadence, and chronology. This is how Jeff told me his story.

Jeff was born in 1957 in Oakland, California. His father was a real-estate appraiser, and his mother was a housewife. Jeff's mom loved music and had an impressive voice. She would sing songs from musicals. This taught her son that music matters and that music helps a person feel better. When Jeff was a kid, he had a trombone that he loved and that he played obsessively. But when he got good enough to play "When the Saints Go Marching In," he quit playing. He figured that was the best he would ever get. Later in his life he donated this trombone to a local elementary school. He is unsure if that was his idea or not.

Jeff had an unhappy family life. He says his father was verbally and, at times, physically abusive. His father may or may not have been struggling with an undiagnosed mental illness. He had a drinking problem. Jeff's mother divorced his father when Jeff was thirteen. Jeff forgave his father. His childhood wasn't the best, but it wasn't the worst. Jeff thinks that problems like this are gifts.

Jeff was *odd*. His word. He shared only three specific anecdotes about his school life. First: In third grade some students from the University of California at Berkeley came to his classroom to teach math.

This, he said, was amazing. This changed his life. Second: Jeff loved his third-grade teacher. He didn't tell me her name. That year, though, Jeff was the teacher's pet. Not the teacher's only pet but one of them. Jeff looked up this third-grade teacher years later and wrote her a letter. She loved him, he said, and she told him that he was a worthwhile person. He didn't always feel worthwhile. Third: Jeff was given an EEG test when he was a child to find out what was wrong with him. The doctors tried to see if there was an organic problem with Jeff's brain. Jeff is unsure about the actual results of the EEG, but knows that they did not find anything "organically" wrong with his brain. "Maybe they determined *it* was a choice," he said, referring to his way of behaving in the world. Jeff was placed in special ed classes for most of fifth grade. Others confirmed what I suspected: Jeff was brutally made fun of throughout his life, both in school and out of school.

Jeff graduated from JFK High School in 1976 and completed almost two years of junior college. There was little in between these moments of time and 1978, when Jeff moved to Davis, to a halfway house for people with mental illness and other disabilities. He thought about suicide. Once he ran away to Canada because he thought the police were after him. They weren't, he realized. During our day together he never confided what label doctors had used to describe his condition, just that he was vaguely aware of some level of mental illness. He now takes medication and believes that God cares for him.

Jeff's life is facilitated by the state. He hasn't worked in years, and the only full-time job he ever had was through a nonprofit organization that specializes in placing people with disabilities in manual labor jobs. "I'm not rich, but I'm not poor," Jeff said to me. He believes that he can be on disability and still be helpful, that people don't have to work for money to be worthwhile. He thinks he does good things. He likes to believe that he gives something to others that is unique. Jeff is growing and learning from life. He loves his partner.

That was it. Jeff's life was like color and brushstrokes without a frame.

As we finished eating at Togo's, I had come to the conclusion that Jeff's behavior definitely fit the autism pattern. I asked him flat out if he was considered autistic or had Asperger syndrome. I would ask this question again later that day and many times thereafter, and I would get the same response every time: "No," Jeff said clearly, without hesitation. I defined the traits. Jeff responded, "I know a guy who is like that, and that is not me."

Jeff then added, out of nowhere, "There is absolutely no evidence that extra dietary salt causes hypertension." We were at an impasse. Lunch was over. Jeff looked at me and said in a way that made me want to cry, "Do you want to see Davis with me?" There were two ways for me to make sense out of my day with Jeff. This was like a "Choose Your Own Adventure" moment.

Option A: Assume Jeff is just uninformed or in denial. Most in my position would say to Jeff, "OK, sure, dude, you say you're not autistic, but you just timed how long it took for us to eat lunch." Option A leads us to the truth with a capital *T.* Option A is grounded in a belief that there is a truth out there about each of us to be discovered and often diagnosed.

Option B: Assume Jeff has the capacity to create his own truth about himself. This is a radical idea. This leads us to the conclusion that the autism story is just that—not a truth but a story that one can use or not use at different times in one's life. Inherent in Option B is the idea that the truth about ourselves is not something to be discovered, but something we make.

But the reality is that it wasn't my choice to make. Jeff had already decided that if I was going to spend the day with him, I was going to understand his truth about himself, not some label placed on him. Sitting with Jeff, I wondered if we could pinpoint the moment in the history of human consciousness when a majority of people stopped thinking of people like Jeff as strange, and started thinking of them as crazy and then sick. In this moment, we as a culture, and as individuals, decided that we knew the truth about people's lives.

As I watched Jeff put away his lunch tray, I thought of something Ludwig Wittgenstein wrote in *Philosophical Investigations.* Wittgenstein is a man claimed by many camps. He has been posthumously diagnosed ADHD, autistic, Asperger syndrome, obsessive-compulsive, and mentally ill. In *Philosophical Investigations* he wrote, " 'Seeing-as' is not part of perception. And for this reason it is *like* seeing, and then again *not* like." Perhaps Ludwig got it right: Seeing someone *as* anything, while like seeing, is not quite seeing them at all.

I would learn by the end of my time with Jeff that he resisted all *seeing-as* when it came to himself. At one point after our day together, I suggested to him that maybe he was in fact an eccentric. I explained to him that the category of an eccentric had been used in the past to describe many people who were now labeled mentally ill. I personally believe that this category of eccentric is a much more humane way to make sense out of people like Jeff. Jeff, however, wasn't quite convinced. "I like eccentric," Jeff said, then quickly added, "but I have an article about eccentrics. It is interesting that you mentioned it. I can copy it [that article]. It is asking how do you define eccentricity and the idea of how many are there. I was wondering if I was an eccentric. I didn't determine anything because I didn't do it rigorously. Some say that they [eccentrics] get in front of automobiles, but automobiles don't bother me. I never got in front of an automobile."

For Jeff there was no seeing himself as anything. What does it mean to stop seeing Jeff as anything other than Jeff? The answer to this question had been in front of me all day. Jeff said it again, what he had been asking me to do since I had arrived: "I want you to see some different places around Davis. I want to show you the places I hang out." The rest of my day would be the story of option B. The rest of my day would be an attempt to see how Jeff made the truth about himself. "OK," I said. "Let's see Davis."

My day with Jeff was almost over but we were back at the beginning.

"I like to be prepared," Jeff said as we walked down Main Street. He pointed to the bag that he had packed with books and notepads back at his apartment. "I got this backpack for thirty dollars." Jeff's backpack was overflowing. It was a heavy load that he carried with him everywhere he went. Jeff and I had no plan, nowhere to go, and nowhere to be. In front of us were two stops—a coffee shop and Kinko's. In between these stops were stories about the people Jeff knew and loved. All of this was timed, of course. These were places Jeff visited daily, unfailingly. I liked that. Often the topography of who we are is not a story, is not constituted in language, but in the concrete things we do, the places we visit, and the people we know and love.

Walking to the coffee shop, our first stop, it was apparent that Jeff knew almost everyone in town. We didn't get more than ten feet without someone waving to Jeff or Jeff waving to someone. "I can see enough of them to recognize them, so when I see someone I know I say hi." Jeff loves Davis, and he shows his love with facts: *Davis has almost sixty thousand people. Davis is known for progressive biking laws. Its population ranks among the most highly educated in the country.* These facts are the kinds of things that make sense to Jeff.

For Jeff to tell me his story our first stop had to be the coffee shop and the first chapter was in the bag that Jeff had carried with him all day. When we arrived, Jeff heaved his backpack on the table and took out its contents. I thought of something Freud once said: To live a meaningful life, all human beings need work and love. In Jeff's bag was his version of these things: books, journals, and a calculator. Jeff's bag was a window into a meaningful life created by an HP48GX calculator, a math group, and the writing of lists and poetry.

The first notebook Jeff pulled out of his backpack had a long title: *This wonderful book is used to explore my good computing projects and ideas.* When I asked him to tell me about the book, he stared back very intensely. "Do you like metric units?" he asked. To be honest, I have no particular passion for metric units or anything resembling them. But Jeff did. He loved the idea of math and loved his calculator. Everyone I spoke with about Jeff emphasized the role math played in his life. The calculator was not just a tool; it was a way Jeff made sense out of his world. "The HP48GX, it's a power computer," Jeff said to me. "I can do anything that I imagine, within reason."

The calculator ordered, measured, and controlled Jeff's life. Using the calculator, he tabulated his weekly expenditures. He calculated, often down to the second, his uses of his time. Using the calculator, he compensated for the fact that he couldn't do paper-and-pencil math. It allowed him to stretch his thinking. These are all Jeff's words. I believe Jeff's timing and calculator have helped him become mindful like a Buddhist. Where I live now in New York City, every morning a group of Buddhist monks walk in a straight line to the temple. These monks seem to count each step, every morning, every day. Everyone I spoke with said that Jeff lived in the present and taught others to do the same. The HP48GX was certainly a powerful tool.

Although, by his own admission, Jeff is not really very good at math, the practice of it connects him to other people. For the past five years, Jeff has organized a monthly lunch with mathematicians from the University of California at Davis. In case you leap to any unfounded conclusion about the makeup of this group, it should be duly noted that this is *not* a group of other HP48GX experts. These are academic mathematicians. The cofounder of this group and most consistent member is a professor named Tom Sallee. Professor Sallee's area of expertise is convexity and combinatorial geometry, especially polytopes and their properties. He is one of those guys who engage in passionate Internet conversations that start with lines like, "I never miss your talks at Asilomar, which are always the high point of the weekend for me. As a result, I was terribly upset to read your attack on my approach to previewing the Pythagorean Theorem."

The history of this group is a history of Jeff's effort to connect. He created this group out of nothing, all on his own. One day, Jeff showed up at Professor Sallee's office. He was not a student at the university; he just wanted to talk about math. The professor humored Jeff for fifteen minutes then chased him out. Jeff came back. Jeff asked Professor Sallee out to lunch. Eventually Jeff invited others to join the discussion. Though Jeff has a limited capacity to participate in the conversation, these men genuinely respect his passion for math and value his presence and contributions. Tom describes Jeff's lunches as one of the highlights of his month.

Within Jeff's math group, he isn't considered strange or disabled. According to one member, named Don Chakerian (another convexity expert), the group is known for the camaraderie that exists among the members. "There is always a good chemistry," Don said, then asked, "Is it the way Jeff selects people or because of his presence? You know, Jeff keeps the jokes coming." Jokes? In all my time with Jeff I had never heard him make a linguistic utterance that was remotely in the universe of a joke. Then again, I don't love metric units or convex shapes.

When Jeff was finished telling me about math and his group, I realized that he had shared, in his way, something deeply personal about who he was. Jeff told me that he is naturally shy. I think this is an understatement. I think Jeff is puzzled by normal human interactions. He has had to work so very hard to learn how to connect to people. Jeff had taught himself to connect and has truly created a tribe for himself. For a man whose cognitive bent led him to withdraw from others, this math group was a monumental accomplishment that I deeply admired.

After half an hour, Jeff put his math notebook away and looked me in the eye. "One thing about math is that it is repeatable," he said. "It means that you can verify and check things." He paused and tried to take in a breath, but he was too excited; his voice took off: "The reason I like people is that you can't predict what they will do. If I had to give up people or math, I would give up math." Later, Jeff would make the same point, expanding upon his moral philosophy. "I don't think anything is more important than being good to people. Things are only important in a different way. People, we all need things, but that is not the point. Being good to people is one of the points of my life. The computers extend my thinking. People extend my loving."

We had just started going through Jeff's other notebooks when he announced, "You have thirty minutes before you leave."

"What about the other books?" I asked him.

"Oh," he said. "These are just things I do."

"Like what?"

"Collect things, write poems."

"Can I see them?"

Jeff nodded his head but looked at his watch. "We don't have much time," he said.

"I can leave later."

This didn't seem to work for Jeff. "I have another idea," he said as he stood up and packed his bag. He said we needed to go to Kinko's. "I want to give you a book of wisdom."

Jeff and I were bathed in the fluorescent light of Kinko's in downtown Davis, California. I was exhausted and ready to go home, but Jeff was bent over a black-and-white copier, sorting through hundreds of small pieces of paper that he had excavated from this backpack. He checked his watch to time the efficiency of each copy. This went on for well over thirty minutes, until Jeff was confronted with an existential dilemma. The timer he set at the start of our day was counting down the minutes I had left until I had to leave. He looked at his watch, and then he looked at the stack of papers. There was simply not enough time left to copy everything he wanted to copy.

I don't know what went through his mind, but Jeff chose to keep copying. When he was done, he walked up to me and handed me a stack of copied papers and then heaved his backpack onto his small frame. "Thank you," I said. He smiled, then bent his head toward his armpit and took a deep inhale. "I need to take a shower," he said, and then he pivoted on his left foot and walked out the door.

It was a courageous and selfless act for Jeff to violate his time structure to give me what he copied. Thoughtlessly, I did not read this material until months later, when I was back in New York, and I sat down to sort through all that I had gathered on the road. Jeff's packet was buried deep in a messenger bag that held my notes from the trip. When I opened Jeff's bundle, I laid it out on the floor of my office with coffee cups holding the pages down. I read it, cover to cover, twice.

Jeff's book of wisdom consists of inspirational quotes he collected from other books and newspapers, his original poetry, lists, and charts. It is one of the most beautiful things anyone has ever given me. I added headings to the book, which is reproduced here without commentary.

COLLECTIONS

PRAY AS IF
EVERYTHING DEPENDED
ON GOD.
ACT AS IF
EVERYTHING DEPENDED
ON YOU.

—ABRAHAM JOSHUA HESCHEL
"FROM THE BOOK NAMED ON THE PREVIOUS PAGE"

ALL THAT HAS
OFFENDED ME I FORGIVE.
WITHIN AND WITHOUT,
I FORGIVE. THINGS PAST,
THINGS PRESENT, THINGS
FUTURE, I FORGIVE.
I FORGIVE EVERYTHING
AND EVERYBODY WHO CAN POSSIBLY
NEED FORGIVENESS
OF THE PAST OR THE PRESENT.
I FORGIVE POSITIVELY
EVERYONE. I AM FREE
AND THEY ARE FREE, TOO.
ALL THINGS ARE
CLEARED UP NOW
BETWEEN US NOW
AND FOREVER.

COPIED ON MONDAY
6-16-2002 AT 1:10 PM DURING A MEAL WITH ARTHUR H. AT BAKERS
☐ IT'S FROM DR. PONDER'S POSTERITY DECREES BROCHURE

POETRY

I LOVE PROGRAMMING

I LOVE MY COMPUTER
IT'S FUN TO HAVE A MACHINE
THAT I CAN GROW INTO.
MY ONLY LIMITATIONS ARE
MY IMAGINATION, CREATIVITY
AND MY INTELLECT.
IT'S FINE AS A HOBBY

4.54 PM   MONDAY
C-VILLE   SEP 15, 2003

MY LABORER JOB

I LIKE MY LABORER JOB TODAY
I'M PROUD TO HAVE WORKED.
THOSE MINIATURE HORSES SURE
ARE CUTE.
SUE WAS FUN TO WORK FOR.
IT'S NICE TO WORK OCCASIONALLY
IT'S NICE TO GET $7.33 PER HOUR.
I'LL DO IT AGAIN.
LABORER WORK IS GREAT
THE SMALL HORSES WERE
ALIVE

MONDAY   TOGOS
5:30 PM   SEPT 15, 2003

MY GROWING INTELLECT

AT AGE 46, I'M GLAD
TO BE ABLE TO DO MY
CREATIVE WORK AND TO
DO SOME LONGER PROJECTS
AS I WISH TO.
IT IS GREAT TO BE GROWING.
I LOVE MY HP MACHINES.
I AM PROUD TO BE BRILLIANT.
I'M GREATFUL FOR MY
UCD MATH PROFESSOR FRIENDS.

5:40 P.M.   SEP 15, 2003
MONDAY   TOGOS

THE BEST THINGS IN MY LIFE.

I HAVE THE BEST GIRLFRIEND.
  ANDREA.
I HAVE THE BEST OTHER FRIENDS

ALL OF THEM.
I HAVE THE BEST POCKET COMPUTER
 HP MACHINES
I HAVE A GREAT PAYEE.
  SHE IS VERY HELPFUL
I HAVE A GREAT PSYCHOLOGIST.
  SHE IS WONDERFUL

LISTS

3:30 P.M.
AFTERNOON WED.   2.26.2003

SOME THINGS THAT BRING HOPE
  01 A KID WAVING AT ME
  02 SMOOTH JAZZ MUSIC
  03 LOVE SONGS
  04 A FRIEND'S KIND WORD
  05 ANDREA'S SMILE
  06 DOING SOMETHING "RIGHT"
  07 GETTING LOVE.
  08 GIVING LOVE.
  09 BEING HAPPY
  10 ANY FRIEND'S SMILE.
  11 INNOCENCE
  12 LOVE FROM MY HEART
  13 TALKING WITH A FRIEND
  14 CALLING A FRIEND
  15 TAKING A'S SUGGESTION.
  16 MAKING A LIST LIKE THIS

#11 8:04 P.M. 7-16-2003 WEDNESDAY

POOL THINGS I DO WELL
  CALL FRIENDS
  BE A FRIEND

APPRECIATE

PROGRAM HP CALCULATORS

DO ALGEBRA

KEEP JOURNALS.

EXCERPT LIST JOURNALS.

CREATE LIST JOURNALS.

GET HELP FROM THERAPY.

EARN A LITTLE MONEY.

RIDE A BIKE.

WRITE POETRY.

CELEBRATE.

EMOTE.

INTUIT.

KEEP SOME KINDS OF RECORDS.

READ THINGS.

WRITE TO PEOPLE.

IMAGINE THINGS

FOLLOW THE SPIRIT.

BE KIND

BE GENEROUS

3:55 P.M. 9-26-2003 FRIDAY

WHAT MAKES ME FEEL ALIVE

SEX

COMPUTING

BEING SMART

BEING INTUITIVE

BEING CLEVER

SOLVING PROBLEMS

BEING LOVING

HAVING GOOD FRIENDS

OPERATING AN HP

KNOWING ANDREA

12-15-2002 NOON SUNDAY A.C.

WAYS I COULD BE MORE.LOVING.OR RESOLUTION
1) FOCUS ON POSITIVE THINKING
2) BE PROACTIVE

2:45 PM 12-25-2002

1 I HEAR THE SPIRIT
2 I CAN BE WRONG
3 I CAN APOLOGIZE.
4 I CAN SAY "I DON'T KNOW."
5 I CAN SAY "I FORGOT."
6 I CAN BE IMPERFECT.
7 I CAN CHOOSE TO BE HAPPY
8 I CAN BE RESOLUTE.
9 I CAN BE A WRITER.
10 I CAN FORGIVE EVERYONE
11 I CAN BE VERY POSITIVE
12 I AM A LAY MINISTER
13 I CAN BE PEACEFUL

CHARTS

DATE

D.O.W	**2002**	**WHO**
TUE	11-19	ANNET J
TUE	11-19	LYNDA J
TUE	11-19	DUANE K
TUE	11-19	TOM S
WED	11-20	JOHN V
THURS	11-21	DAVID P
MON	11-25	JACKIE'S
FRI	11-29	MONICA
FRI	11-29	RICK HEIN
FRI	11-29	JEFF HEIN
MON	12-2	CYNN C
MON	12-2	CAREN L

SAT?	12-7?	ABHI A
MON	12-9	TOM J
THU	12-12	JIM-CENARIOS
FRI	12-13	ABHI'S ROOMMATE
TUE	12-16	MARK JEBBUI
TUE	12-16	MARIA TEBBUT
TUE	12-24	DEB STONER
TUE	12-24	FRED
MON	12-2?	JOSHUA SUMMIT
TUE	12-31-02	RICHARD ELLIS
TUE	12-31-02	JANET PARKER

This has been a strange story, hasn't it? After my initial readings of Jeff's book of wisdom, I read through it again thirty or forty times. The book changed for me and changed Jeff for me. At first, many of the writings in Jeff's book of wisdom were, like Jeff, a bit strange. I perceived them as insights into or from the mind of the other.

But are they really that strange, that other?

In my library at home, Jeff's book of wisdom shares space with a book called *The List: The Uses and Pleasures of Cataloging.* This book is by a Yale-educated Ph.D. and documents the literary uses of listing. Jeff follows other great listers such as Emerson, Whitman, Melville, and Thoreau. The list itself might be one of the foundations of thought. Jeff's book of wisdom shares space with the *Oxford Book of Light Verse,* a genre-shattering collection of common poetry compiled by W. H. Auden. I see little difference between Jeff's poetry and many of the works in these pages. Jeff's book of wisdom shares space with an issue of *Harper's Magazine* that includes a reading about a group of ancient Greek philosophers who devoted themselves to memorizing simple phrases such as "avoid the weasel," "mind the teeth when you jump off a wagon."

Are you still confused about Jeff? You should be. I've given up on trying to place Jeff in a story, label, or diagnosis. No, I don't see Jeff's writing as anything. I've corrected myself. Seeing-as is not a part of seeing. What I can tell you is what I learned from Jeff, and that is this: If you watch the strange, the other, the bizarre long enough, if you really see these people, you will find familiar pieces of yourself in their experiences. Empathy may be our only hope. I found in Jeff not just something familiar but also a better way to live.

The only way I know how to end Jeff's story is with two more lists. The first is short and easy to remember. It is titled "Things Not to Share—at First."

There is nothing on this list.

The second:

HOW ANDREA LOVES ME
   ASKS OFTEN HOW I'M FEELING
   THANKS ME WHEN I HELP HER
   PRAISES ME
   TELLS ME THE TRUTH
   LETS ME SHOP FOR HER
   STROKES MY FACE

None of this is hard to understand. None of this is strange.

16

What Is Left, After What One Isn't
Is Taken Away, Is What One Is

DAVIS, CA—CULVER CITY, CA

My original plan for ending my journey was to leave the short bus in front of my old elementary school and walk away.

First, Miles and I had to figure out what it meant to go home. During my time with Jeff, I had left Miles with the Manuses, friends of mine from my lecturing days. They were an eccentric, subversive family. They lived in the heart of Republican El Dorado county, a white-picket-fence, SUV-driving, Iraq war–supporting suburb of Sacramento. But in the midst of this conservative world, the Manuses had carved out a quietly subversive life. Cathy was a radical education activist. Her oldest son, Derek, was dyslexic and growing up could hardly read. Cathy had argued that reading was irrelevant to Derek's education. Cathy's younger son, Aaron, was openly gay and had been for most of high school. To me, the Manuses had found a way to answer the question that both Miles and I had been asking ourselves: How do we find a place, as ourselves, as exceptional people, in the world?

Miles didn't want to leave the Manuses. When I came back from my day with Jeff, I found him sitting on the floor of Aaron's room. Aaron had recently dropped out of high school and enrolled in a local junior college. "I love it," I heard Aaron telling Miles. "You know, shit just changes when you are out of high school." Miles nodded his head and smiled at Aaron. They spent the rest of the night talking about San Francisco, the Fulsom leather fair—a massive leather/gay rally in SF—and life outside the narrow halls of conformity called school.

Before we left the next morning, Miles and Aaron exchanged phone numbers. Miles had connected with Aaron. Miles had found a tribe in slacker Olympia, Washington, and with the Manuses he found another sort of inspiration.

Before we left El Dorado, I stopped to fill up Bob Henry. It was fitting that our last stop on the short bus was a shitty gas station in the heart of a conservative suburb of Sacramento. Next to us was a man in a black Porsche wearing an expensive watch and gesticulating wildly as he spoke about buying and selling something. Miles looked at the man, and then over at me, pumping the gas, then back at the man. "That is America," he screamed. Miles was right. With appropriate irony, he quickly added, "and I'm going inside to get a Starbucks."

I was feeling a little sentimental. This was one of the last tanks of gas that I would ever put into Bob Henry. Miles was leaving; in less than two hours he would be home, and soon he would have to decide if he was going back to school. I just sat there all alone in BH. I wasn't so sure about leaving Bob Henry. The short bus represented terrible experiences, sure. But this wasn't a short bus anymore. I realized that it no longer represented special education to me, as it had four months ago. Special education, the concept of disability, had been purged from this bus. Bob Henry was something wholly new; it held the stories of exceptional and beautiful humanity. Maybe it always had, but the transformation was something that I had to create. Maybe that was the real lesson of all the miles and stories. I thought of something Jeff had said to me before I left, "Anything can be made useful. Everything is worthwhile. Everyone is worthwhile." Disability and normalcy are ideas we create as a culture and society and something we can transform. "Sweet, sweet Bob Henry!" I yelled out loud into the bus. "Sweet Bob Henry."

At that moment, Miles came back. "Are you talking to the bus, dude?" he asked. There was no denying it. "Yeah," I replied. "You got a problem with it?" I said as I smiled. "Nah," Miles said. Then he added, without his signature sarcasm: "Sweet Bob Henry." Miles climbed in and handed me a cup of coffee. "I've spent my last dime on caffeine," Miles said. "You of all people, Jon, you have to respect that." I looked closely at Miles. The kid was wearing the same black raver pants and the same black shirt and the same pretentious beret as when I had picked him up. But he looked a little less the lost hurt kid. Most of us don't search for who we are; most people become who they are told they should be. Not Miles. "Miles," I said. "You need to know, dude," I said over the roar of the freeway, "there is absolutely nothing about you that I don't respect."

Our drive to Petaluma, California, Miles's hometown, was fast and easy. I could feel the fog building in the bay, and I imagined the high pressure of the Sacramento River sucking all of those gray clouds inland. There was not much more for us to talk about, and as I drove I watched Miles through the rearview mirror. He would have to decide soon whether he was going to try and make it in the so-called normal world or create his own.

Miles had a long hard fight in front of him, and I had so much behind me that perhaps I had not escaped. But Miles and I had come to the same place in our ride on the short bus. We both needed new stories to keep ourselves going.

"You're home," I said to Miles an hour later as we pulled into Petaluma.

"I know," Miles said in a voice tinged with resignation.

I stopped the bus a little short of his house so we could talk. "Miles," I said, preparing for a cheesy good-bye. I wanted to tell him how much he inspired me. I wanted to tell him that normal people just don't exist. I wanted to tell him that everything would be OK. But Miles rolled his eyes at me, like he had done a hundred times over the past ten days. Yet this time, I realized that Miles wasn't just being a pain in the ass. Miles was not Miles anymore. He had changed his name to Alec. I had forgotten, ignoring his most courageous act of self-invention.

"Alec," I said. "I want you to know that I'm there for you in New York. Anytime, man, just get on a plane if you need to leave." I extended my hand to shake good-bye. Alec didn't say anything. He brushed my hand aside and gave me a hug.

The next day, I was alone. All that was left was one last stop in San Francisco, where I would have lunch with my uncle Bill, my mother's older brother and a conservative Catholic priest. I hadn't seen him since he presided over my brother Billy's wedding in 1996. At the time, I was still playing soccer. I was the dumb jock who wanted to be something else but didn't know what or how.

My uncle and I never had a relationship. I have maybe five memories of him, most of them covered in a film that coated all my memories of San Francisco like sunscreen to protect me from the harmful rays of my grandmother's drunken rages. The fact that I did not have a relationship with Bill was not really my fault. My mom left San Francisco in 1977, the year that I was born, and left Uncle Bill behind, both literally and psychologically. My mom rarely visited Bill, and he never visited her. I think for Mom, Uncle Bill embodied the past, the chaos of a life she was trying to leave behind. Bill helped raise my brother and two sisters when my mom was (depending on the source) either fighting for the workers' liberation or drinking with hippies. For my siblings, Bill was something good in life when good things were few and far between.

I could have built a relationship with my uncle. Through the years I visited San Francisco maybe ten times, but I never called him. I'm not sure why. God knows, as I've struggled, I could have used Uncle Bill's presence and experience. He is an irreverent man. When he watched my brother and sisters when they were little kids, he used to act like he was blind and scream, in crowded public places, "Children, children, please don't leave a poor blind priest. Please, you bastards!"

The thing is, Bill made even me uneasy. Bill lived in the Castro, an odd (legendarily gay) neighborhood for an extremely conservative Catholic priest. He had become a priest after toying with the idea of becoming an academic. He had studied Sanskrit and spoke Latin. He was a certified genius. Bill, though, so conservative that he was radical, was an outsider even in his church. He held Mass only in Latin, believed the previous six popes to be illegitimate, and was, in general, a bit of an ecclesiastical freak. I never knew what happened to Bill, but

I knew that he, like Icarus, flew too close to the sun. He was always sort of a warning to me of what could happen if I was too different. I could end up alone.

Uncle Bill had lived in the same one-room apartment, on the second floor of the Most Holy Redeemer, since the early 1960s. When I arrived there, an old woman buzzed me into the rectory. She had probably been the same young woman who had greeted my mom and me when I was a little boy. "He'll be right down, young man," she said to me.

I thanked her and stood to the side.

"Is something wrong?" she asked.

"No. Why?"

"Well, son, you're pacing."

She was right; I was pacing in tight little circles. This was the first time that I had ever visited Bill on my own. Bill was that figure that many of us have in our family: the "special" uncle, the one we don't talk about because he doesn't fit the myth of an all-American normal family. But Bill was my family. I needed to do this to be able to go home.

"Jonathan!" Uncle Bill yelled as he descended the stairs dressed in black with only a sliver of white from his priest collar. Bill was almost sixty-five years old, but he still had all his hair. "Jonathan," he said again, "did you meet my boy?" He was pointing to a young Latino man sitting behind a desk. "This is my pool boy, Juan." Bill snapped his fingers. "Juan! Drinks for the father and the young man." Juan laughed. Bill was completely out of control and insane but still a hell of a good time.

Before lunch, Bill and I spent an hour in his apartment. "You remember Pepsi?" Bill asked, referring to the old border collie that sat at my feet. I did, I said. I knew Pepsi when she was younger. "Did you know that she was originally trained as a service dog for the hard of hearing and the elderly?" Bill asked. "No," I said. "That's fascinating."

"Fascinating? Jonathan, who are you kidding?" He then got down on all fours and addressed the dog to her face. "Yes," Bill said to Pepsi in a high-pitched voice. "Yes, yes, you were, weren't you? You were trained to recognize the sound of the phone or a knock on the door and take the person to the sound. But you were so fat and crazy when you heard the noise you leaped onto the elderly person's chest, yes you did, didn't you, knocking them down, yes you did, didn't you?" I burst out laughing.

"Oh you think that's funny, don't you? Well, I'm not kidding. Pepsi was such a fat bastard that she broke one old broad's hip!"

"Have you ever seen the *Silly Symphonies?*" Bill asked me. I shook my head no. It should be noted that Uncle Bill is an animation freak. He loves Disney movies, with the huge caveat that he refuses to watch or acknowledge the existence of any form of animation produced after 1946. "What? You haven't seen the *Silly Symphonies?*" Bill screamed. "That is a travesty that I will take it upon myself to rectify!" And, with that, he got up and rummaged around to find the *Silly Symphonies* laser disc. Yes, laser disc. It should also be noted that although Uncle Bill has taken, and lived for forty years, a vow of poverty, he has a passion for his big-screen TV that took up the entire living room.

Bill and I never made it to lunch. We sat in his room, talking for all of the afternoon. Mostly about things neither here nor there, about the things that two strangers have to get out of the way so they won't be strangers anymore. Throughout the conversation, I couldn't help but notice how much he and I looked alike. He was pale, had red hair and an upturned Irish nose. No one in my family looked like me, except Uncle Bill.

Our conversation eventually turned to my trip and to why I had come to see him. "You know I'm almost done," I said to him. "But the problem is that I still don't know what I've learned about being different, or being normal, or anything really."

"Normal?" Bill said. "That is important. Did you know that I was hospitalized when I was about your age?" I had no idea. Bill went on to explain that he had had a nervous breakdown in his late twenties. He spent a significant amount of time hospitalized. "I learned something really important about normal then," he said, and looked directly at me. "I learned that sickness is really normal. That sickness is a part of health. I learned that normal is so much bigger than we think."

Uncle Bill had seemed to miss the point, I thought. I had just spent four months of my life living out of a short bus, interrogating the idea of normalcy, and all he could say was "normal is bigger than you think"? No shit.

Perhaps Bill could see my doubt. Bill looked at me very seriously. "When you realize that sickness is normal you're free. You can stop trying to be other than as you are." Pepsi jumped on Bill's lap. He put his face close to hers and whispered, "You little fat bastard." I looked around his room. I saw Bill's medication for depression on the nightstand next to his bed. I saw his bizarre collection of animation films. But he was right; this realization had freed him to not be ashamed of who he was. And after three months of traveling, what wasn't normal to me? Having forty-seven chromosomes was normal. Cursing in sign language was normal. Twenty-four hours of stand-up comedy was normal. A burning city in the desert was normal.

I drove all the way around the United States to find a simple truth close to home.

I looked at him closely. I could see my family in his face. Bill had never left San Francisco. He had visited my grandmother every day until she died. In our family there had always been a silent war against where we came from, against who we are, but Bill wasn't fighting this war.

"How about another movie?" Uncle Bill asked.

"Sure," I said. "I would love that." Bill looked at me, "We should have done this a long time ago." I agreed and then added, "But at least we are doing it now."

California State Highway 1 is famous for its rugged, dangerous beauty. It was the road I would take from San Francisco to L.A. Highway 1 was also the road my family took out of San Francisco when I was a year old, chasing an idea of a better life. One was also the number of days left in this trip.

About an hour out of San Francisco, I pulled to the side of the road to call my Mom before I lost cell phone reception in Big Sur, to let her know that I would be home soon. The phone rang a few times, and then my father, of all people, answered. I was shocked. You have to understand, my dad never answers the phone. My dad is scared of people. In the past ten years this may have been the first time he picked up.

"Hey, man," I said. "Mom around?" I always asked for my mom.

"No, she's with Conor."

"Cool. Just tell her I called. I'm going to be home tomorrow."

This, much to my surprise, was not the end of the conversation. My father, a man of few words, asked me, "So how is the trip going?"

I was floored. Let me put it this way: If a monk could live in a winery, I would say that my father lived a sort of monastic existence. For the past ten years my father and I hadn't talked about much of anything. He had never, on his own accord, called me. I grew up thinking that my father was ashamed of me because I wasn't smart and then later on because I wasn't good enough at soccer. After I quit soccer, I suspected he never forgave me and saw it as a failure. But perhaps things were changing or had changed: *How's the trip going* sounded like a bona fide question one human might ask another.

"Fine," I said, curtly. There was silence on the other end of the phone. My dad sounded tired and sad. I had no idea what he thought about the trip or my plans. We hadn't had much of a relationship in the past few years, or, really, ever. But now he was suddenly chatty. "OK, maybe you'll tell me about it when you get home," he said.

I had misunderstood my father for most of my life. My dad had always carried with him what I considered a bone-crushing anxiety. He used to carry around a briefcase of raw food and hard-boiled eggs. He obsessively turned off all the lights in the house to save electricity even while other people were reading. He has kept almost every newspaper clipping on health-related issues since 1970. In college there were no phone calls from him, no letters, no visits, just random newspaper clippings in the mail.

I used to just hate these things about my dad. And he despised the fact that I couldn't read. For years, we had spun each other around and around in a brutal cycle. I decided that it didn't have to be that way anymore.

"Well, if you have time, I could tell you a little bit about the trip now, Dad," I said. "I would love that," he replied. So I did. I told him all of it.

When I was finished, there was silence on the end of the phone. He was so strange, all his life; he must have felt so ashamed. "You know," he said over the phone, "I'm proud of you."

"Yeah, I hope it makes a good book. I hope people like it." Those were the types of things I thought my dad was proud of: Brown, books, achievement. Those were the things I learned to be proud of.

"No," my dad said, "you're not listening to me. I'm proud of you."

After I said good-bye to my dad, I sat in Bob Henry for a while. My dad had never said that to me. The fog rolled in off the coast and covered Highway 1. It was so deep and thick that it felt as if the ocean was exhaling part of its soul. I sat and listened to the foghorns off the coast. Had I been *that* wrong about myself? For so long I thought my worth was in what I achieved. I thought that all that mattered in this story was that I had overcome. I started this trip chasing a horizon, and now it was gone and I was left with myself in the bus. I read that the photographer Diane Arbus once said that what is left, after what one *isn't* is taken away, is what one *is*.

There were no more stops. There were no more stories. There was nothing left to discover. There was nothing left to change. I wondered what was left of me.

I spent my last night on the road in La Ventana Inn, an expensive hotel in Big Sur. Not only did I max out the last of my credit cards, I want it known that I made a very memorable, poor-white-trash entrance into this five-star establishment that would have made my family proud. After I parked, I got out of the bus, only to hear a very strange noise less than five feet from me. A wild turkey, maybe three feet tall, emerged from the fog. The turkey and I made eye contact; the turkey spread its wings and let out a sound that I took to be a warning. It was a warning. It lowered its beak. I ran. The turkey chased me. I screamed. I ran and yelled all the way to the front desk.

"There is a wild turkey chasing me," I said, out of breath, to the man behind the desk.

He laughed, which was hardly comforting.

"Did you hear me?" I said. "You're not concerned."

"I am very sorry, sir. The turkeys only chase you if you run. It thought you were another turkey."

Was this some sort of existential service the hotel provided? "Is this part of your new spa services line here at the hotel? Pay five hundred dollars for an existential lesson?"

He didn't get it. I rephrased it. "So the turkey was chasing itself?"

"Yes, it was."

I got good and drunk that night, as one should upon finishing something. I sat and finished my bottle of wine and listened to the turkeys chase each other in the night. The pool, I was told, was clothing optional, a throwback to Big Sur's hippie days. The weather was cold and clear, and it was fall; summer had split out the back door. I decided it was a fine night for a swim.

I decided to ignore the clothing-optional suggestion. I walked out into the pool fully clothed. I was wearing the jeans that I wore every day on the bus and an old thrift-store shirt that I had gotten at Brown that said *Survivor* on it. I walked out into the pool and watched myself shudder in the water mixing with the radiant light of the moon. I looked at my reflection in the shimmering water. I looked different. I looked older. I had put my youth into this trip, and on the other end was a sense of myself as more singular and solid than I had ever had when chasing normalcy. I wasn't a striver; maybe I had been, but I wasn't anymore. These last three months, and for most of life, I had been searching.

Standing in the pool, I decided I couldn't leave Bob Henry in front of my elementary school. His home was with me. These experiences were me, this community was me, was perhaps the best part of who I am. What a dim world we would live in without people like Brent, Kent, Ashley, Cookie, Katie, and Jeff.

I was, I am, and I always will be a short-bus rider.

I took a deep breath, and I lowered myself down and felt the water rush over me. I held my breath and let the water, like a baptism, wash off all the sweat and dust and dirt from the last three months. I stood up, weighed down by my soggy clothes. I felt renewed, I felt light, I felt . . . like I was being stared at.

It turned out that I was not alone. While I was underwater, a group of ten middle-aged people had joined me at the pool. Nor was the clothing-optional policy a superficial homage to the past, but a living, pasty, and flabby reality. I stood in the middle of the pool fully clothed.

Ten of my fellow human beings stood at the end of the pool butt naked. I was outnumbered. I, of course, was the freak again. On my last night on the short bus, a group of ten naked middle-aged people were *staring*. At me.

I couldn't win.

"Hey," I yelled to the naked gaggle of people staring. "Cut me some slack. I'm a short-bus rider."

author's note

The short bus is a vehicle that has been and is still used to transport students with disabilities to special education settings. The short bus is also a symbol of difference and disability in our culture. For the majority of individuals appearing in this book, myself included, the short bus was not a pervasive physical reality but a symbol of oppressive experiences.

The prologue of *The Short Bus* is a condensed rendering of my time lecturing from September 2000 to August 2001. Bobby and Clay have been renamed in order to conceal the identity of individuals who shared their experiences with no expectation of ever appearing in print.

The body of *The Short Bus* documents a four-month, 35,000-mile journey from May to October 2003. All the characters are real, though some names have been changed. These name changes are *not* noted and will be left to the reader's imagination.

Lastly, all profiles of individuals are subjective renderings of their experience. My writing should by no means be considered the truth or final word about anyone. Each person is welcome and encouraged to tell his or her own story in its own way.

If more short-bus stories were told, the world would be a better place.

acknowledgments

I've been working on this book for more than six years. It never would have come close to happening without the following people:

My wife, Becky. For the past nine years she has been directly responsible for the person that I've become. Moreover, she has supported me from day one with this project. Since then we have moved for this book, planned our vacations for this book, rearranged our lives for this book. She has read every word, at least twenty times. This is as much her book as it is mine. I love her unconditionally.

To Brent, Sarah, Kent, Butch, Ashley, Deborah, Matt, John, Cookie, Chad, Cully, Katie, Candee, Miles, Jeff, Uncle Bill, and Bob Henry. This is your book. Thank you. To all the others who responded to my insane e-mail calling all short-bus riders: The world would be a better place if your stories were told. To all short-bus riders—and people oppressed by normalcy in our society—thank you for your courageous resistance.

To mom, dad, brother Billy, sister Michelle. I would be nowhere if it wasn't for where I came from. Kelly, you have believed in me from the beginning. You helped make the journey even better than I thought it could be. Thank you.

My agent, Jill Kneerim. She decided to represent me when I was a twenty-one-year-old punk. She had the vision to believe in this book before I could. Thank you!

All the folks at Henry Holt, present and past, especially my editor, George Hodgman. I've learned more about writing, thinking, and communicating from George than I did in all my time at an Ivy League university. But the greatest gifts George gave me were time and patience. I think of myself kind of like those monkeys who, if given enough time pounding at a typewriter, will compose a Shakespearean play. This ain't Shakespeare, but George gave me the time, space, and support to get what was in my head onto the page. A gift for a dyslexic writer that I can never repay. Thank you.

To Supurna Banerjee—an amazing assistant and partner in this process. And to Maggie Richards, Eileen Lawrence, Claire McKinney, Dana Trombley, and Richard Rhorer. An amazing marketing team, who have believed in this book from the beginning, thank you. I'll thank you in advance for getting me on *Oprah*.

And to Deborah Brody, the editor who had the vision to acquire this book. I sat in her office after drinking way too much caffeine and described how I was going to drive around the United States in a bus I did not have, to talk with people I did not know. Vision might not be a strong enough word. Thank you!

Friends and assorted colleagues. They are in no particular order or category. David Flink, a brother, colleague, mentor, friend. Christopher Klonecke, for taking the ride with me and being such a big supporter of the book. My Brown transfer crew: David Pinkowitz, Ben Holzer, and honorary member Dan Weiner. You all helped me see myself differently, when all I saw was a stupid soccer player. Thank you. Thank you Linda and Jerry Golden for your unconditional support and your kindness to the different ragged crews dragged into your home over the years. To the families who made all this happen in the first place: Leah Davis, Cathy, Steve, Derrick, and Aaron Manus, Miriam Gerstenblith, Miriam Whitehouse, Sherry Davidowitz. The folks at PEN, Dewey and Julie, Moira in New Zealand and my traveling crew, all my other hosts. Thank you LeDerick for having a voice and a story. Thank you to all the Eye-to-Eye members around the country for giving me hope—Ann Schneider, Gail Propp, Peggy Ogdon, Harold Koplewicz, Linda Sirow, Dan Thiebauld, Lisa Goldschmidt, Brad Truding. Thank you John McKnight for helping me see the world differently. Thank you Eli Wolff for helping me grow as a disability rights activist. Thank you Mike MacDonald for writing and talking me through second-book hell. And, lastly, thank you Ned Hallowell for changing my life many times over.

about the author

JONATHAN MOONEY graduated from Brown with an honors degree in English. A recipient of the distinguished Truman Fellowship for graduate study in the fields of creative writing and disability studies, he is also the coauthor of *Learning Outside the Lines*. Jonathan is the president of Project Eye-to-Eye, a nonprofit mentoring and advocacy organization for students with learning disabilities. He lives in New York City with his wife, Rebecca, and can be contacted at jonathanmooney.com.